ANGEL
&FAITH

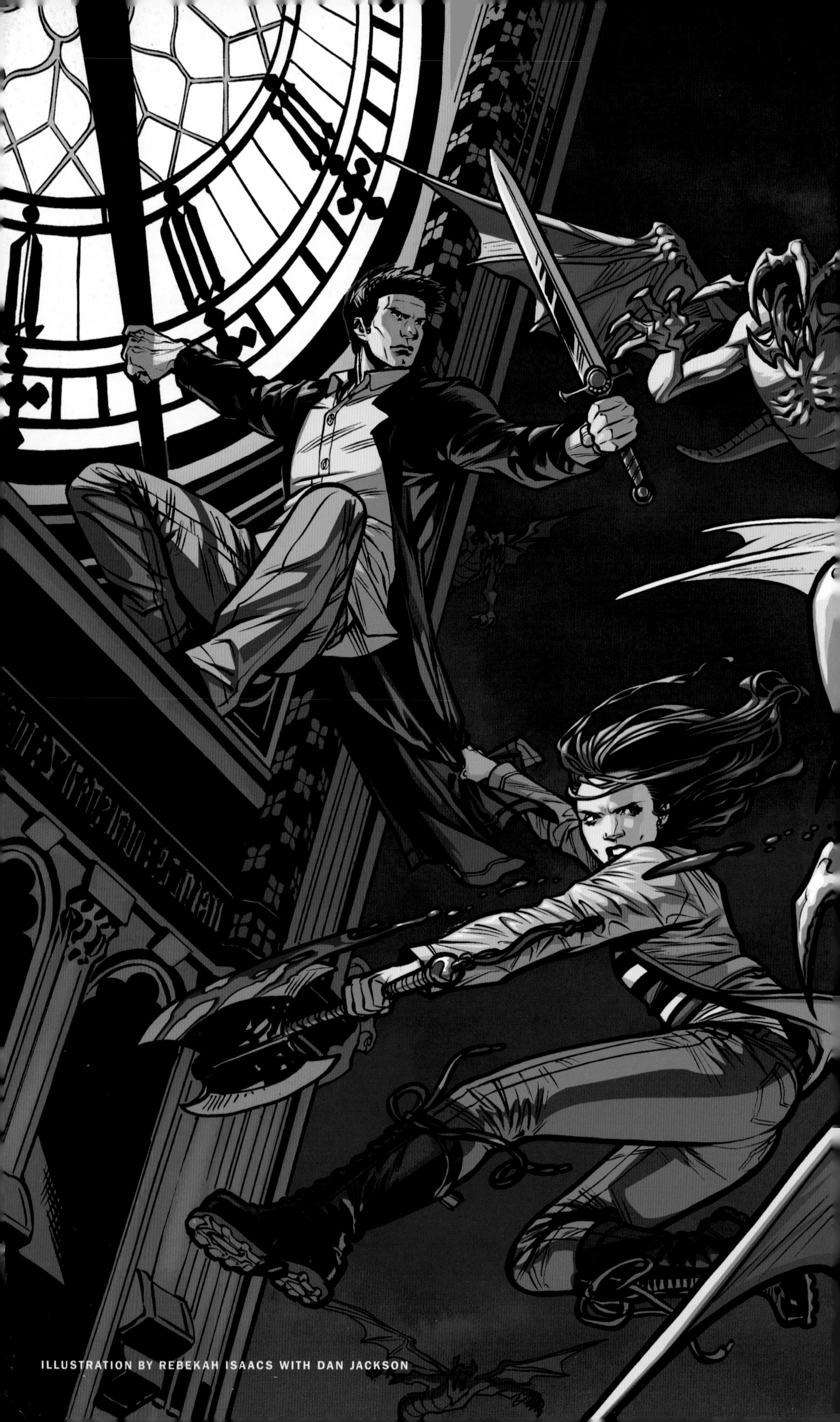

ILLUSTRATION BY REBEKAH ISAACS WITH DAN JACKSON

ANGEL &FAITH

SEASON 9 · VOLUME 5

WHAT YOU WANT, NOT WHAT YOU NEED

SCRIPT
CHRISTOS GAGE

ART
REBEKAH ISAACS

COLORS
DAN JACKSON

LETTERS
RICHARD STARKINGS *& Comicraft's*
JIMMY BETANCOURT

COVER ART
STEVE MORRIS

EXECUTIVE PRODUCER
JOSS WHEDON

DARK HORSE BOOKS

PRESIDENT & PUBLISHER
MIKE RICHARDSON

EDITORS
SCOTT ALLIE & SIERRA HAHN

ASSISTANT EDITOR
FREDDYE LINS

COLLECTION DESIGNER
JUSTIN COUCH

Published by Dark Horse Books
A division of Dark Horse Comics, Inc.
10956 SE Main Street
Milwaukie, OR 97222

DarkHorse.com
International Licensing: (503) 905-2377

To find a comics shop in your area, call the
Comic Shop Locator Service toll-free at
(888) 266-4226.

First edition: February 2014
ISBN 978-1-61655-253-4

10 9 8 7 6 5 4 3 2 1
Printed in China

This story takes place during *Buffy the Vampire Slayer* Season 9, created by Joss Whedon.

Special thanks to Lauren Winarski at Twentieth Century Fox, and Daniel Kaminsky.

NEIL HANKERSON Executive Vice President • TOM WEDDLE Chief Financial Officer • RANDY STRADLEY Vice President of Publishing • MICHAEL MARTENS Vice President of Book Trade Sales • ANITA NELSON Vice President of Business Affairs • SCOTT ALLIE Editor in Chief • MATT PARKINSON Vice President of Marketing • DAVID SCROGGY Vice President of Product Development • DALE LaFOUNTAIN Vice President of Information Technology • DARLENE VOGEL Senior Director of Print, Design, and Production • KEN LIZZI General Counsel • DAVEY ESTRADA Editorial Director • CHRIS WARNER Senior Books Editor • DIANA SCHUTZ Executive Editor • CARY GRAZZINI Director of Print and Development • LIA RIBACCHI Art Director • CARA NIECE Director of Scheduling • TIM WIESCH Director of International Licensing • MARK BERNARDI Director of Digital Publishing

This volume reprints the comic-book series *Angel & Faith* #21–#25 from Dark Horse Comics.

ANGEL &FAITH™

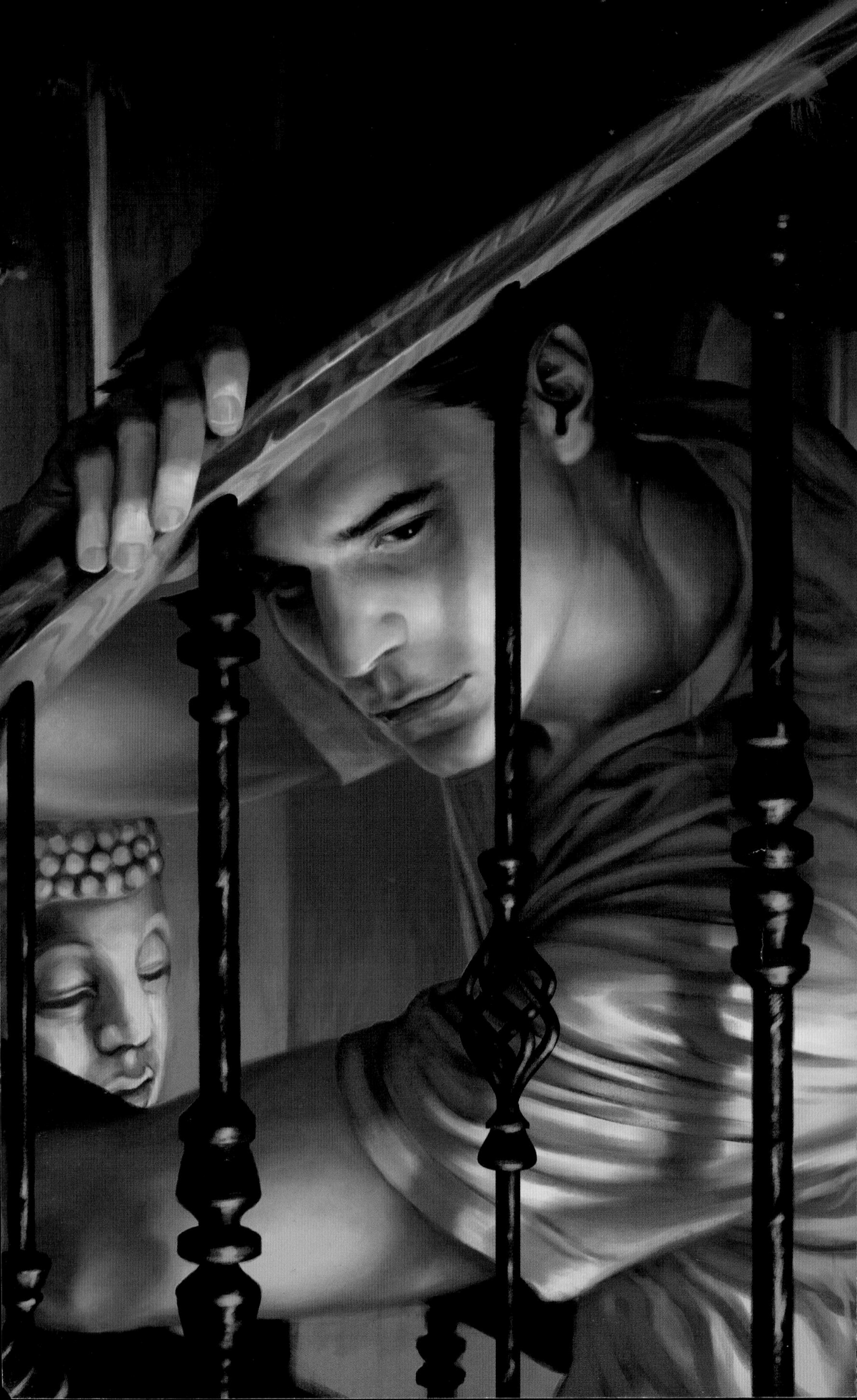

WELL, IT SEEMS YOUR GRAND PLAN HAS COME TOGETHER NICELY.

YOU HAVE THE CORPSE OF RUPERT GILES, RESTORED TO VITALITY IF NOT LIFE BY THE *CROWN OF COILS.*

YOU HAVE HIS *SOUL,* FULLY REASSEMBLED AND CONTAINED WITHIN THE *ESSUARY.*

WHAT YOU WANT, NOT WHAT YOU NEED

ALL THAT REMAINS IS TO BRING THEM *TOGETHER.*

AND WHILE I STILL THINK IT'S A TERRIBLE IDEA, I'M EAGER TO HEAR HOW YOU PLAN TO DO IT IN A WORLD WHERE SPELLS NO LONGER FUNCTION.

THERE *IS* A PLAN, I HOPE? I'M SPENDING ENTIRELY TOO MUCH TIME STOPPING MY CATS FROM USING MY POOR FRIEND AS A *SCRATCHING POST.*

HOME OF ALASDAIR COAMES.

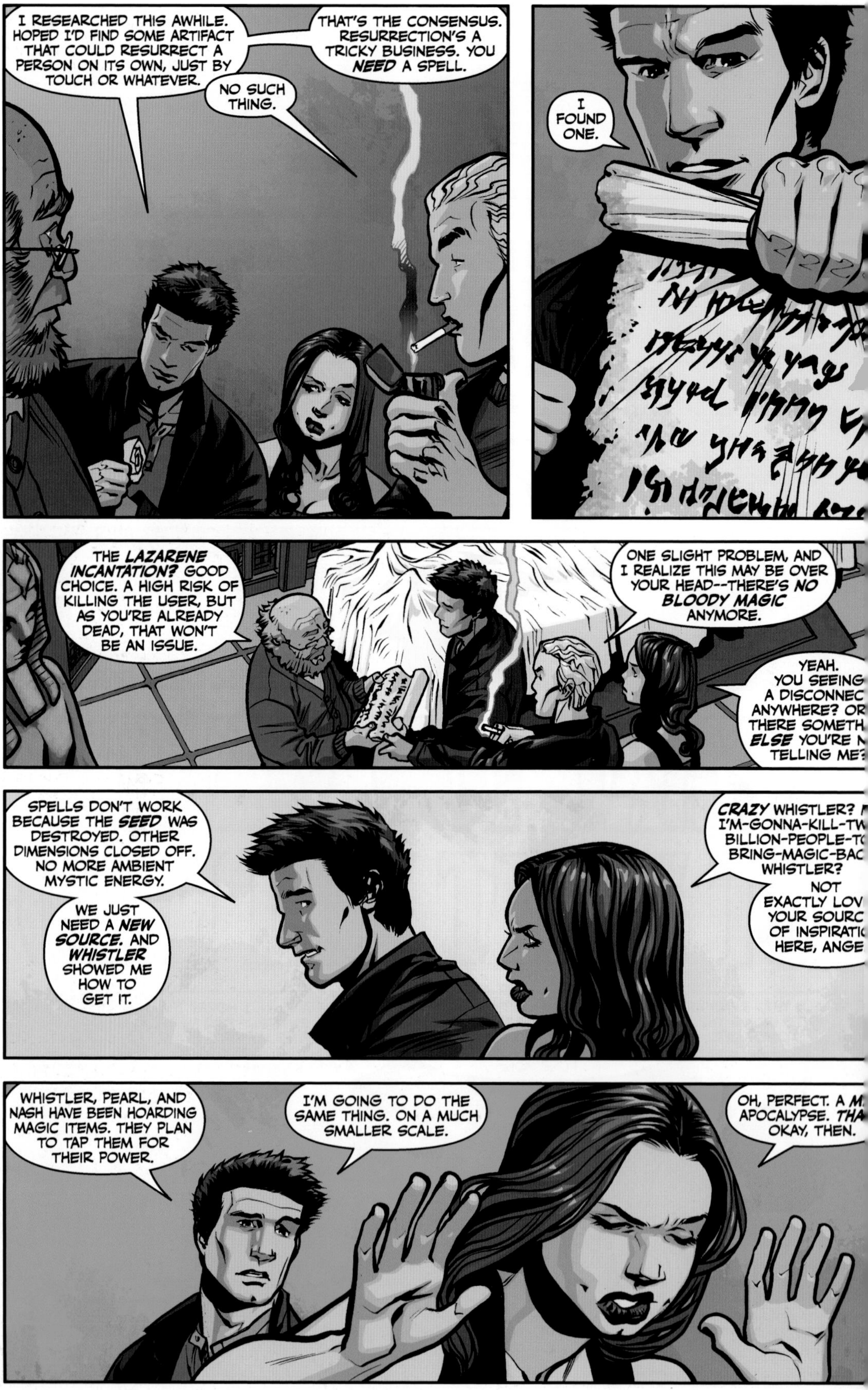
I RESEARCHED THIS AWHILE. HOPED I'D FIND SOME ARTIFACT THAT COULD RESURRECT A PERSON ON ITS OWN, JUST BY TOUCH OR WHATEVER.
NO SUCH THING.
THAT'S THE CONSENSUS. RESURRECTION'S A TRICKY BUSINESS. YOU *NEED* A SPELL.
I FOUND ONE.
THE *LAZARENE INCANTATION?* GOOD CHOICE. A HIGH RISK OF KILLING THE USER, BUT AS YOU'RE ALREADY DEAD, THAT WON'T BE AN ISSUE.
ONE SLIGHT PROBLEM, AND I REALIZE THIS MAY BE OVER YOUR HEAD--THERE'S *NO BLOODY MAGIC* ANYMORE.
YEAH. YOU SEEING A DISCONNEC ANYWHERE? OR THERE SOMETH *ELSE* YOU'RE N TELLING ME?
SPELLS DON'T WORK BECAUSE THE *SEED* WAS DESTROYED. OTHER DIMENSIONS CLOSED OFF. NO MORE AMBIENT MYSTIC ENERGY.
WE JUST NEED A *NEW SOURCE.* AND *WHISTLER* SHOWED ME HOW TO GET IT.
CRAZY WHISTLER? I'M-GONNA-KILL-TW BILLION-PEOPLE-TO BRING-MAGIC-BAC WHISTLER?
NOT EXACTLY LOV YOUR SOURC OF INSPIRATI HERE, ANGE
WHISTLER, PEARL, AND NASH HAVE BEEN HOARDING MAGIC ITEMS. THEY PLAN TO TAP THEM FOR THEIR POWER.
I'M GOING TO DO THE SAME THING. ON A MUCH SMALLER SCALE.
OH, PERFECT. A M APOCALYPSE. *THA* OKAY, THEN.

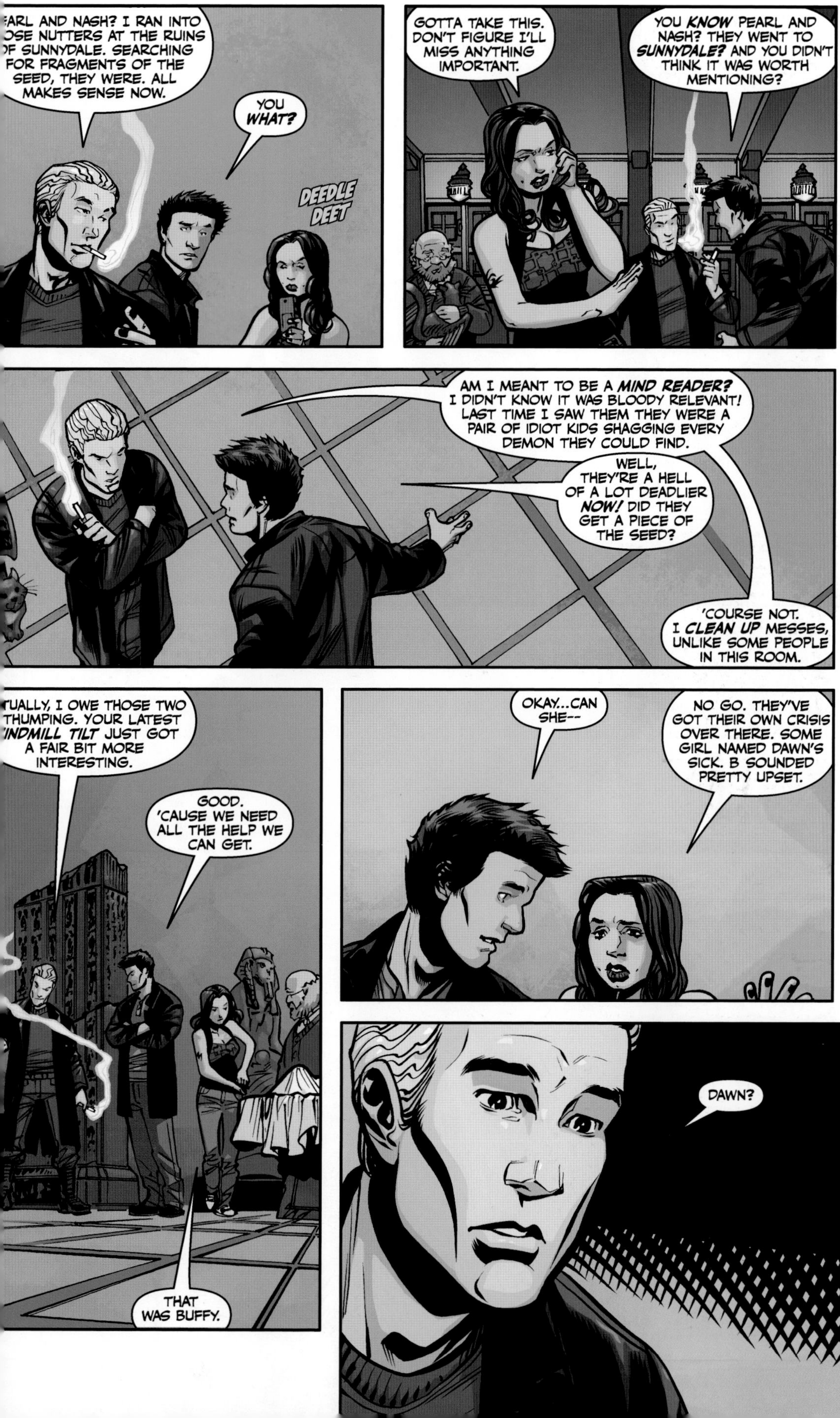
EARL AND NASH? I RAN INTO
OSE NUTTERS AT THE RUINS
OF SUNNYDALE. SEARCHING
FOR FRAGMENTS OF THE
SEED, THEY WERE. ALL
MAKES SENSE NOW.
YOU WHAT?
DEEDLE DEET
GOTTA TAKE THIS. DON'T FIGURE I'LL MISS ANYTHING IMPORTANT.
YOU KNOW PEARL AND NASH? THEY WENT TO SUNNYDALE? AND YOU DIDN'T THINK IT WAS WORTH MENTIONING?
AM I MEANT TO BE A MIND READER? I DIDN'T KNOW IT WAS BLOODY RELEVANT! LAST TIME I SAW THEM THEY WERE A PAIR OF IDIOT KIDS SHAGGING EVERY DEMON THEY COULD FIND.
WELL, THEY'RE A HELL OF A LOT DEADLIER NOW! DID THEY GET A PIECE OF THE SEED?
'COURSE NOT. I CLEAN UP MESSES, UNLIKE SOME PEOPLE IN THIS ROOM.
TUALLY, I OWE THOSE TWO THUMPING. YOUR LATEST INDMILL TILT JUST GOT A FAIR BIT MORE INTERESTING.
GOOD. 'CAUSE WE NEED ALL THE HELP WE CAN GET.
THAT WAS BUFFY.
OKAY...CAN SHE--
NO GO. THEY'VE GOT THEIR OWN CRISIS OVER THERE. SOME GIRL NAMED DAWN'S SICK. B SOUNDED PRETTY UPSET.
DAWN?

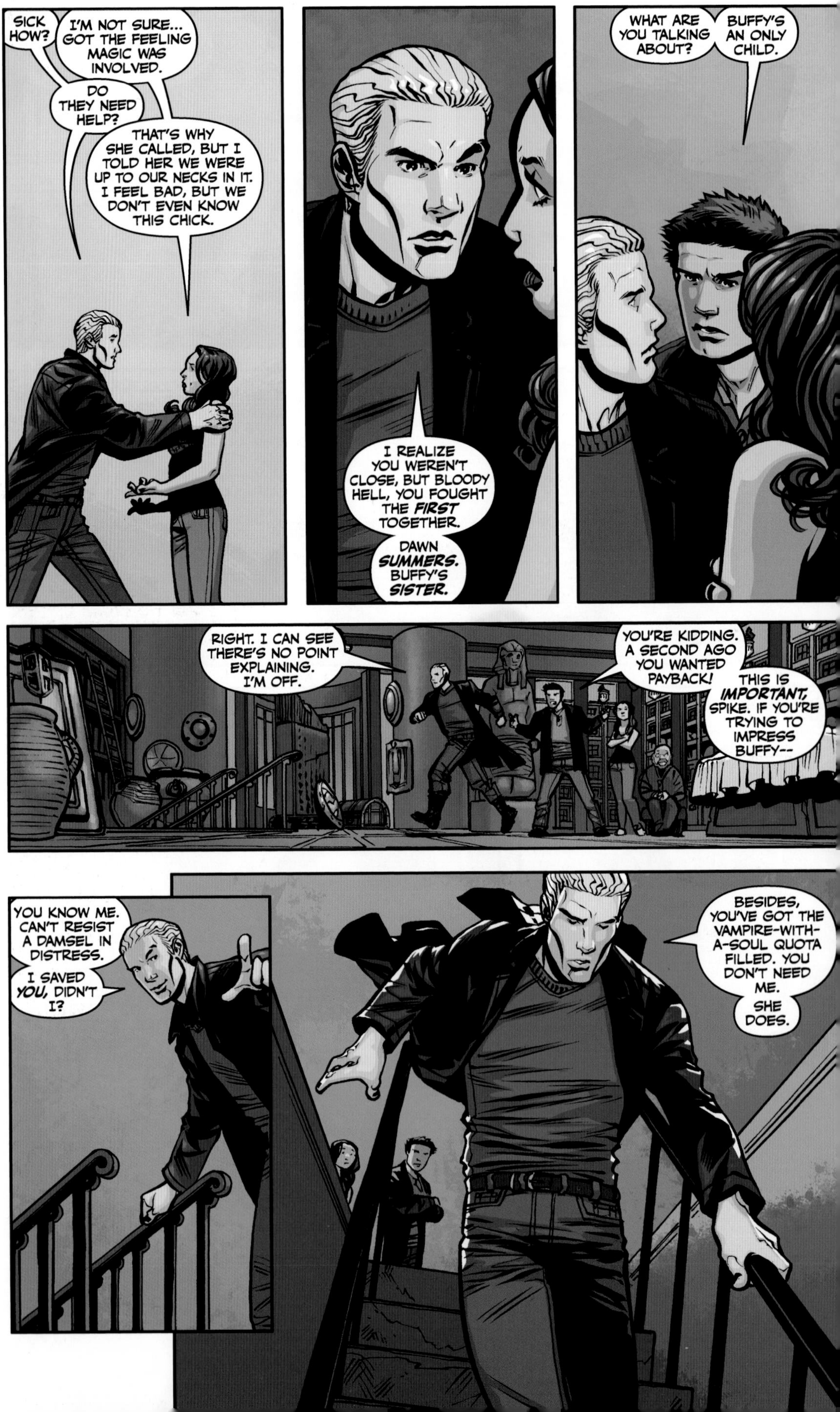
SICK HOW?
I'M NOT SURE... GOT THE FEELING MAGIC WAS INVOLVED.
DO THEY NEED HELP?
THAT'S WHY SHE CALLED, BUT I TOLD HER WE WERE UP TO OUR NECKS IN IT. I FEEL BAD, BUT WE DON'T EVEN KNOW THIS CHICK.
I REALIZE YOU WEREN'T CLOSE, BUT BLOODY HELL, YOU FOUGHT THE *FIRST* TOGETHER.
DAWN ***SUMMERS.*** BUFFY'S ***SISTER.***
WHAT ARE YOU TALKING ABOUT?
BUFFY'S AN ONLY CHILD.
RIGHT. I CAN SEE THERE'S NO POINT EXPLAINING. I'M OFF.
YOU'RE KIDDING. A SECOND AGO YOU WANTED PAYBACK!
THIS IS ***IMPORTANT,*** SPIKE. IF YOU'RE TRYING TO IMPRESS BUFFY--
YOU KNOW ME. CAN'T RESIST A DAMSEL IN DISTRESS.
I SAVED ***YOU,*** DIDN'T I?
BESIDES, YOU'VE GOT THE VAMPIRE-WITH-A-SOUL QUOTA FILLED. YOU DON'T NEED ME.
SHE DOES.

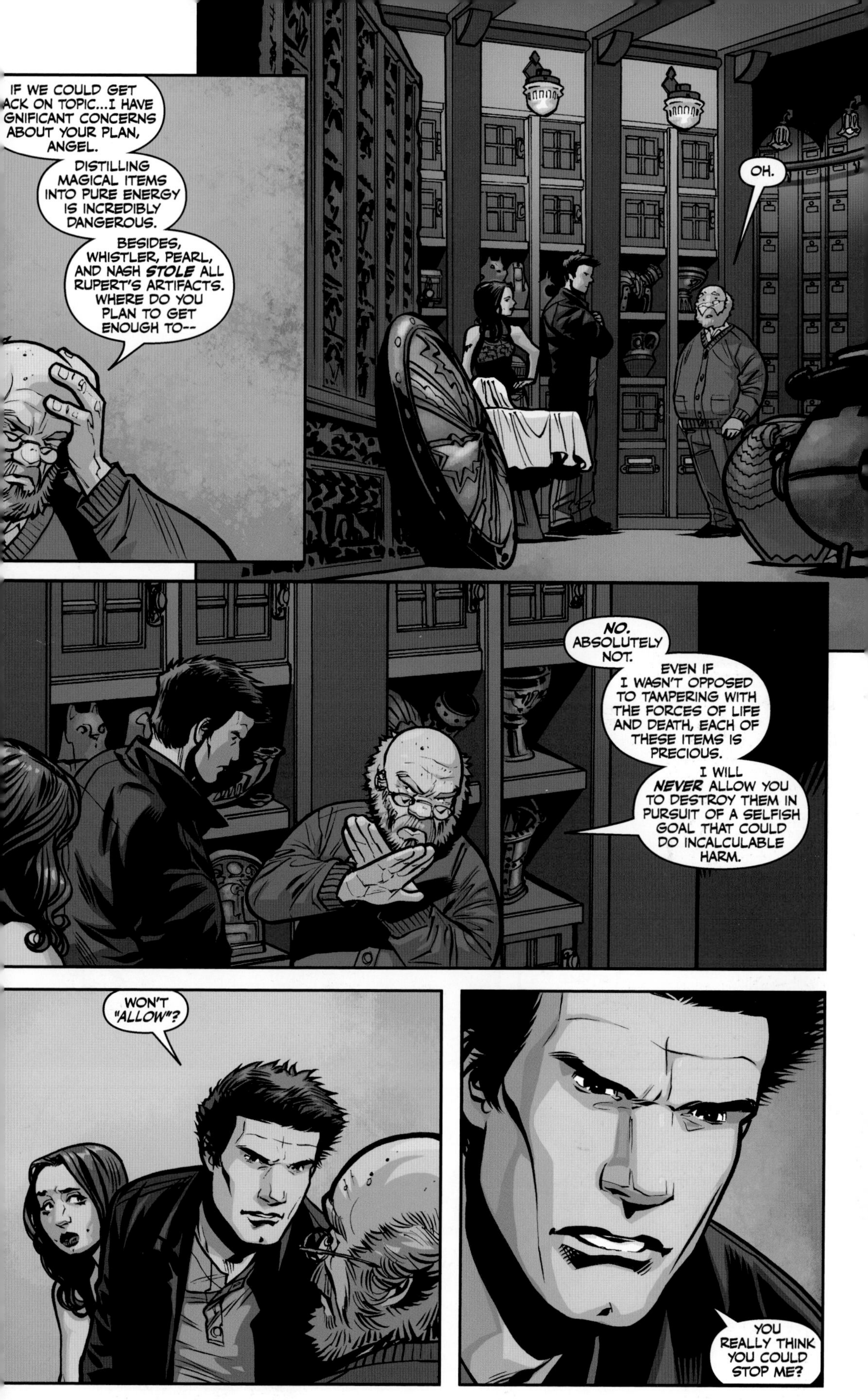
IF WE COULD GET ACK ON TOPIC...I HAVE GNIFICANT CONCERNS ABOUT YOUR PLAN, ANGEL.
DISTILLING MAGICAL ITEMS INTO PURE ENERGY IS INCREDIBLY DANGEROUS.
BESIDES, WHISTLER, PEARL, AND NASH STOLE ALL RUPERT'S ARTIFACTS. WHERE DO YOU PLAN TO GET ENOUGH TO--
OH.
NO. ABSOLUTELY NOT.
EVEN IF I WASN'T OPPOSED TO TAMPERING WITH THE FORCES OF LIFE AND DEATH, EACH OF THESE ITEMS IS PRECIOUS.
I WILL NEVER ALLOW YOU TO DESTROY THEM IN PURSUIT OF A SELFISH GOAL THAT COULD DO INCALCULABLE HARM.
WON'T "ALLOW"?
YOU REALLY THINK YOU COULD STOP ME?

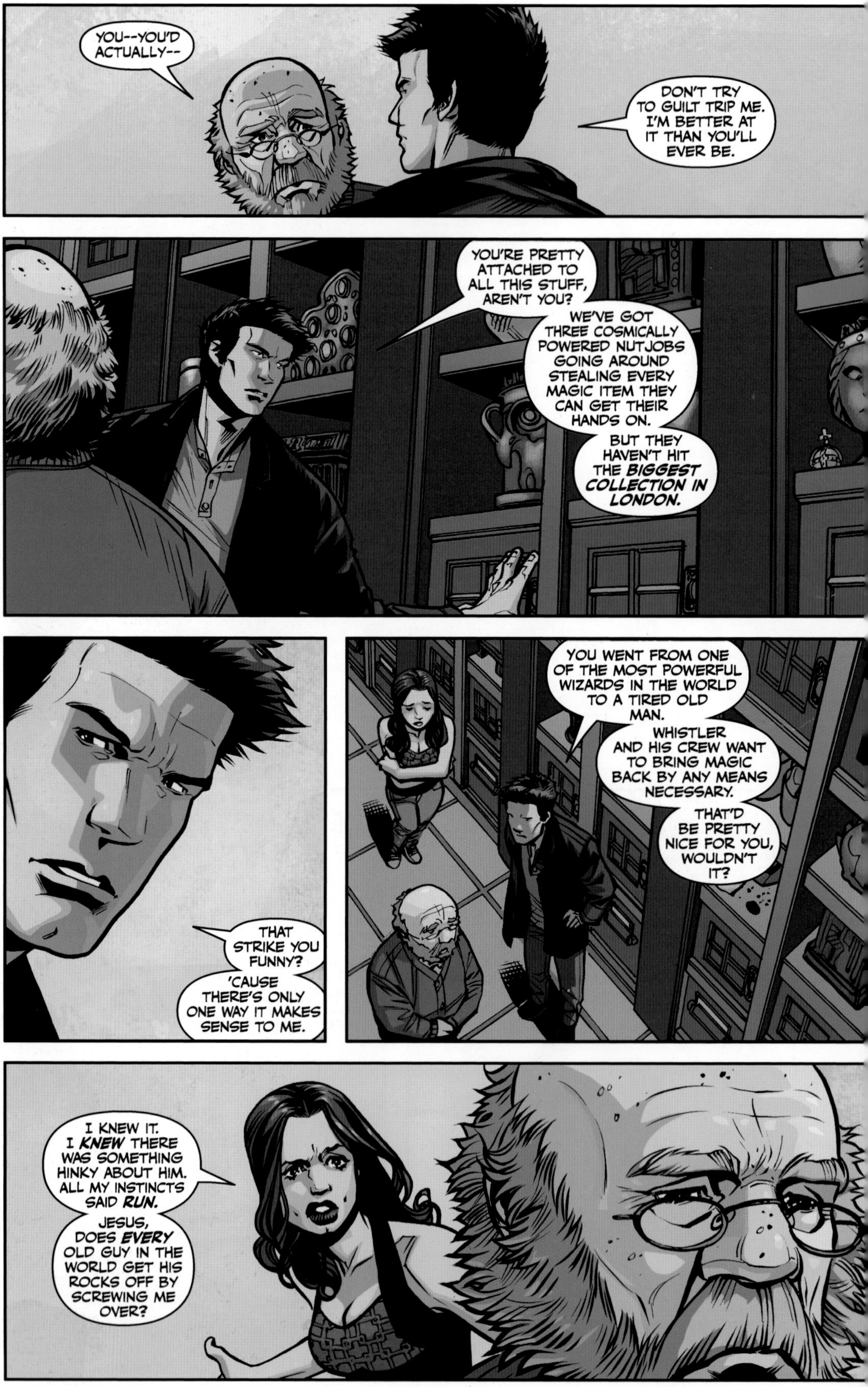
YOU--YOU'D ACTUALLY--
DON'T TRY TO GUILT TRIP ME. I'M BETTER AT IT THAN YOU'LL EVER BE.
YOU'RE PRETTY ATTACHED TO ALL THIS STUFF, AREN'T YOU?
WE'VE GOT THREE COSMICALLY POWERED NUTJOBS GOING AROUND STEALING EVERY MAGIC ITEM THEY CAN GET THEIR HANDS ON.
BUT THEY HAVEN'T HIT THE *BIGGEST COLLECTION IN LONDON.*
THAT STRIKE YOU FUNNY?
'CAUSE THERE'S ONLY ONE WAY IT MAKES SENSE TO ME.
YOU WENT FROM ONE OF THE MOST POWERFUL WIZARDS IN THE WORLD TO A TIRED OLD MAN.
WHISTLER AND HIS CREW WANT TO BRING MAGIC BACK BY ANY MEANS NECESSARY.
THAT'D BE PRETTY NICE FOR YOU, WOULDN'T IT?
I KNEW IT. I *KNEW* THERE WAS SOMETHING HINKY ABOUT HIM. ALL MY INSTINCTS SAID *RUN.*
JESUS, DOES *EVERY* OLD GUY IN THE WORLD GET HIS ROCKS OFF BY SCREWING ME OVER?

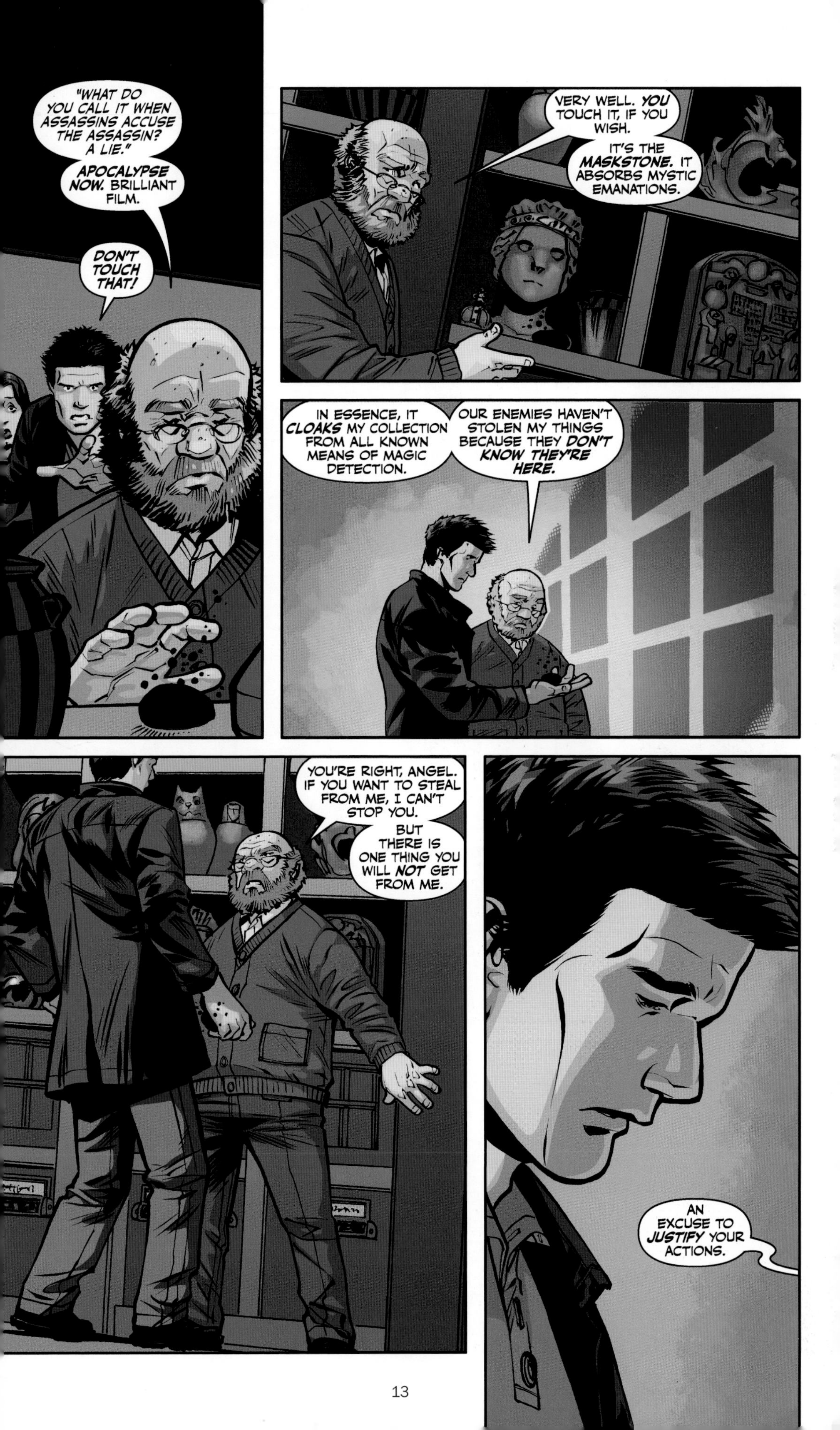
"WHAT DO YOU CALL IT WHEN ASSASSINS ACCUSE THE ASSASSIN? A LIE."
APOCALYPSE NOW. BRILLIANT FILM.
DON'T TOUCH THAT!
VERY WELL. YOU TOUCH IT, IF YOU WISH.
IT'S THE MASKSTONE. IT ABSORBS MYSTIC EMANATIONS.
IN ESSENCE, IT CLOAKS MY COLLECTION FROM ALL KNOWN MEANS OF MAGIC DETECTION.
OUR ENEMIES HAVEN'T STOLEN MY THINGS BECAUSE THEY DON'T KNOW THEY'RE HERE.
YOU'RE RIGHT, ANGEL. IF YOU WANT TO STEAL FROM ME, I CAN'T STOP YOU.
BUT THERE IS ONE THING YOU WILL NOT GET FROM ME.
AN EXCUSE TO JUSTIFY YOUR ACTIONS.

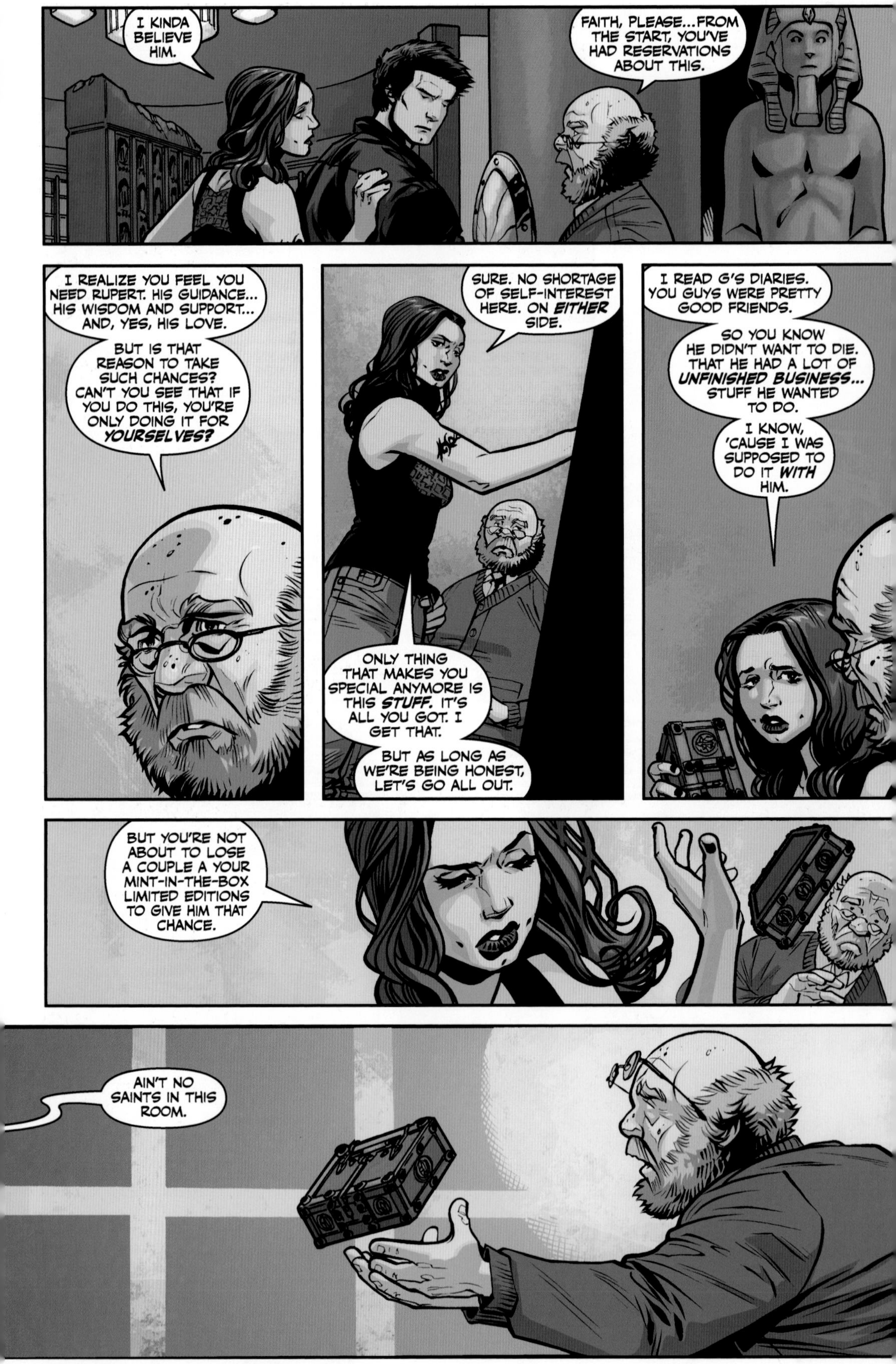
I KINDA BELIEVE HIM.
FAITH, PLEASE...FROM THE START, YOU'VE HAD RESERVATIONS ABOUT THIS.
I REALIZE YOU FEEL YOU NEED RUPERT. HIS GUIDANCE... HIS WISDOM AND SUPPORT... AND, YES, HIS LOVE.
BUT IS THAT REASON TO TAKE SUCH CHANCES? CAN'T YOU SEE THAT IF YOU DO THIS, YOU'RE ONLY DOING IT FOR YOURSELVES?
SURE. NO SHORTAGE OF SELF-INTEREST HERE. ON EITHER SIDE.
ONLY THING THAT MAKES YOU SPECIAL ANYMORE IS THIS STUFF. IT'S ALL YOU GOT. I GET THAT.
BUT AS LONG AS WE'RE BEING HONEST, LET'S GO ALL OUT.
I READ G'S DIARIES. YOU GUYS WERE PRETTY GOOD FRIENDS.
SO YOU KNOW HE DIDN'T WANT TO DIE. THAT HE HAD A LOT OF UNFINISHED BUSINESS... STUFF HE WANTED TO DO.
I KNOW, 'CAUSE I WAS SUPPOSED TO DO IT WITH HIM.
BUT YOU'RE NOT ABOUT TO LOSE A COUPLE A YOUR MINT-IN-THE-BOX LIMITED EDITIONS TO GIVE HIM THAT CHANCE.
AIN'T NO SAINTS IN THIS ROOM.

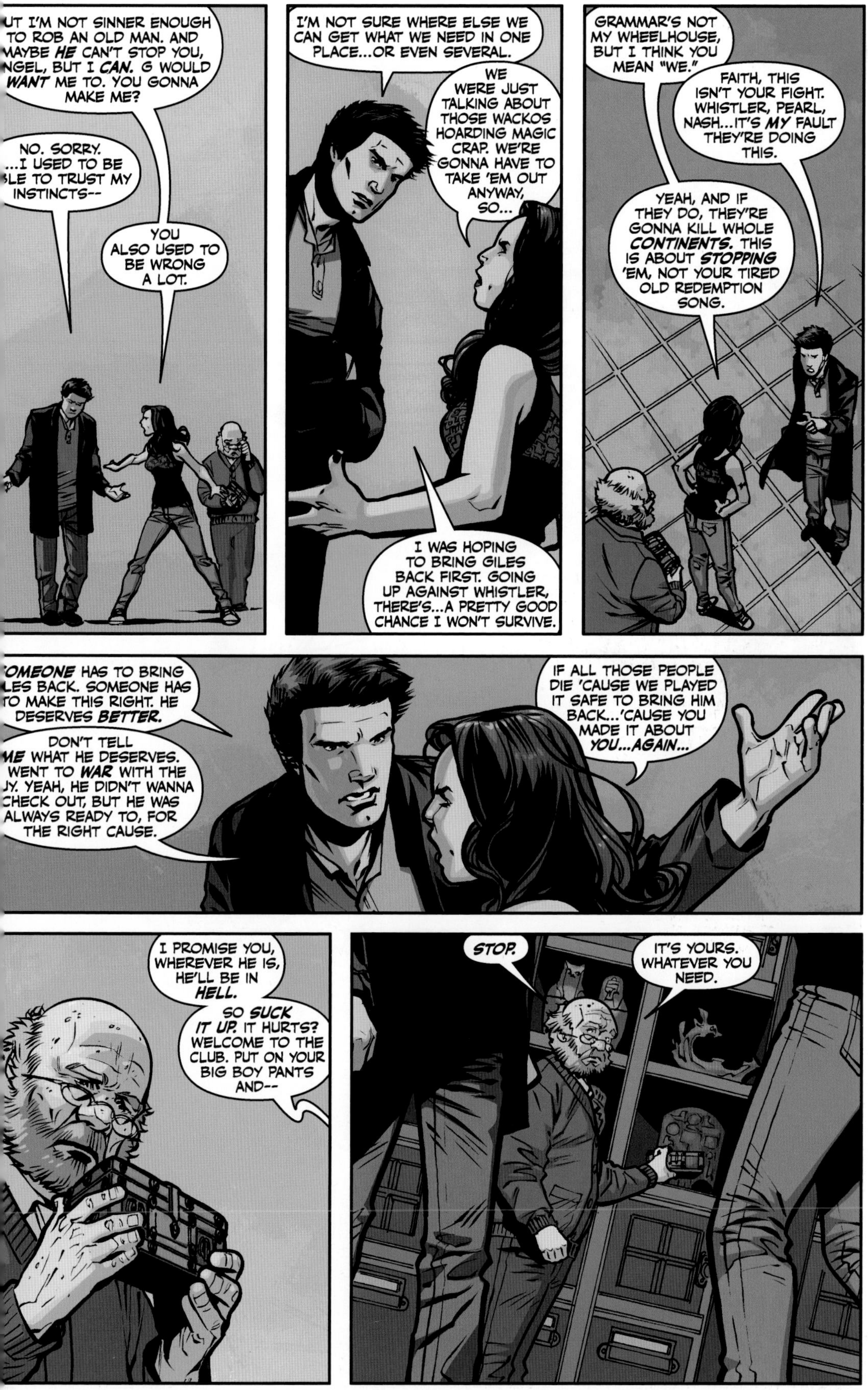
UT I'M NOT SINNER ENOUGH TO ROB AN OLD MAN. AND MAYBE HE CAN'T STOP YOU, NGEL, BUT I CAN. G WOULD WANT ME TO. YOU GONNA MAKE ME?
NO. SORRY. ...I USED TO BE BLE TO TRUST MY INSTINCTS--
YOU ALSO USED TO BE WRONG A LOT.
I'M NOT SURE WHERE ELSE WE CAN GET WHAT WE NEED IN ONE PLACE...OR EVEN SEVERAL.
WE WERE JUST TALKING ABOUT THOSE WACKOS HOARDING MAGIC CRAP. WE'RE GONNA HAVE TO TAKE 'EM OUT ANYWAY, SO...
I WAS HOPING TO BRING GILES BACK FIRST. GOING UP AGAINST WHISTLER, THERE'S...A PRETTY GOOD CHANCE I WON'T SURVIVE.
GRAMMAR'S NOT MY WHEELHOUSE, BUT I THINK YOU MEAN "WE."
FAITH, THIS ISN'T YOUR FIGHT. WHISTLER, PEARL, NASH...IT'S MY FAULT THEY'RE DOING THIS.
YEAH, AND IF THEY DO, THEY'RE GONNA KILL WHOLE CONTINENTS. THIS IS ABOUT STOPPING 'EM, NOT YOUR TIRED OLD REDEMPTION SONG.
OMEONE HAS TO BRING LES BACK. SOMEONE HAS TO MAKE THIS RIGHT. HE DESERVES BETTER.
DON'T TELL ME WHAT HE DESERVES. WENT TO WAR WITH THE JY. YEAH, HE DIDN'T WANNA CHECK OUT, BUT HE WAS ALWAYS READY TO, FOR THE RIGHT CAUSE.
IF ALL THOSE PEOPLE DIE 'CAUSE WE PLAYED IT SAFE TO BRING HIM BACK...'CAUSE YOU MADE IT ABOUT YOU...AGAIN...
I PROMISE YOU, WHEREVER HE IS, HE'LL BE IN HELL.
SO SUCK IT UP. IT HURTS? WELCOME TO THE CLUB. PUT ON YOUR BIG BOY PANTS AND--
STOP.
IT'S YOURS. WHATEVER YOU NEED.

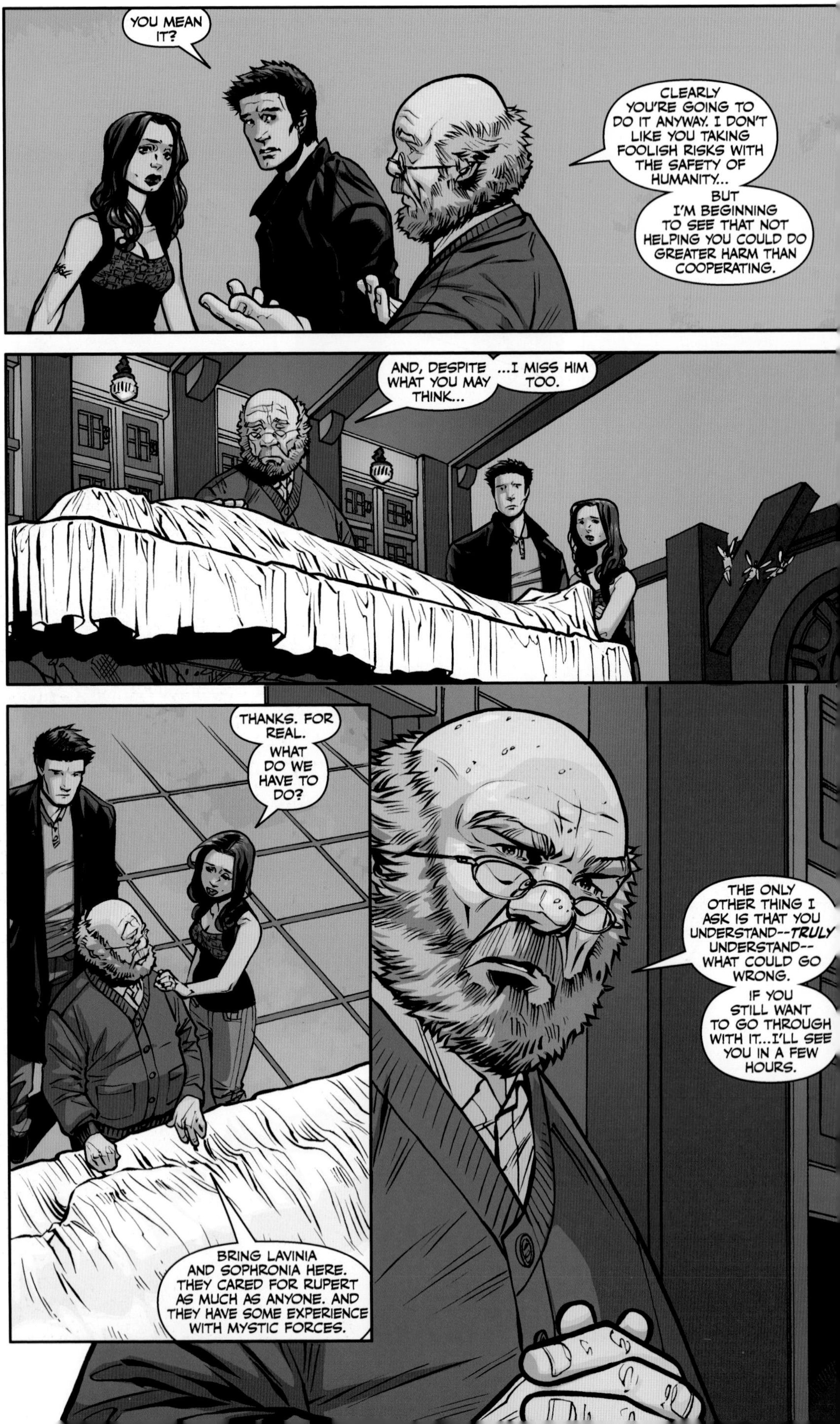

YOU MEAN IT?
CLEARLY YOU'RE GOING TO DO IT ANYWAY. I DON'T LIKE YOU TAKING FOOLISH RISKS WITH THE SAFETY OF HUMANITY...
BUT I'M BEGINNING TO SEE THAT NOT HELPING YOU COULD DO GREATER HARM THAN COOPERATING.
AND, DESPITE WHAT YOU MAY THINK...
...I MISS HIM TOO.
THANKS. FOR REAL.
WHAT DO WE HAVE TO DO?
BRING LAVINIA AND SOPHRONIA HERE. THEY CARED FOR RUPERT AS MUCH AS ANYONE. AND THEY HAVE SOME EXPERIENCE WITH MYSTIC FORCES.
THE ONLY OTHER THING I ASK IS THAT YOU UNDERSTAND--*TRULY* UNDERSTAND--WHAT COULD GO WRONG.
IF YOU STILL WANT TO GO THROUGH WITH IT...I'LL SEE YOU IN A FEW HOURS.

HOME OF FAITH LEHANE.

LADIES... ...WE NEED TO TALK.

THEN IT'S FINALLY TIME. SPLENDID.

I'LL START THE RITUAL, SO THE DEATH CURSE HITS ME. BUT I DON'T HAVE ANY EXPERIENCE CASTING SPELLS, SO...

ALASDAIR WILL TAKE OVER. OF COURSE. AND IF HE SHOULD FALTER, SOPHIE OR I COULD STEP IN.

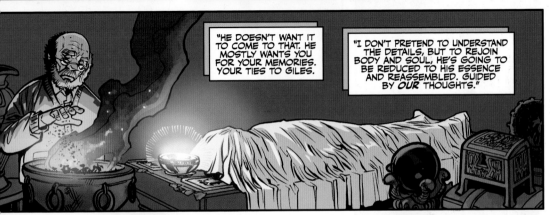

"HE DOESN'T WANT IT TO COME TO THAT. HE MOSTLY WANTS YOU FOR YOUR MEMORIES. YOUR TIES TO GILES."

"I DON'T PRETEND TO UNDERSTAND THE DETAILS, BUT TO REJOIN BODY AND SOUL, HE'S GOING TO BE REDUCED TO HIS ESSENCE AND REASSEMBLED. GUIDED BY *OUR* THOUGHTS."

"'S CRUCIAL WE DON'T .OSE OUR FOCUS, OR HE COULD JUST... DISPERSE.

ANGEL...I REALIZE I CAN APPEAR FLIGHTY AND IMMATURE. BUT I WANT YOU TO LISTEN AND BELIEVE ME WHEN I TELL YOU THIS.

I THINK YOU, OF ALL PEOPLE, WILL UNDERSTAND.

MY SISTER AND I ONCE DESTROYED OUR NEPHEW'S LIFE.

IF WE ARE GIVEN A CHANCE TO RECTIFY THAT DEED...

...THERE IS *NO POWER ON EARTH* THAT IS GOING TO STOP US.

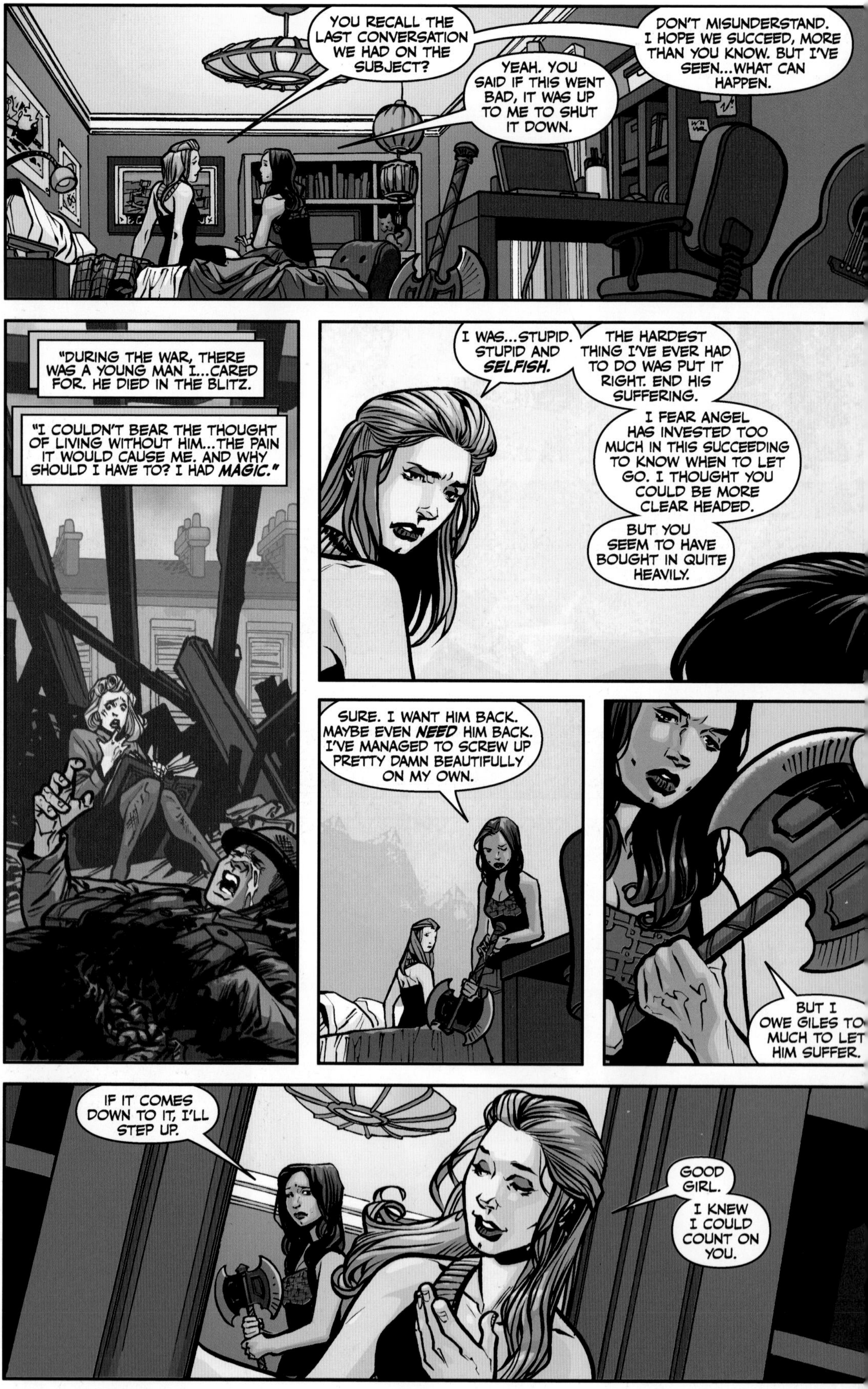
YOU RECALL THE LAST CONVERSATION WE HAD ON THE SUBJECT?
YEAH. YOU SAID IF THIS WENT BAD, IT WAS UP TO ME TO SHUT IT DOWN.
DON'T MISUNDERSTAND. I HOPE WE SUCCEED, MORE THAN YOU KNOW. BUT I'VE SEEN...WHAT CAN HAPPEN.
"DURING THE WAR, THERE WAS A YOUNG MAN I...CARED FOR. HE DIED IN THE BLITZ.
"I COULDN'T BEAR THE THOUGHT OF LIVING WITHOUT HIM...THE PAIN IT WOULD CAUSE ME. AND WHY SHOULD I HAVE TO? I HAD MAGIC."
I WAS...STUPID. STUPID AND SELFISH.
THE HARDEST THING I'VE EVER HAD TO DO WAS PUT IT RIGHT. END HIS SUFFERING.
I FEAR ANGEL HAS INVESTED TOO MUCH IN THIS SUCCEEDING TO KNOW WHEN TO LET GO. I THOUGHT YOU COULD BE MORE CLEAR HEADED.
BUT YOU SEEM TO HAVE BOUGHT IN QUITE HEAVILY.
SURE. I WANT HIM BACK. MAYBE EVEN NEED HIM BACK. I'VE MANAGED TO SCREW UP PRETTY DAMN BEAUTIFULLY ON MY OWN.
BUT I OWE GILES TOO MUCH TO LET HIM SUFFER.
IF IT COMES DOWN TO IT, I'LL STEP UP.
GOOD GIRL.
I KNEW I COULD COUNT ON YOU.

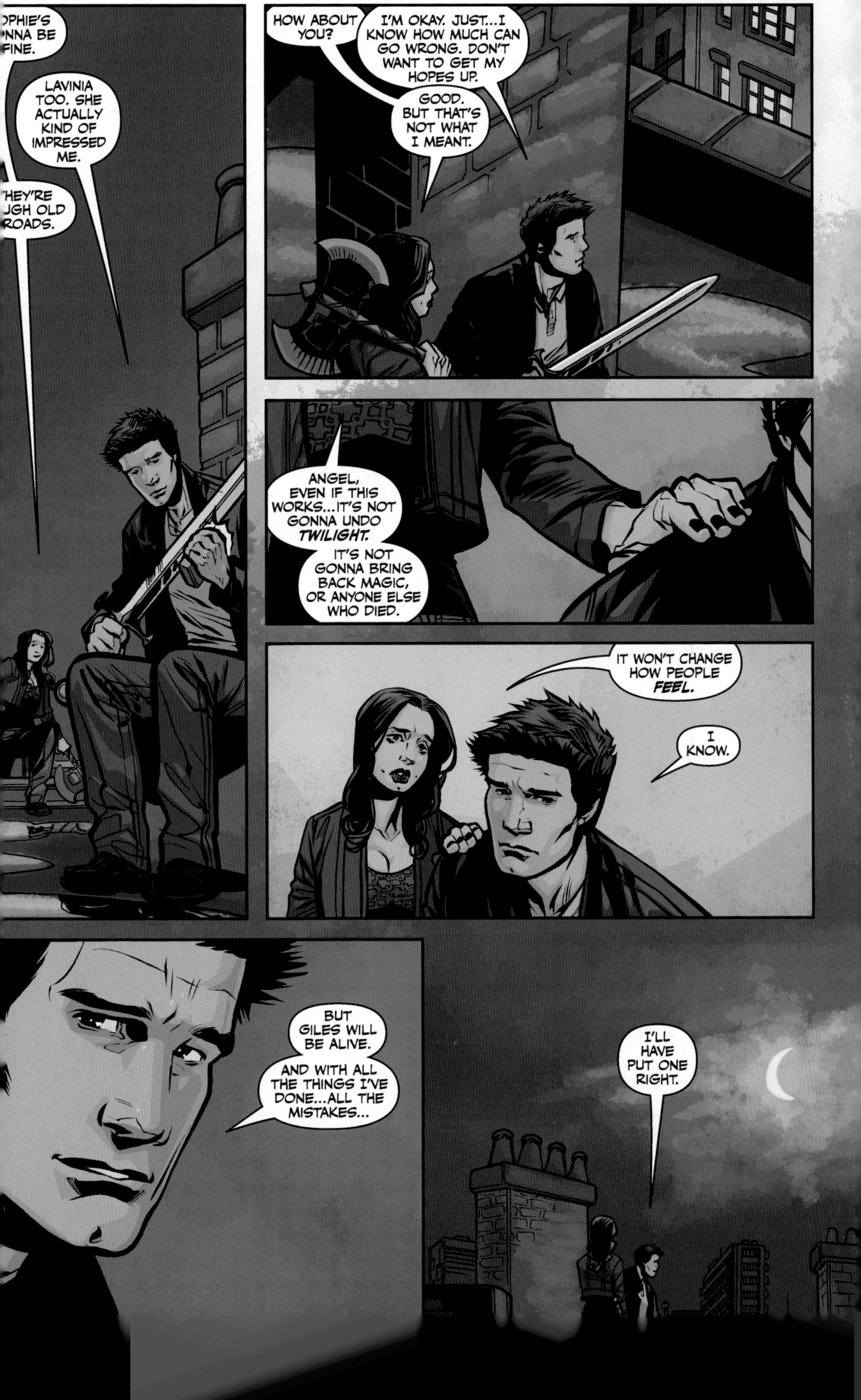
PHIE'S NNA BE FINE.
LAVINIA TOO. SHE ACTUALLY KIND OF IMPRESSED ME.
HEY'RE JGH OLD ROADS.
HOW ABOUT YOU?
I'M OKAY. JUST...I KNOW HOW MUCH CAN GO WRONG. DON'T WANT TO GET MY HOPES UP.
GOOD. BUT THAT'S NOT WHAT I MEANT.
ANGEL, EVEN IF THIS WORKS...IT'S NOT GONNA UNDO *TWILIGHT.*
IT'S NOT GONNA BRING BACK MAGIC, OR ANYONE ELSE WHO DIED.
IT WON'T CHANGE HOW PEOPLE *FEEL.*
I KNOW.
BUT GILES WILL BE ALIVE.
AND WITH ALL THE THINGS I'VE DONE...ALL THE MISTAKES...
I'LL HAVE PUT ONE RIGHT.

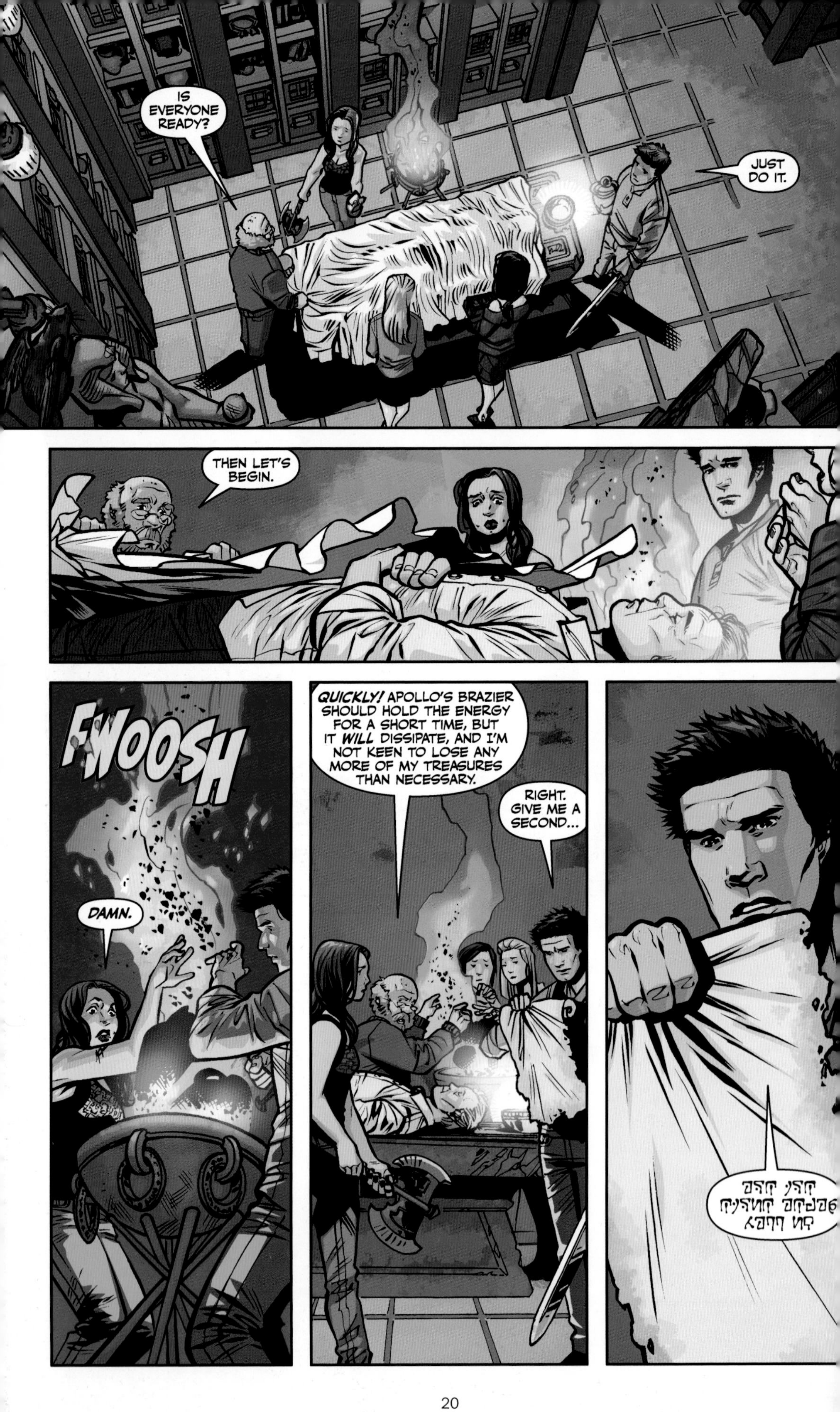
IS EVERYONE READY?
JUST DO IT.
THEN LET'S BEGIN.
FWOOSH
DAMN.
QUICKLY! APOLLO'S BRAZIER SHOULD HOLD THE ENERGY FOR A SHORT TIME, BUT IT WILL DISSIPATE, AND I'M NOT KEEN TO LOSE ANY MORE OF MY TREASURES THAN NECESSARY.
RIGHT. GIVE ME A SECOND...

SOMETHING'S DEFINITELY HAPPENING.

GNNH!

I...THINK THAT WAS SUPPOSED TO KILL ME.

GOOD. NOW GIVE ME THAT. YOUR ARAMAIC IS APPALLING.

I...I THINK IT'S WORKING.

I THINK IT MIGHT ACTUALLY BE--

SKRESSHH

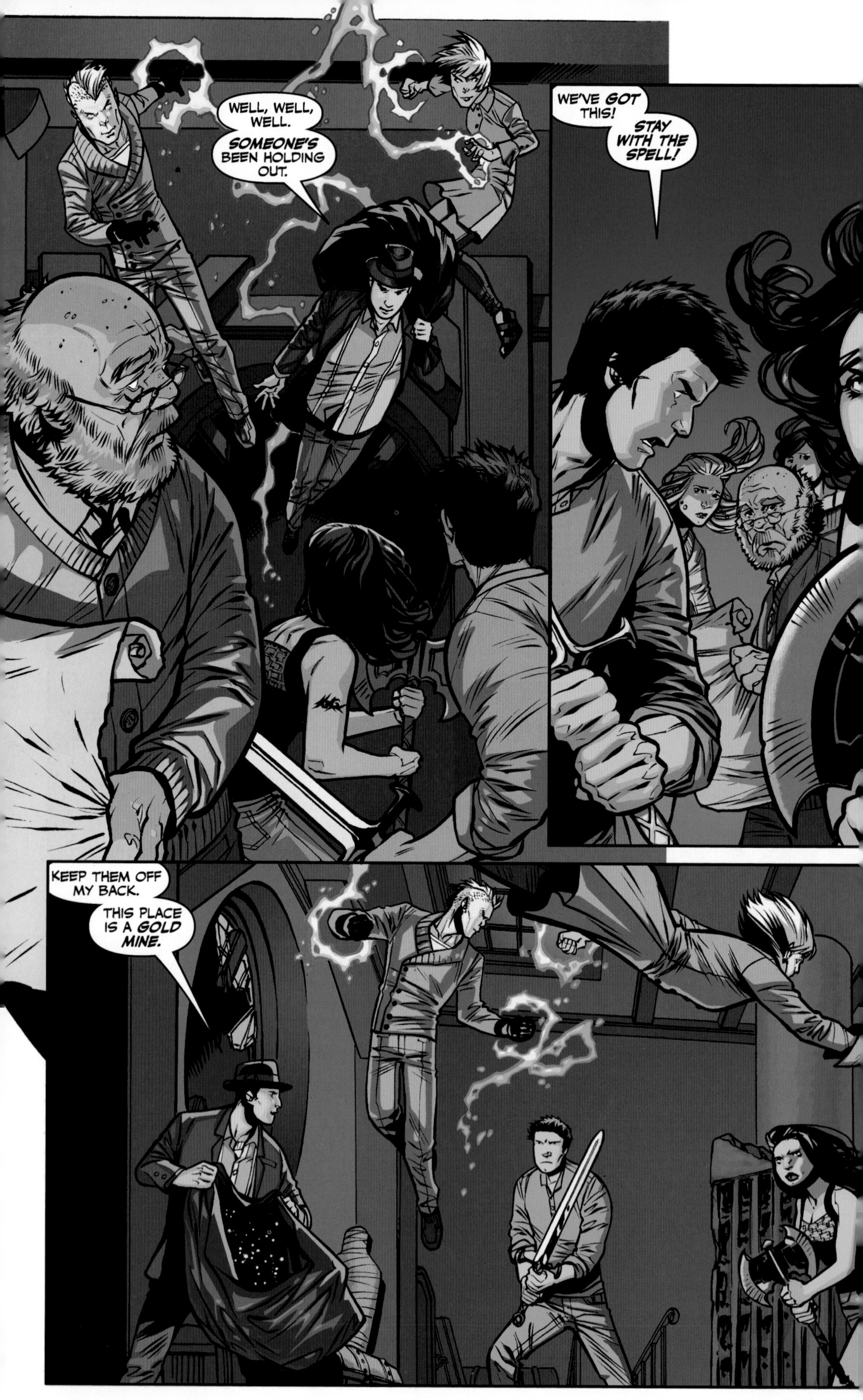
WELL, WELL, WELL. *SOMEONE'S* BEEN HOLDING OUT.
WE'VE *GOT* THIS! *STAY WITH THE SPELL!*
KEEP THEM OFF MY BACK.
THIS PLACE IS A *GOLD MINE.*

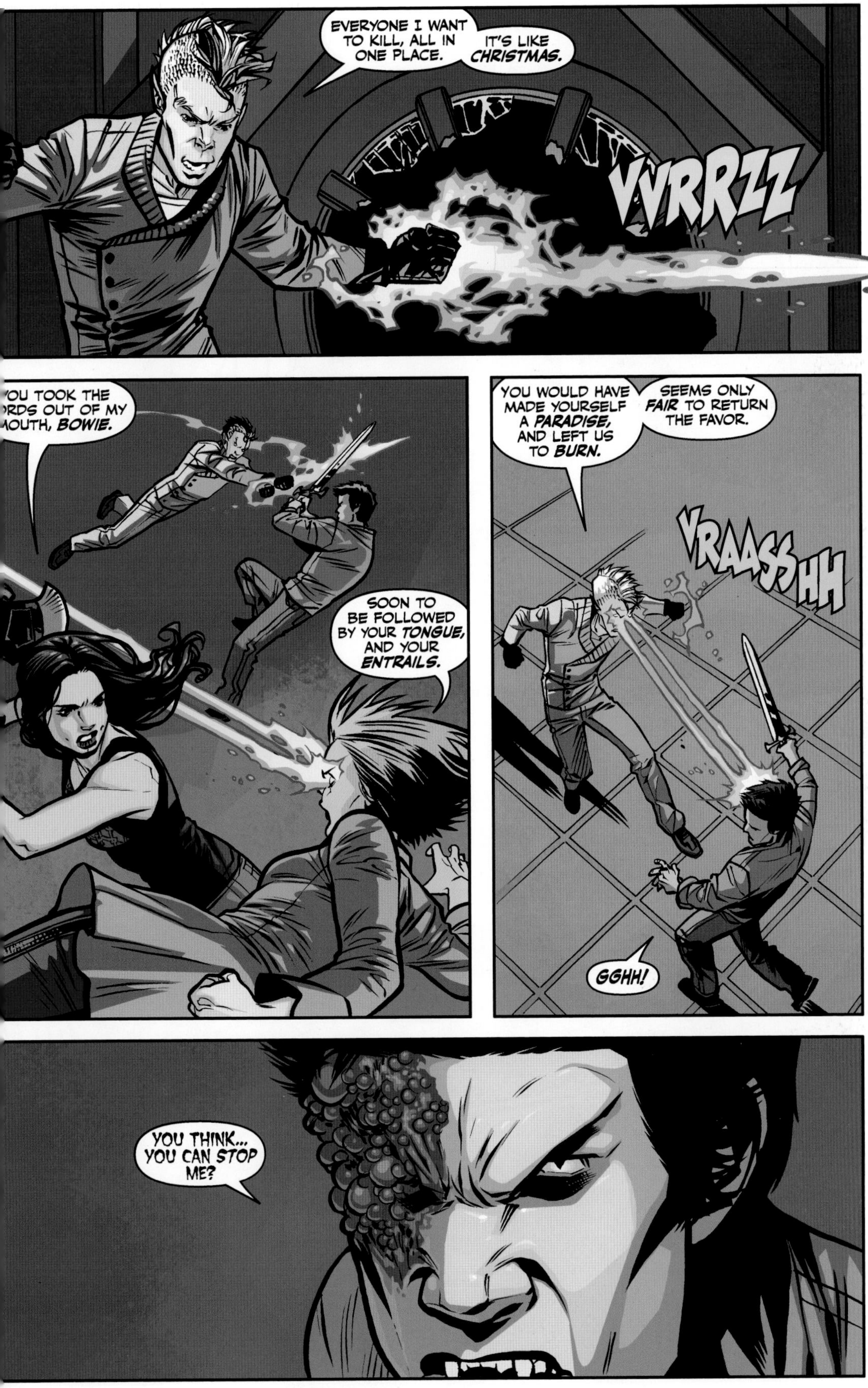
EVERYONE I WANT TO KILL, ALL IN ONE PLACE.
IT'S LIKE CHRISTMAS.
VVRRZZ
YOU TOOK THE ORDS OUT OF MY MOUTH, BOWIE.
SOON TO BE FOLLOWED BY YOUR TONGUE, AND YOUR ENTRAILS.
YOU WOULD HAVE MADE YOURSELF A PARADISE, AND LEFT US TO BURN.
SEEMS ONLY FAIR TO RETURN THE FAVOR.
VRAASSHH
GGHH!
YOU THINK... YOU CAN STOP ME?

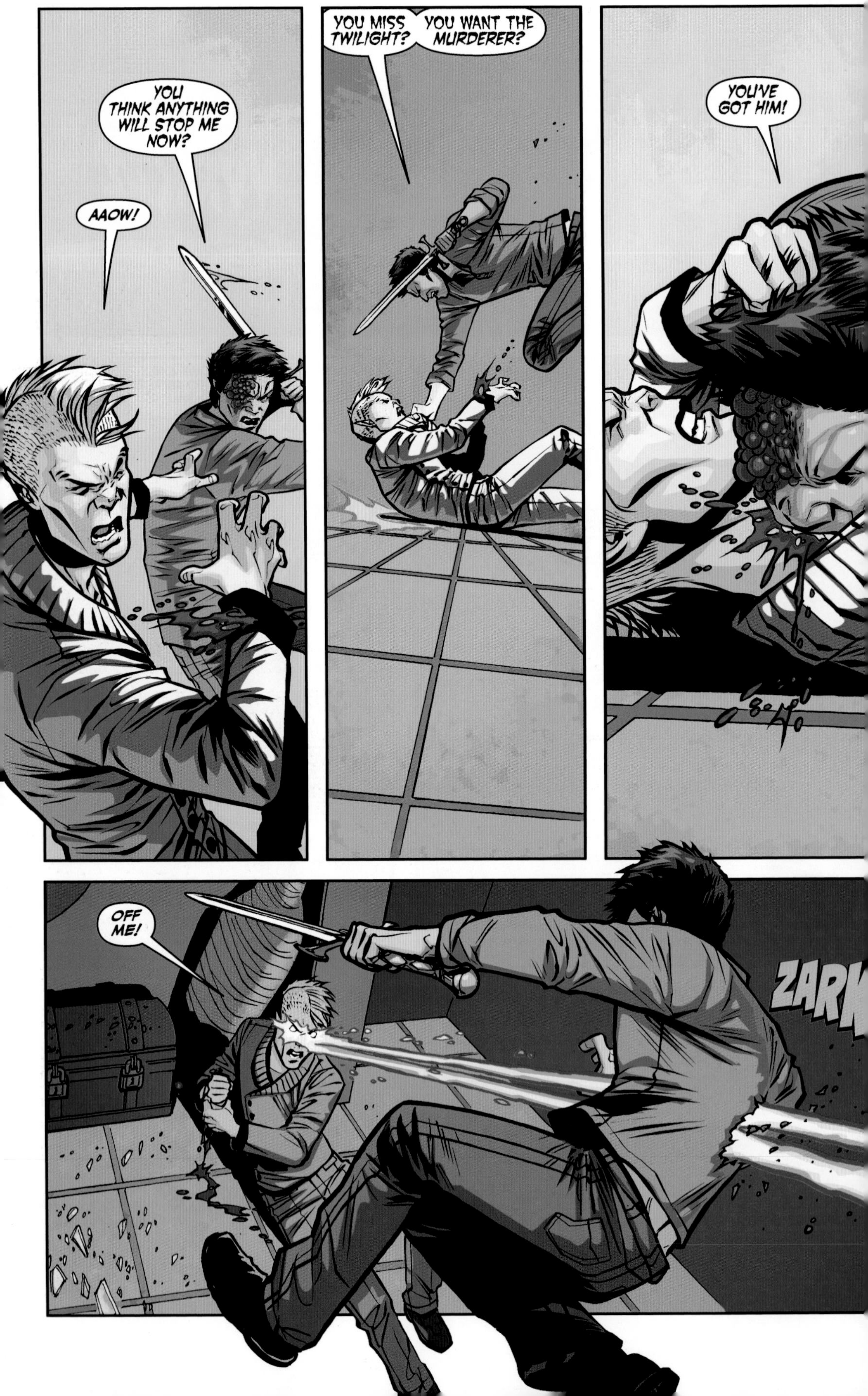
YOU THINK ANYTHING WILL STOP ME NOW?
AAOW!
YOU MISS TWILIGHT?
YOU WANT THE MURDERER?
YOU'VE GOT HIM!
OFF ME!
ZARK

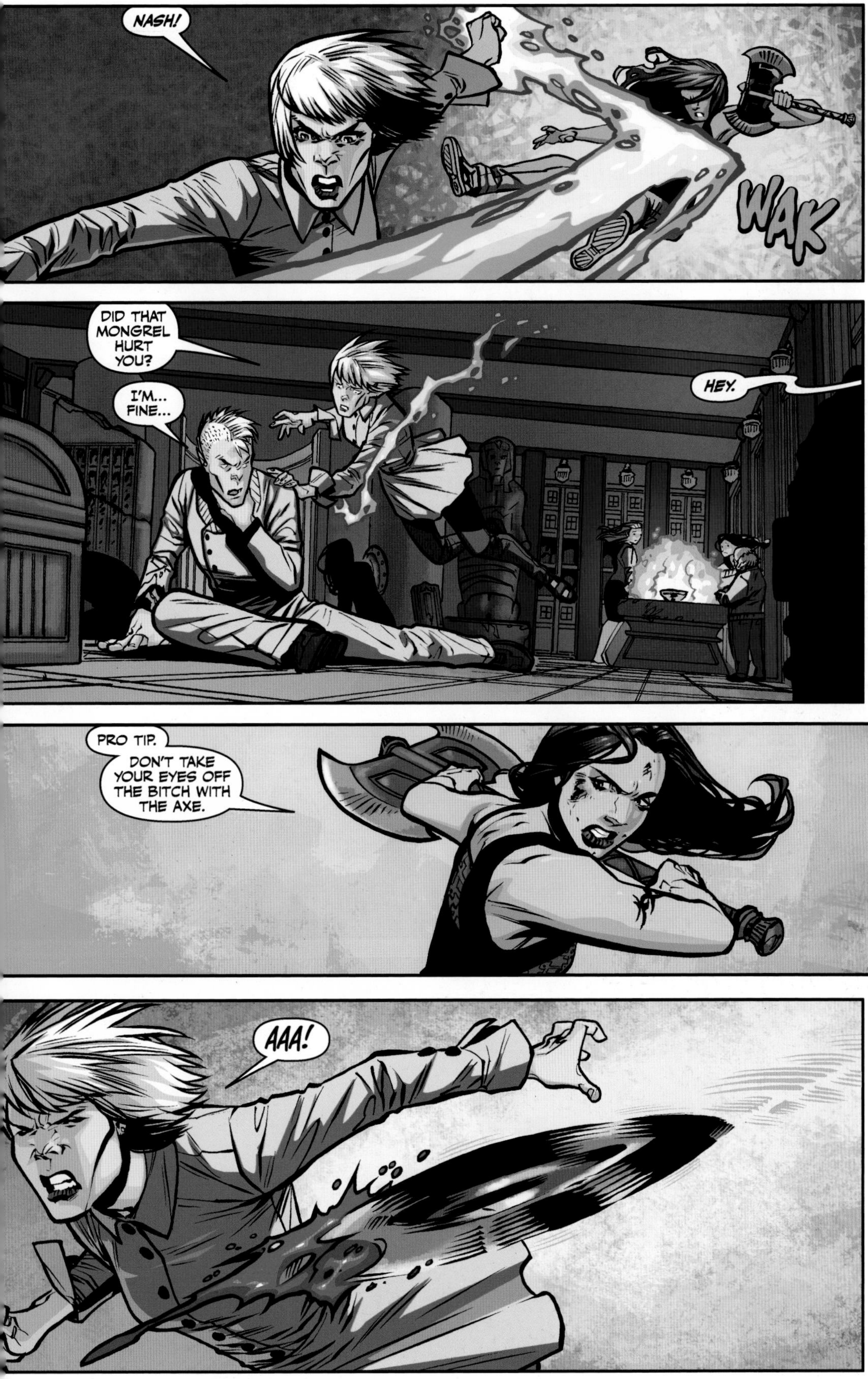

NASH!
WAK
DID THAT MONGREL HURT YOU?
I'M... FINE...
HEY.
PRO TIP.
DON'T TAKE YOUR EYES OFF THE BITCH WITH THE AXE.
AAA!

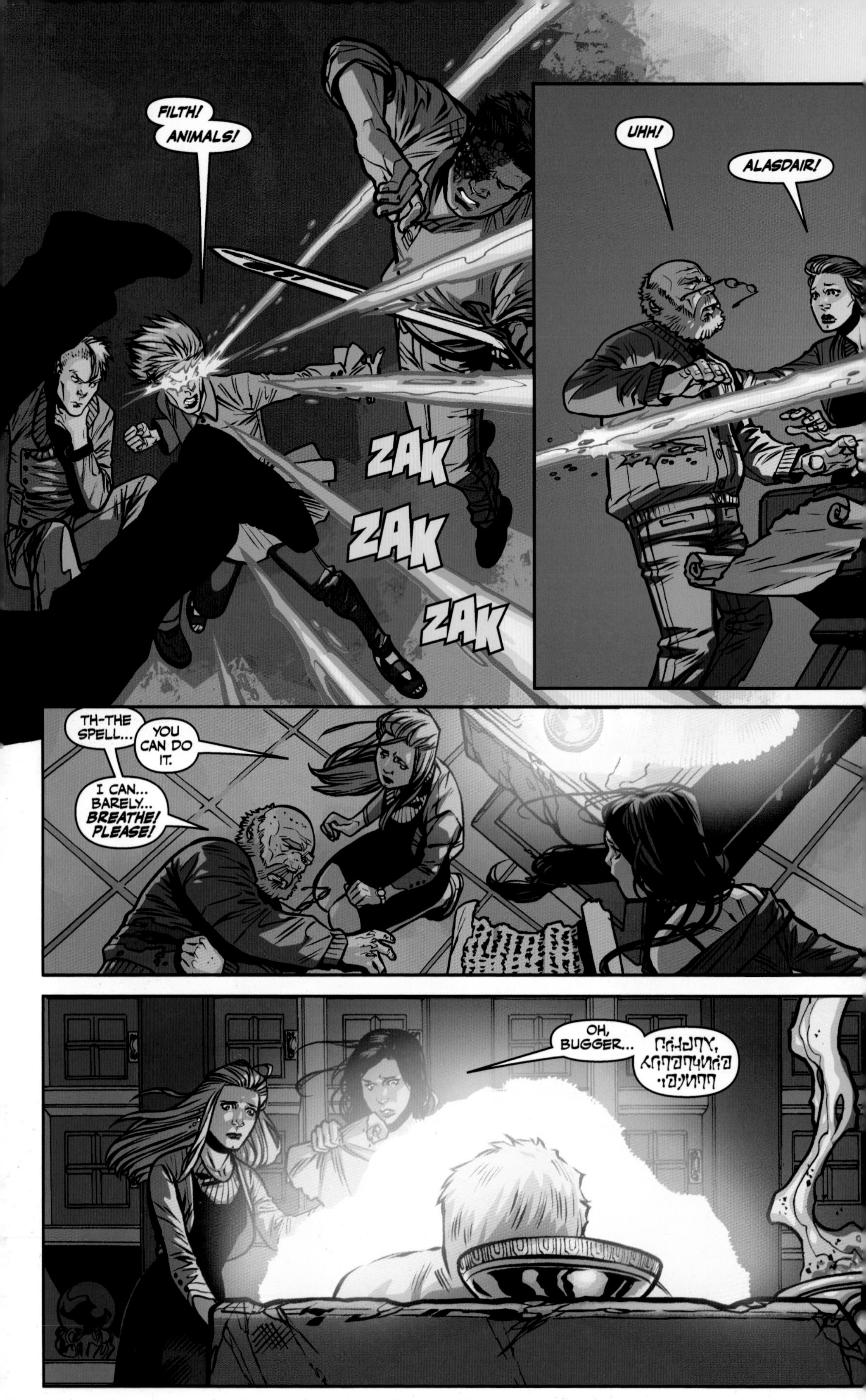
FILTH! ANIMALS!
ZAK
ZAK
ZAK
UHH!
ALASDAIR!
TH-THE SPELL...
YOU CAN DO IT.
I CAN... BARELY... BREATHE! PLEASE!
OH, BUGGER...

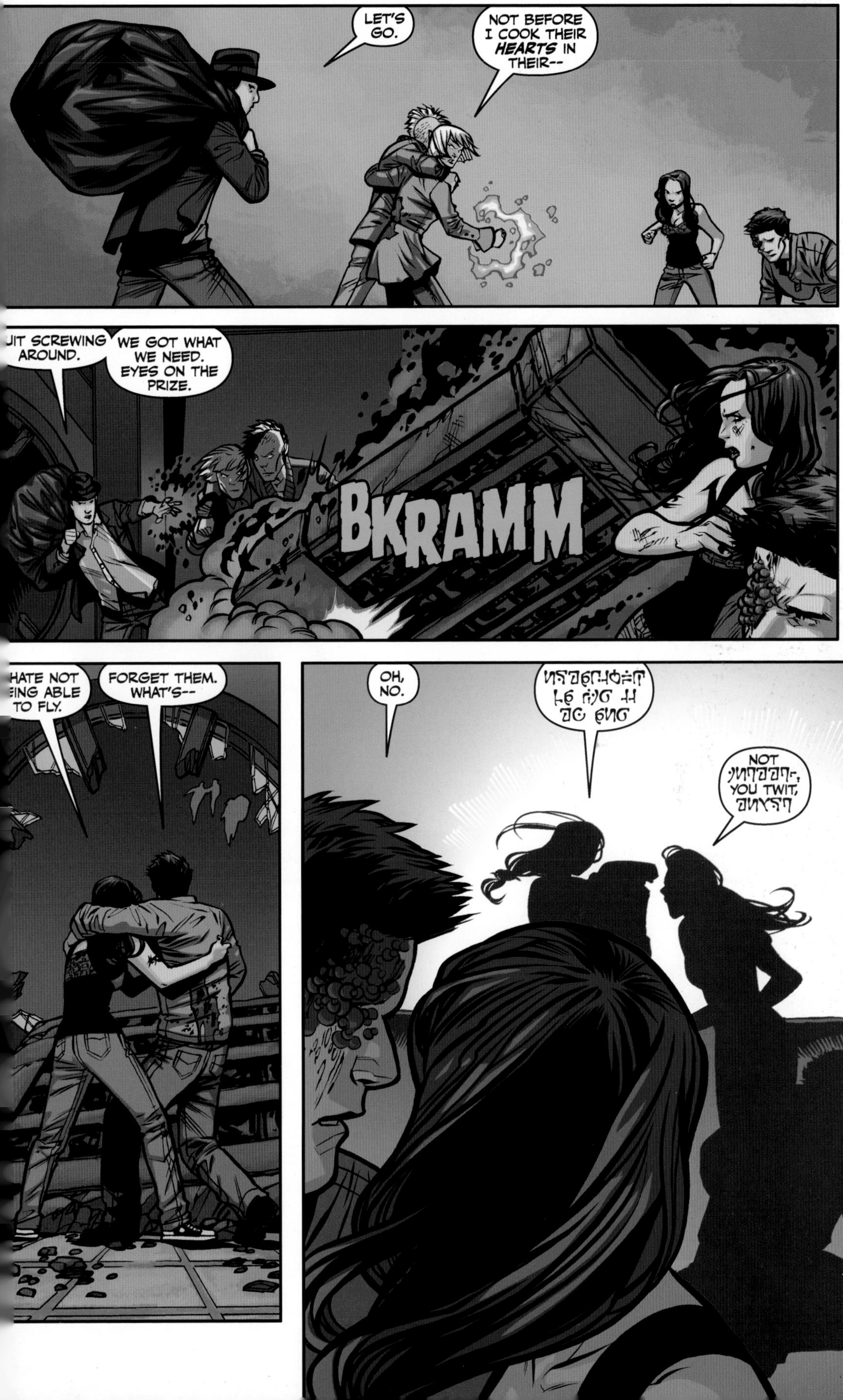
LET'S GO.
NOT BEFORE I COOK THEIR **HEARTS** IN THEIR--
UIT SCREWING AROUND.
WE GOT WHAT WE NEED. EYES ON THE PRIZE.
BKRAMM
HATE NOT EING ABLE TO FLY.
FORGET THEM. WHAT'S--
OH, NO.
NOT
YOU TWIT,

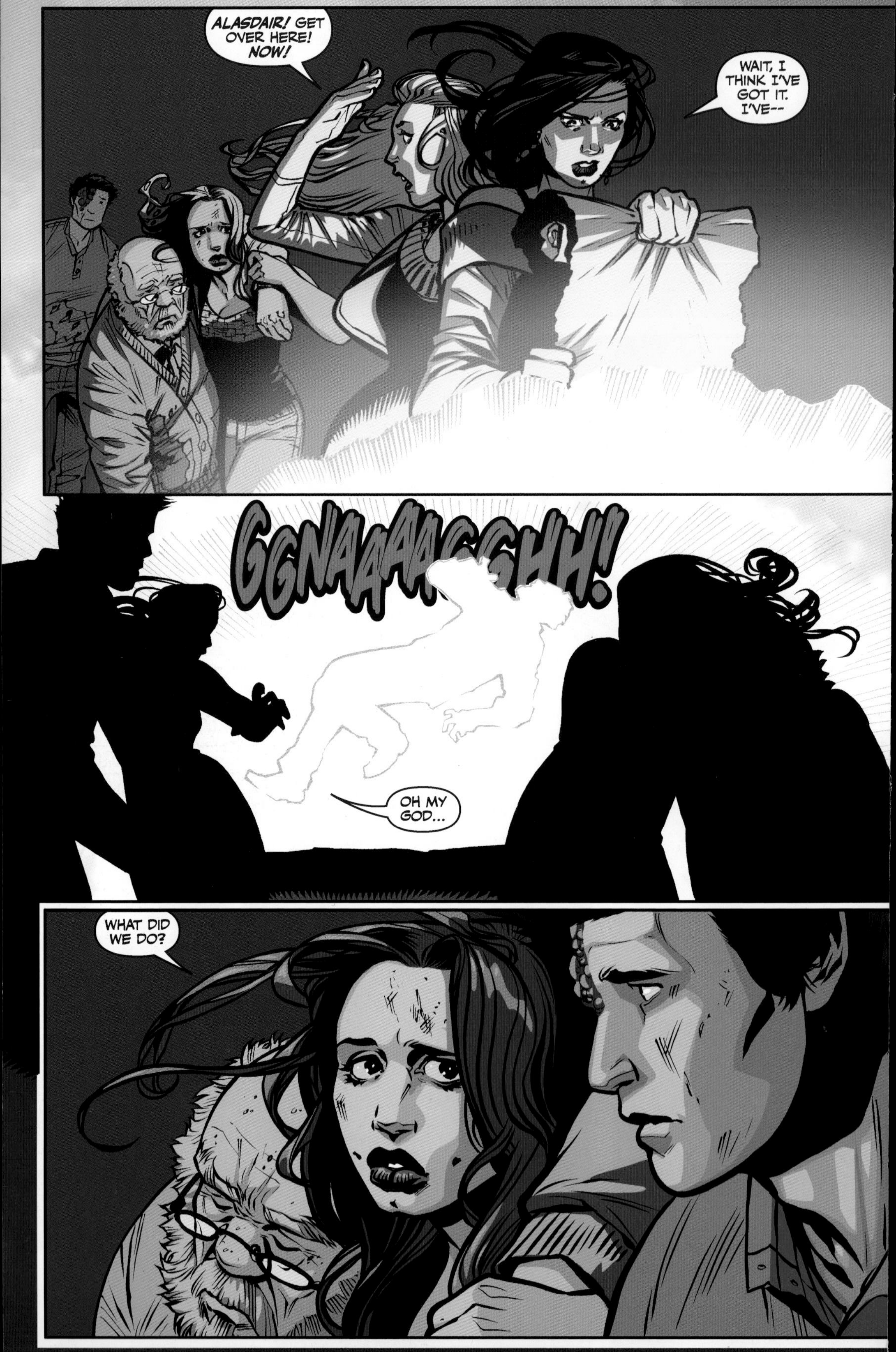
ALASDAIR! GET OVER HERE! NOW!
WAIT, I THINK I'VE GOT IT. I'VE--
GGNAAAAAGGHH!
OH MY GOD...
WHAT DID WE DO?

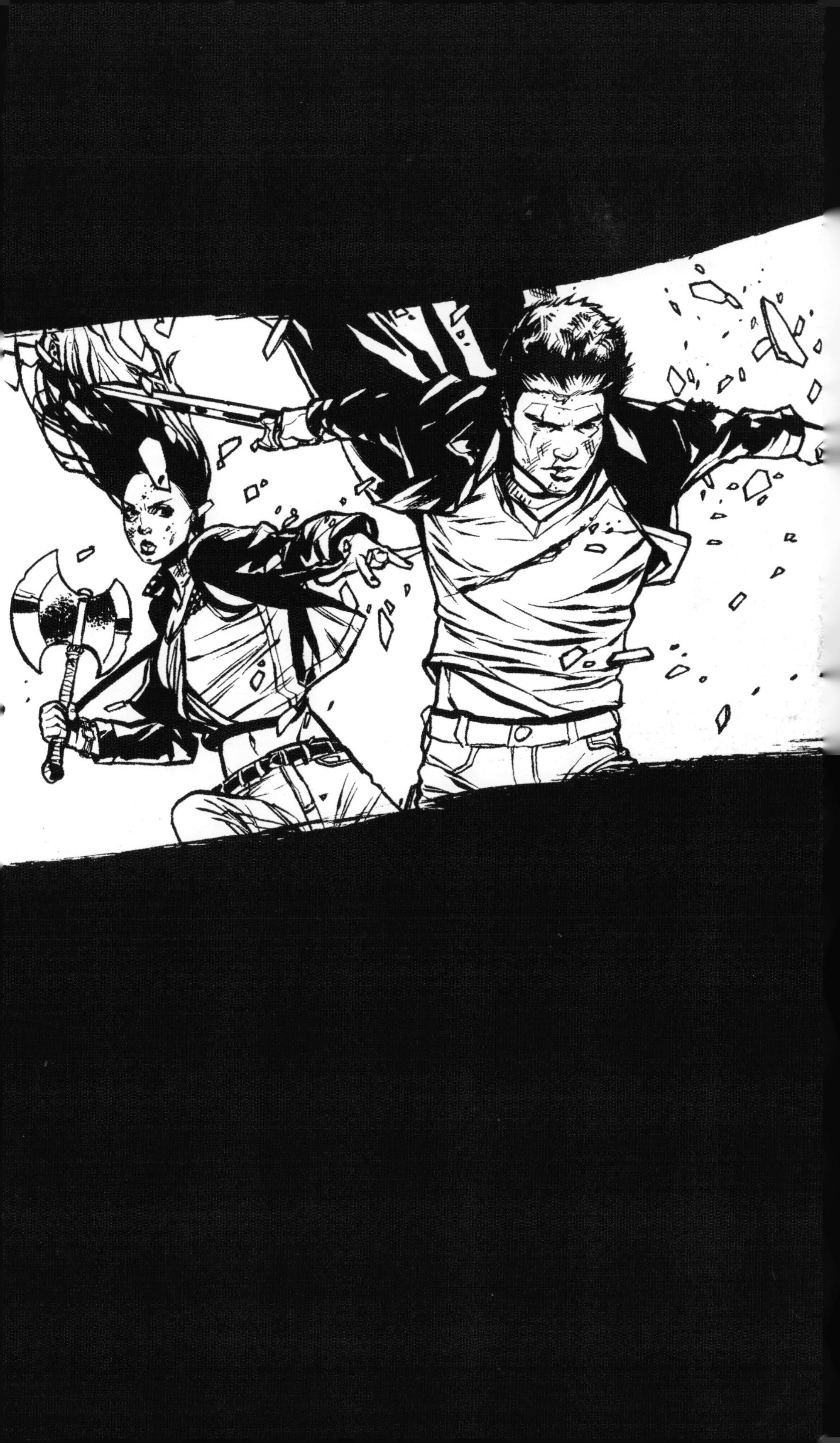

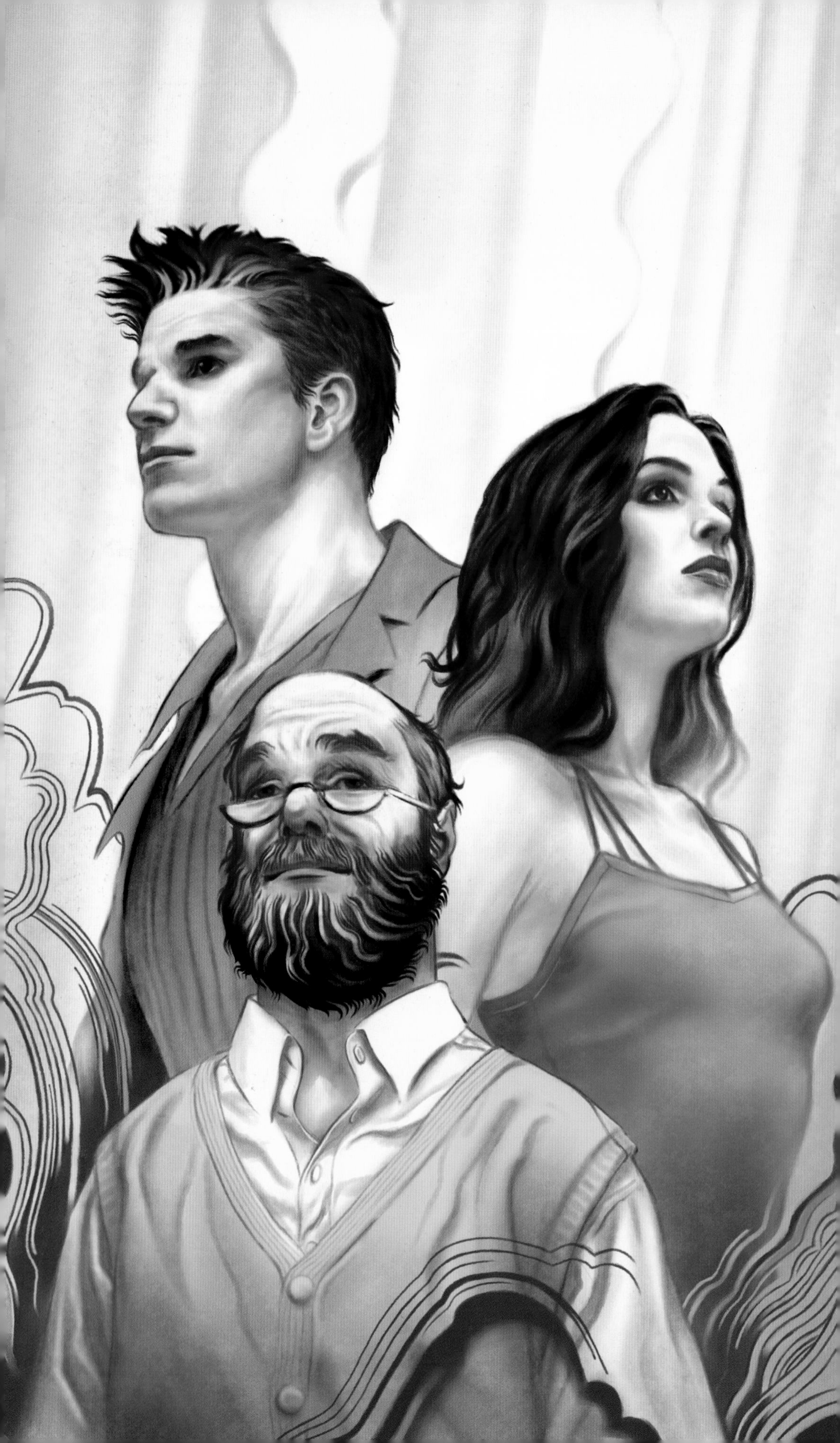

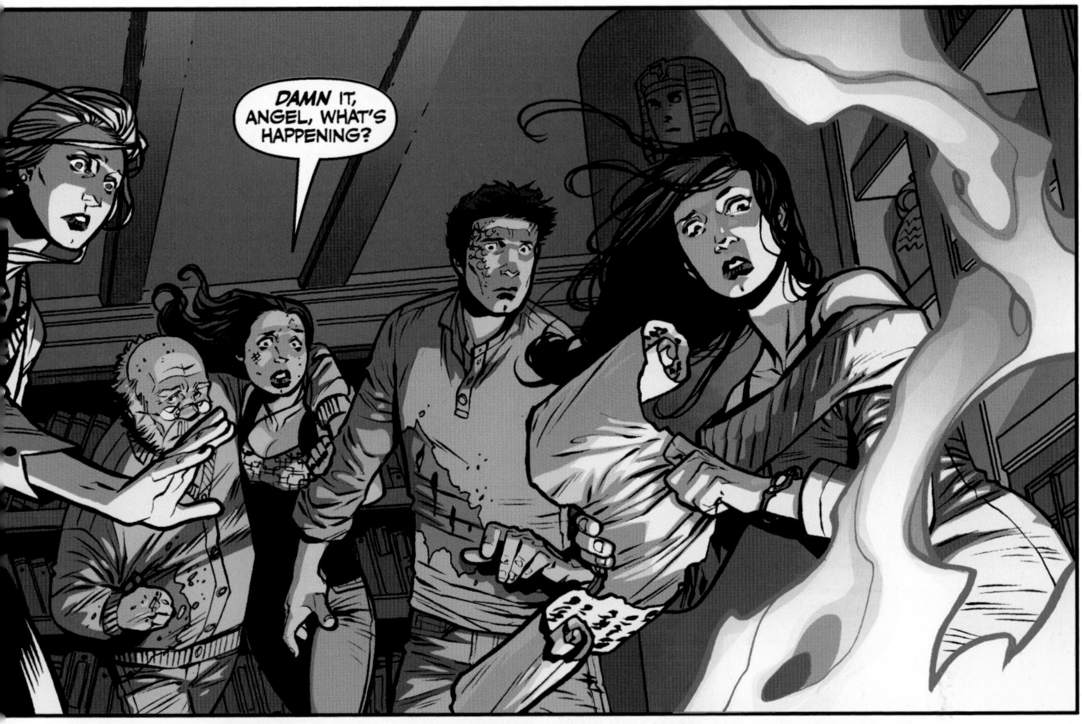
DAMN IT, ANGEL, WHAT'S HAPPENING?

WHAT YOU WANT, NOT WHAT YOU NEED

PART 2

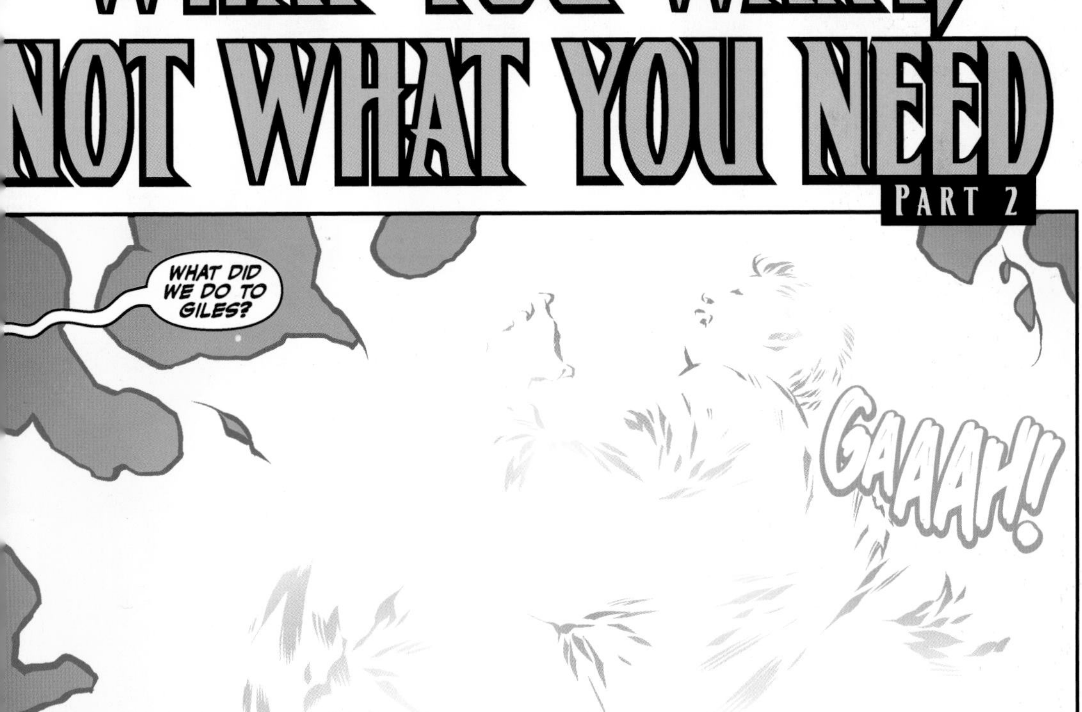
WHAT DID WE DO TO GILES?
GAAAH!

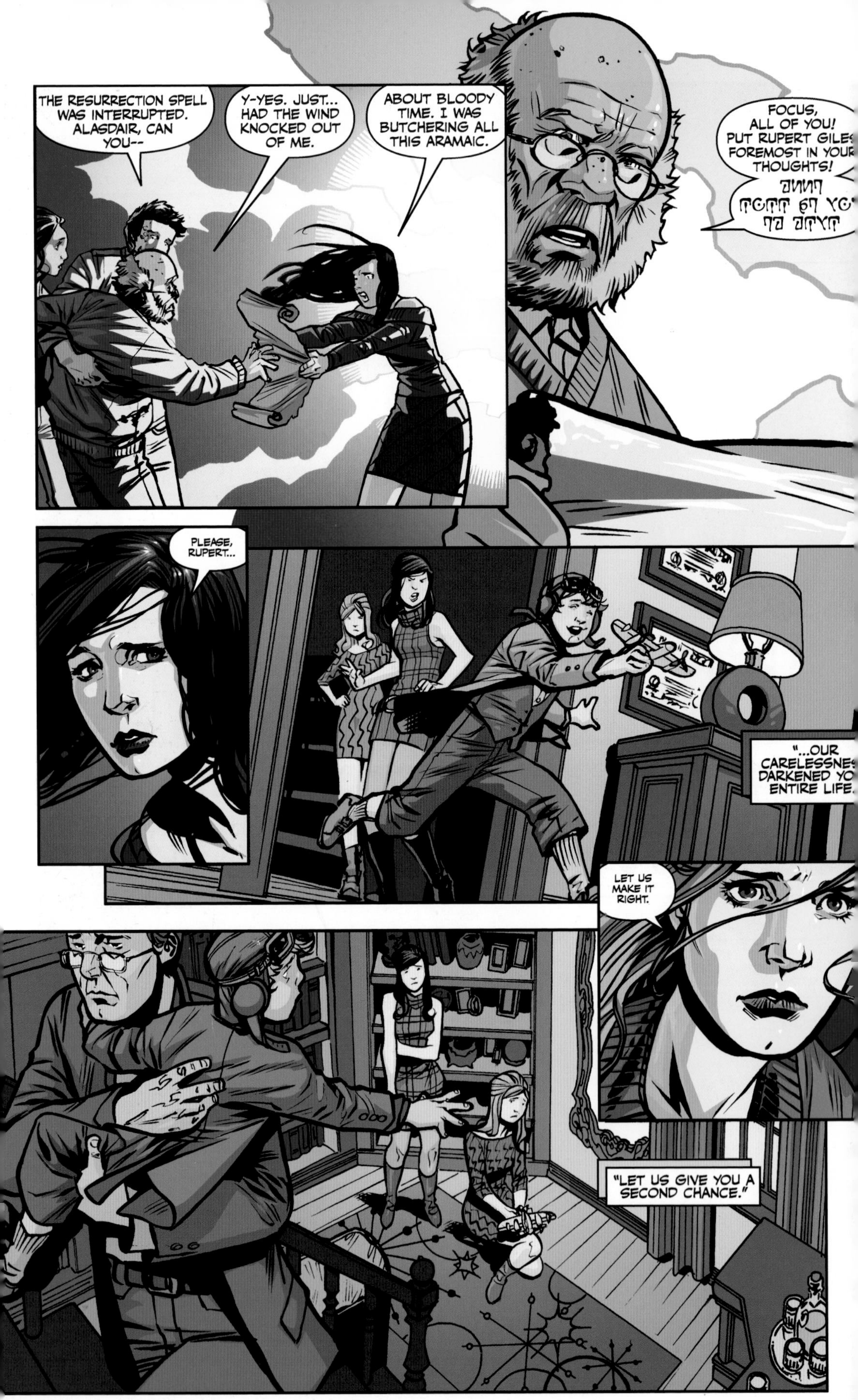
THE RESURRECTION SPELL WAS INTERRUPTED. ALASDAIR, CAN YOU--
Y-YES. JUST... HAD THE WIND KNOCKED OUT OF ME.
ABOUT BLOODY TIME. I WAS BUTCHERING ALL THIS ARAMAIC.
FOCUS, ALL OF YOU! PUT RUPERT GILES FOREMOST IN YOUR THOUGHTS!
PLEASE, RUPERT...
"...OUR CARELESSNES DARKENED YO ENTIRE LIFE.
LET US MAKE IT RIGHT.
"LET US GIVE YOU A SECOND CHANCE."

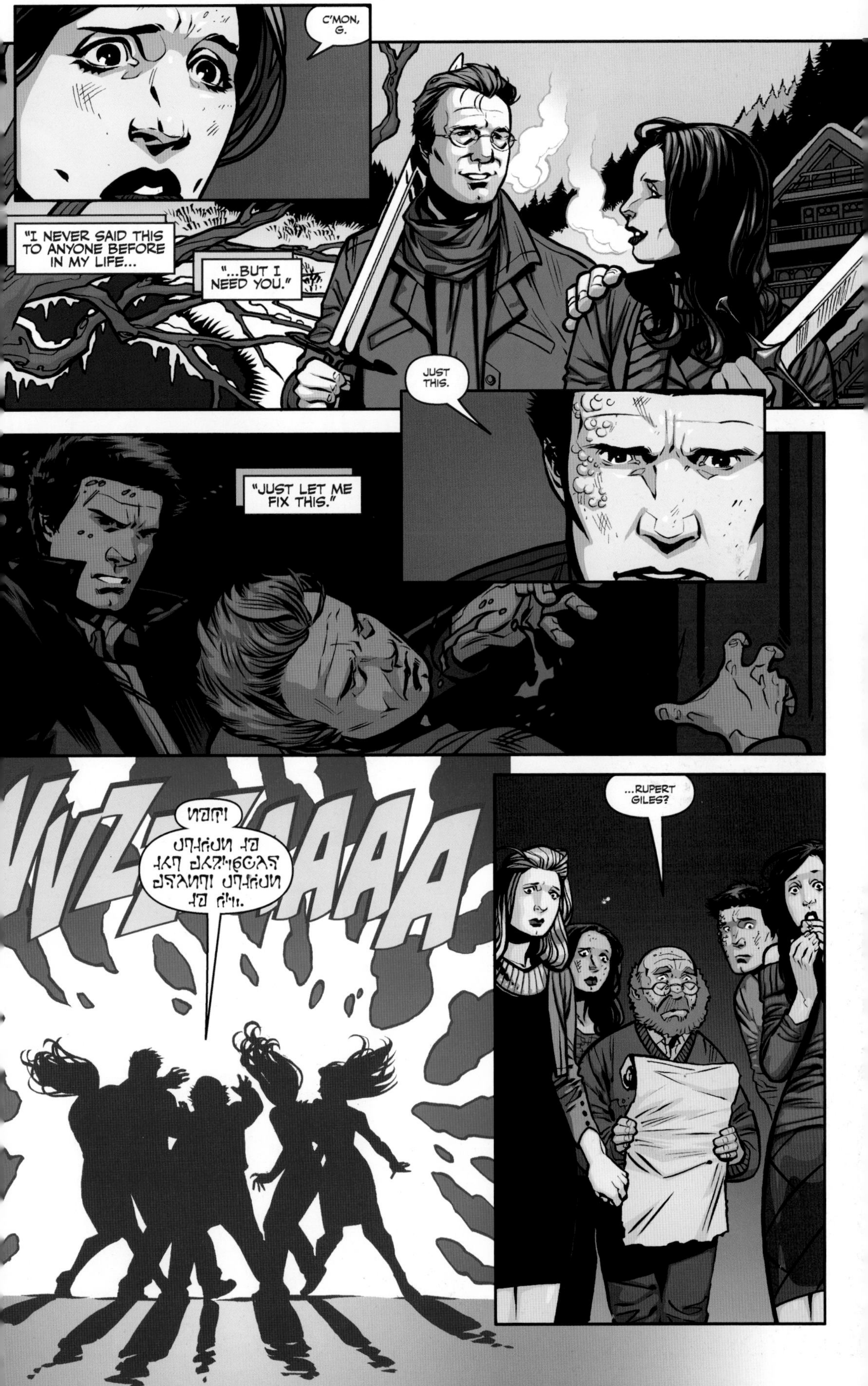
C'MON, G.
"I NEVER SAID THIS TO ANYONE BEFORE IN MY LIFE...
"...BUT I NEED YOU."
JUST THIS.
"JUST LET ME FIX THIS."
...RUPERT GILES?

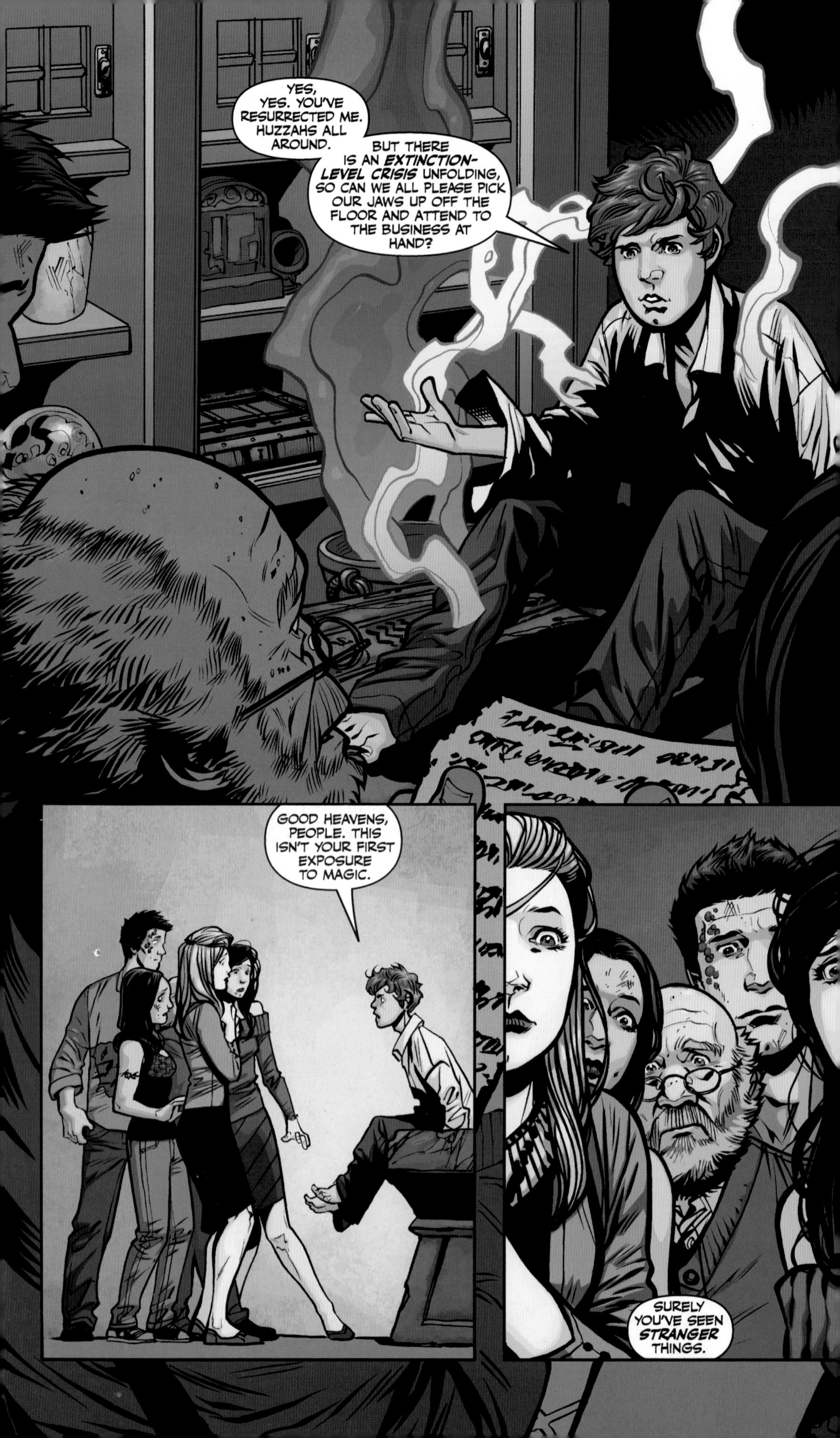
YES, YES. YOU'VE RESURRECTED ME. HUZZAHS ALL AROUND.
BUT THERE IS AN *EXTINCTION-LEVEL CRISIS* UNFOLDING, SO CAN WE ALL PLEASE PICK OUR JAWS UP OFF THE FLOOR AND ATTEND TO THE BUSINESS AT HAND?
GOOD HEAVENS, PEOPLE. THIS ISN'T YOUR FIRST EXPOSURE TO MAGIC.
SURELY YOU'VE SEEN *STRANGER* THINGS.

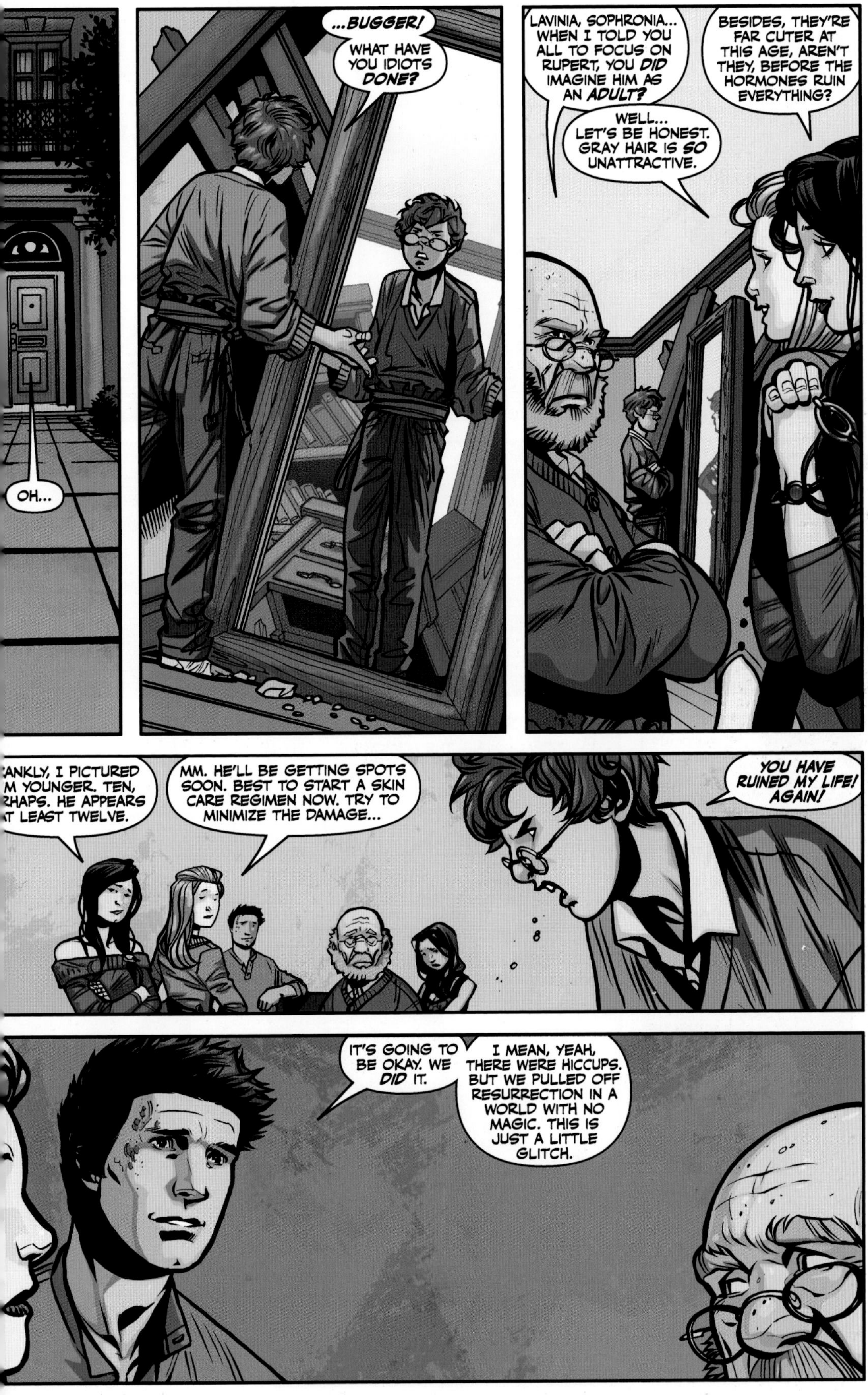
OH...
...BUGGER!
WHAT HAVE YOU IDIOTS DONE?
LAVINIA, SOPHRONIA... WHEN I TOLD YOU ALL TO FOCUS ON RUPERT, YOU DID IMAGINE HIM AS AN ADULT?
WELL... LET'S BE HONEST. GRAY HAIR IS SO UNATTRACTIVE.
BESIDES, THEY'RE FAR CUTER AT THIS AGE, AREN'T THEY, BEFORE THE HORMONES RUIN EVERYTHING?
ANKLY, I PICTURED M YOUNGER. TEN, RHAPS. HE APPEARS T LEAST TWELVE.
MM. HE'LL BE GETTING SPOTS SOON. BEST TO START A SKIN CARE REGIMEN NOW. TRY TO MINIMIZE THE DAMAGE...
YOU HAVE RUINED MY LIFE! AGAIN!
IT'S GOING TO BE OKAY. WE DID IT.
I MEAN, YEAH, THERE WERE HICCUPS. BUT WE PULLED OFF RESURRECTION IN A WORLD WITH NO MAGIC. THIS IS JUST A LITTLE GLITCH.

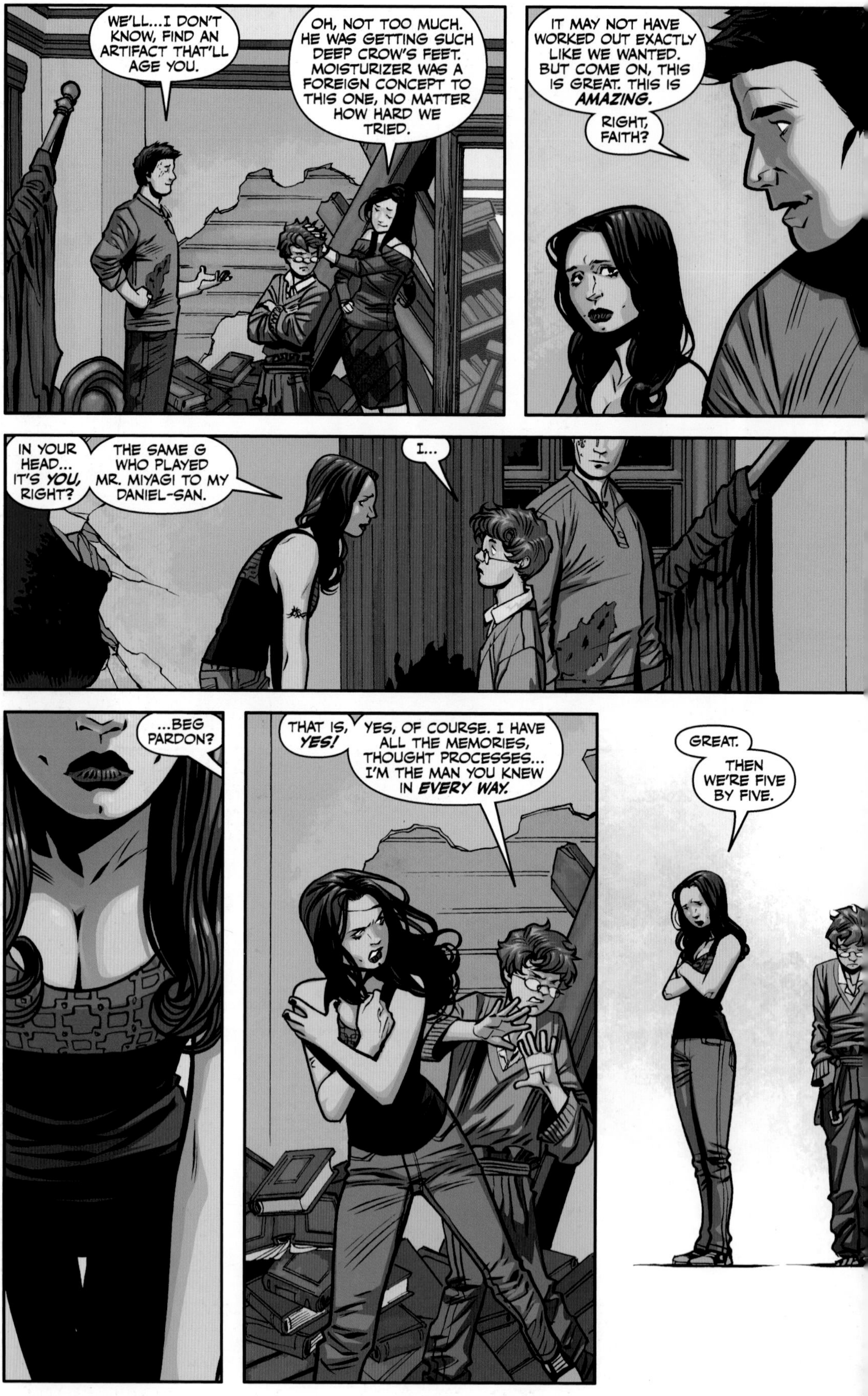
WE'LL...I DON'T KNOW, FIND AN ARTIFACT THAT'LL AGE YOU.
OH, NOT TOO MUCH. HE WAS GETTING SUCH DEEP CROW'S FEET. MOISTURIZER WAS A FOREIGN CONCEPT TO THIS ONE, NO MATTER HOW HARD WE TRIED.
IT MAY NOT HAVE WORKED OUT EXACTLY LIKE WE WANTED. BUT COME ON, THIS IS GREAT. THIS IS AMAZING.
RIGHT, FAITH?
IN YOUR HEAD... IT'S YOU, RIGHT?
THE SAME G WHO PLAYED MR. MIYAGI TO MY DANIEL-SAN.
I...
...BEG PARDON?
THAT IS, YES!
YES, OF COURSE. I HAVE ALL THE MEMORIES, THOUGHT PROCESSES... I'M THE MAN YOU KNEW IN EVERY WAY.
GREAT.
THEN WE'RE FIVE BY FIVE.

SORRY. I KNOW THIS IS HARD FOR YOU. LIKE BUFFY, WHEN SHE CAME BACK.

AT PEACE, THEN ALL OF A SUDDEN--

BUFFY WAS IN *HEAVEN.* YANKED FROM A STATE OF PARADISE BACK INTO A WORLD OF PAIN. THAT DID NOT HAPPEN TO ME.

I WAS ALTERNATELY IN THRALL TO A *DEMON* AND TRAPPED WITHIN *YOU,* CAPTIVE AUDIENCE TO A CENTURY OF *ATROCITIES* AND YOUR SCHIZOPHRENIC MIX OF GUILT AND DELIGHT OVER THEM.

NO, I WOULD HAVE BEEN QUITE GRATEFUL TO YOU FOR TAKING ME AWAY FROM ALL THAT...

...IF NOT FOR THE FACT THAT YOU *KILLED* ME IN THE FIRST PLACE, THEN RESURRECTED ME USING *OBSCENE SORCERY* THE LIKES OF WHICH I'D *NEVER* CONDONE--

--WHILE THERE'S AN *APOCALYPTIC CRISIS* YOU SHOULD BE ATTENDING TO INSTEAD! BUT PUTTING ALL THAT AND EVERYTHING *ELSE* YOU'VE DONE TO ME ASIDE FOR A MOMENT...

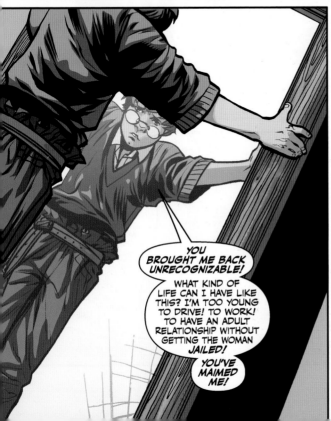

YOU BROUGHT ME BACK UNRECOGNIZABLE!

WHAT KIND OF LIFE CAN I HAVE LIKE THIS? I'M TOO YOUNG TO DRIVE! TO WORK! TO HAVE AN ADULT RELATIONSHIP WITHOUT GETTING THE WOMAN *JAILED!*

YOU'VE MAIMED ME!

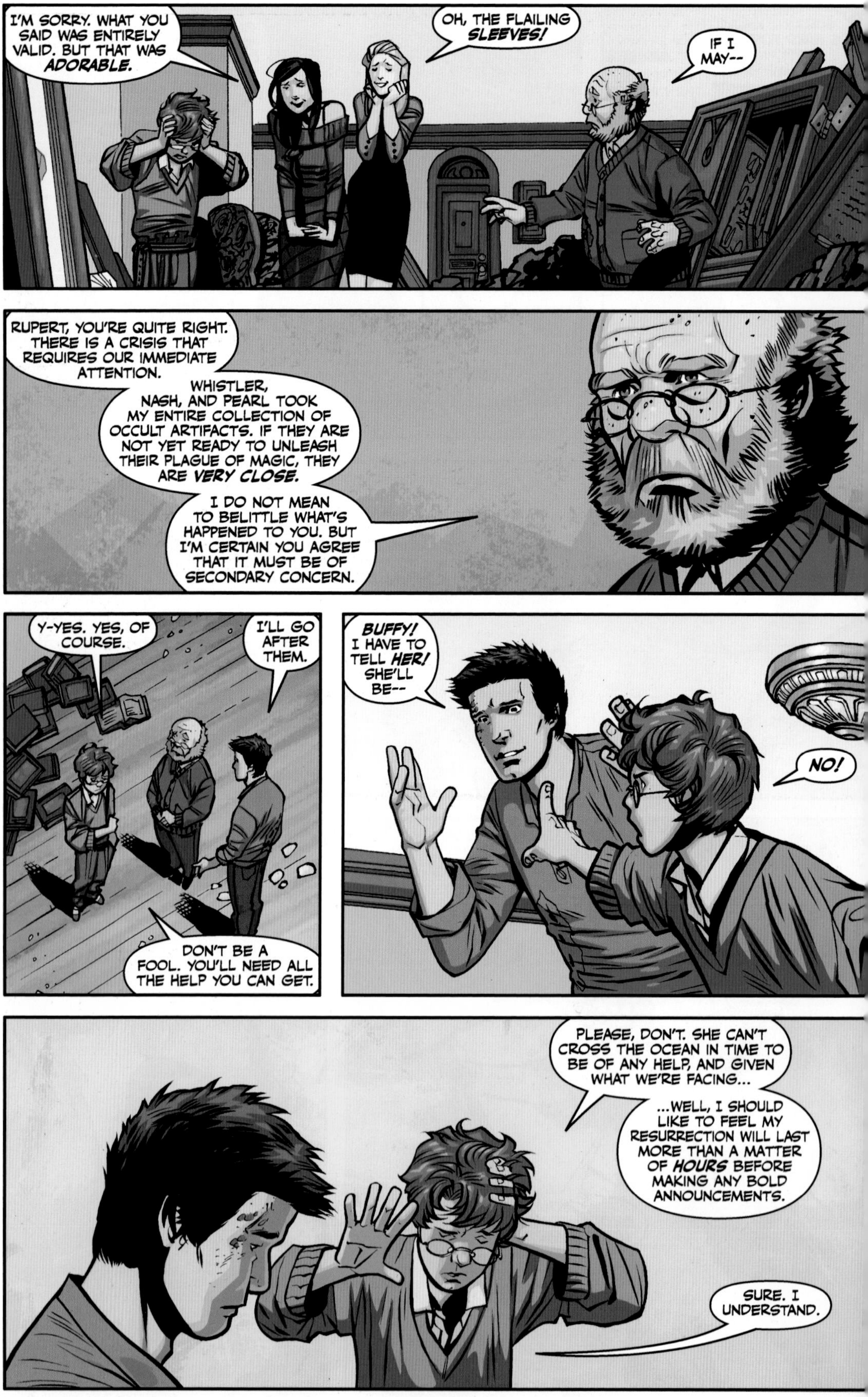
I'M SORRY. WHAT YOU SAID WAS ENTIRELY VALID. BUT THAT WAS *ADORABLE.*
OH, THE FLAILING *SLEEVES!*
IF I MAY--
RUPERT, YOU'RE QUITE RIGHT. THERE IS A CRISIS THAT REQUIRES OUR IMMEDIATE ATTENTION.
WHISTLER, NASH, AND PEARL TOOK MY ENTIRE COLLECTION OF OCCULT ARTIFACTS. IF THEY ARE NOT YET READY TO UNLEASH THEIR PLAGUE OF MAGIC, THEY ARE *VERY CLOSE.*
I DO NOT MEAN TO BELITTLE WHAT'S HAPPENED TO YOU. BUT I'M CERTAIN YOU AGREE THAT IT MUST BE OF SECONDARY CONCERN.
Y-YES. YES, OF COURSE.
I'LL GO AFTER THEM.
DON'T BE A FOOL. YOU'LL NEED ALL THE HELP YOU CAN GET.
BUFFY! I HAVE TO TELL *HER!* SHE'LL BE--
NO!
PLEASE, DON'T. SHE CAN'T CROSS THE OCEAN IN TIME TO BE OF ANY HELP, AND GIVEN WHAT WE'RE FACING...
...WELL, I SHOULD LIKE TO FEEL MY RESURRECTION WILL LAST MORE THAN A MATTER OF *HOURS* BEFORE MAKING ANY BOLD ANNOUNCEMENTS.
SURE. I UNDERSTAND.

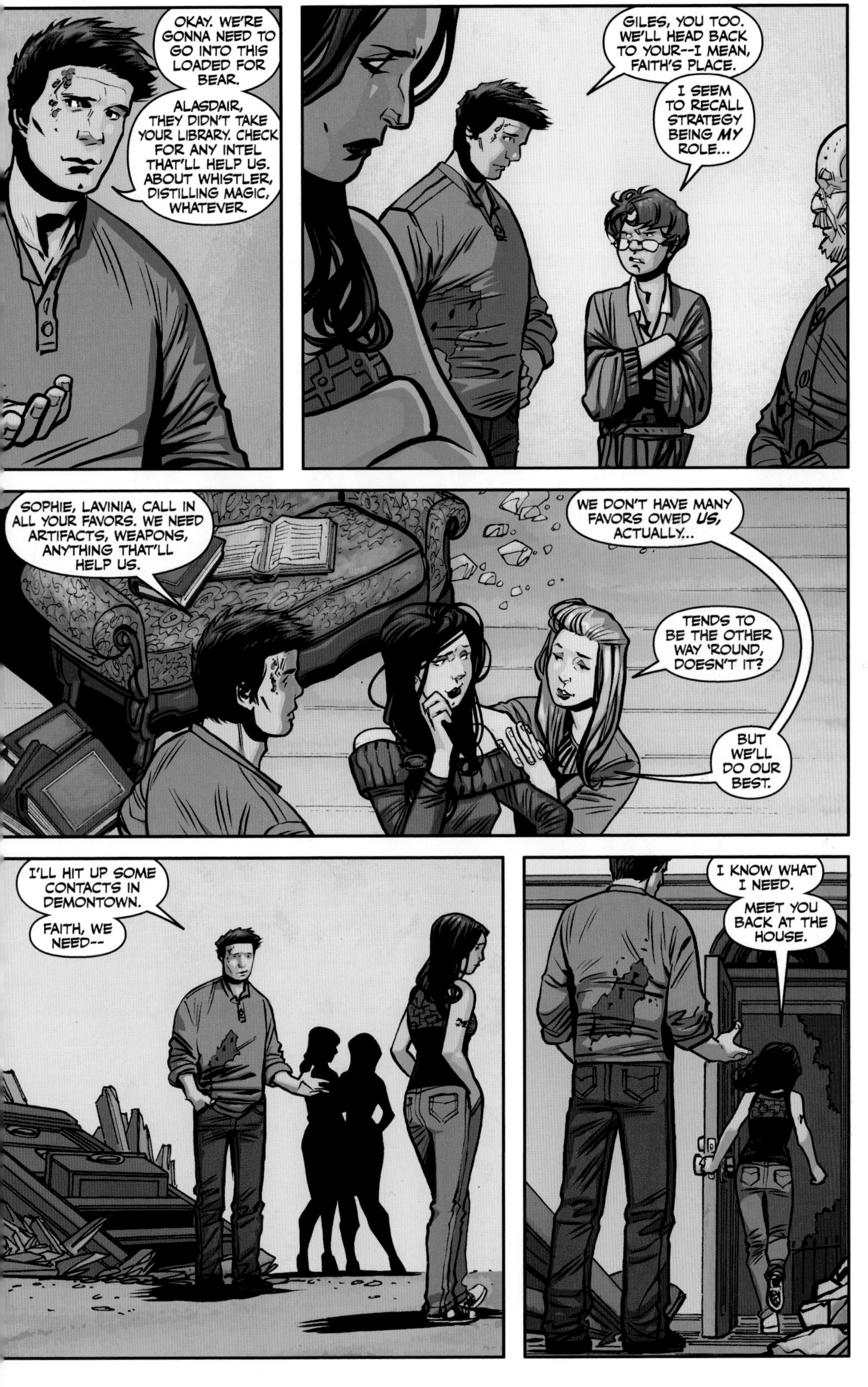
OKAY. WE'RE GONNA NEED TO GO INTO THIS LOADED FOR BEAR.
ALASDAIR, THEY DIDN'T TAKE YOUR LIBRARY. CHECK FOR ANY INTEL THAT'LL HELP US. ABOUT WHISTLER, DISTILLING MAGIC, WHATEVER.
GILES, YOU TOO. WE'LL HEAD BACK TO YOUR--I MEAN, FAITH'S PLACE.
I SEEM TO RECALL STRATEGY BEING *MY* ROLE...
SOPHIE, LAVINIA, CALL IN ALL YOUR FAVORS. WE NEED ARTIFACTS, WEAPONS, ANYTHING THAT'LL HELP US.
WE DON'T HAVE MANY FAVORS OWED *US*, ACTUALLY...
TENDS TO BE THE OTHER WAY 'ROUND, DOESN'T IT?
BUT WE'LL DO OUR BEST.
I'LL HIT UP SOME CONTACTS IN DEMONTOWN.
FAITH, WE NEED--
I KNOW WHAT I NEED.
MEET YOU BACK AT THE HOUSE.

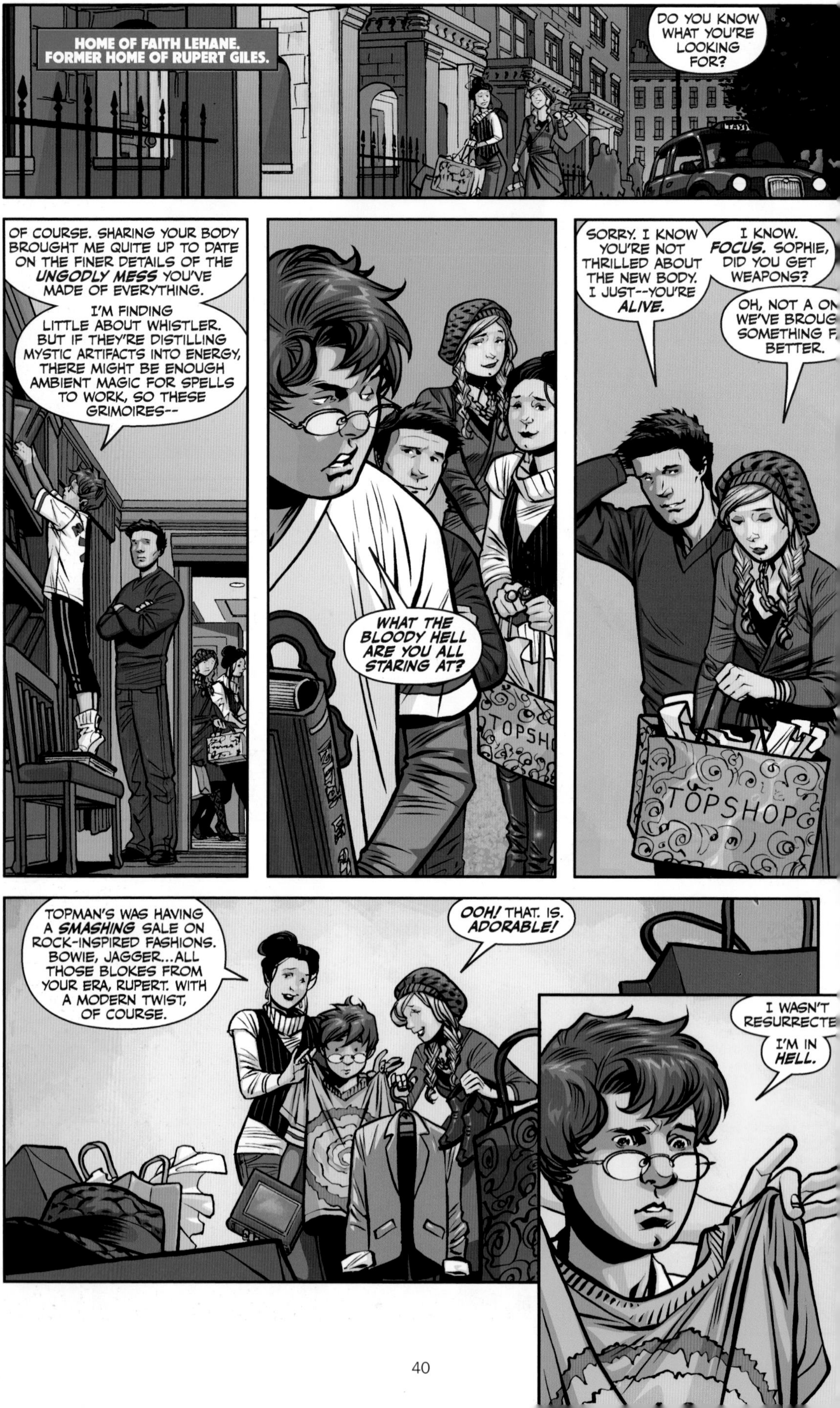
HOME OF FAITH LEHANE. FORMER HOME OF RUPERT GILES.
DO YOU KNOW WHAT YOU'RE LOOKING FOR?
OF COURSE. SHARING YOUR BODY BROUGHT ME QUITE UP TO DATE ON THE FINER DETAILS OF THE UNGODLY MESS YOU'VE MADE OF EVERYTHING.
I'M FINDING LITTLE ABOUT WHISTLER. BUT IF THEY'RE DISTILLING MYSTIC ARTIFACTS INTO ENERGY, THERE MIGHT BE ENOUGH AMBIENT MAGIC FOR SPELLS TO WORK, SO THESE GRIMOIRES--
WHAT THE BLOODY HELL ARE YOU ALL STARING AT?
TOPSHOP
SORRY. I KNOW YOU'RE NOT THRILLED ABOUT THE NEW BODY. I JUST--YOU'RE ALIVE.
I KNOW. FOCUS. SOPHIE, DID YOU GET WEAPONS?
OH, NOT A ON
WE'VE BROUG
SOMETHING F
BETTER.
TOPSHOP
TOPMAN'S WAS HAVING A SMASHING SALE ON ROCK-INSPIRED FASHIONS. BOWIE, JAGGER...ALL THOSE BLOKES FROM YOUR ERA, RUPERT. WITH A MODERN TWIST, OF COURSE.
OOH! THAT. IS. ADORABLE!
I WASN'T RESURRECTE
I'M IN HELL.

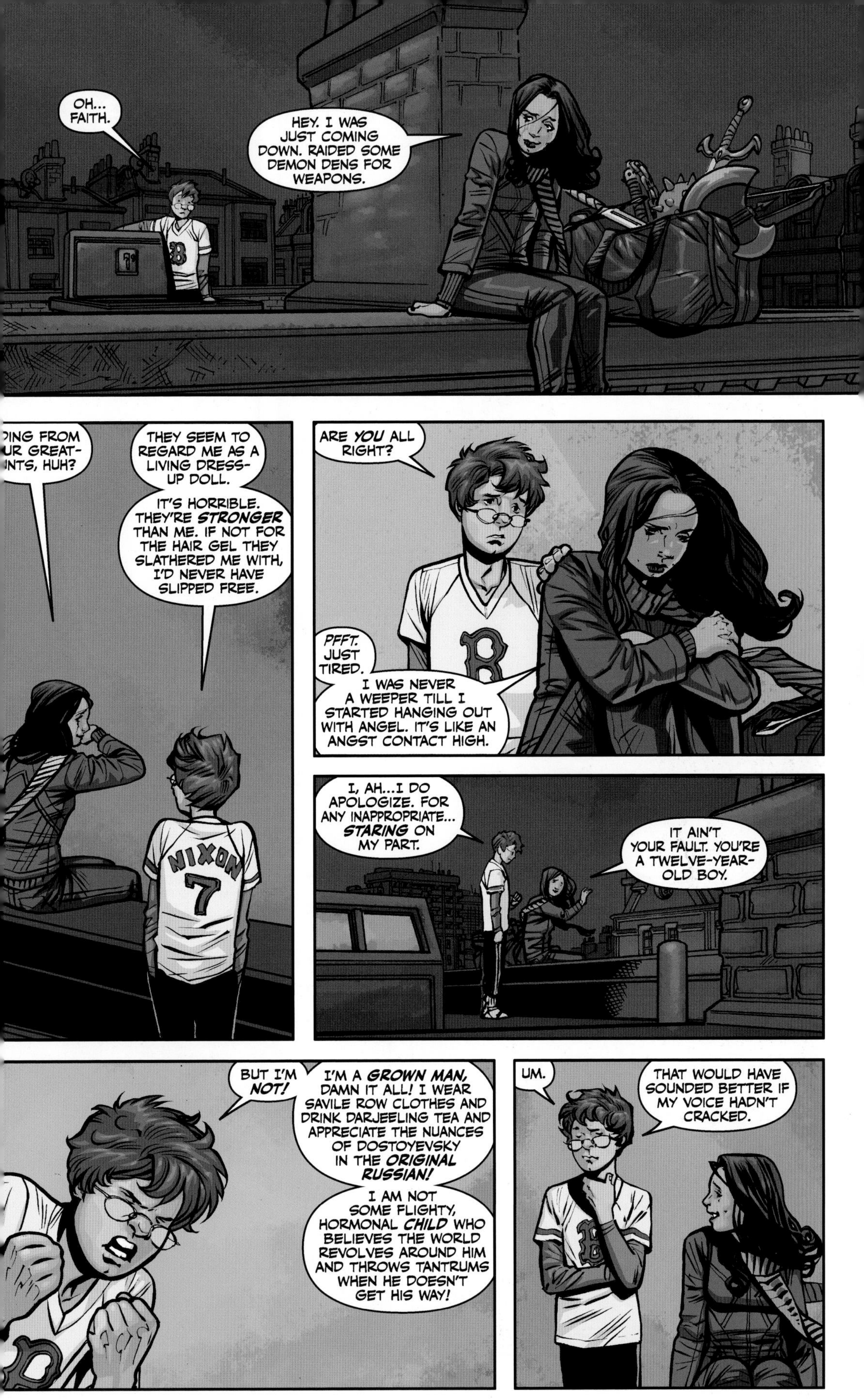

OH... FAITH.
HEY. I WAS JUST COMING DOWN. RAIDED SOME DEMON DENS FOR WEAPONS.
PING FROM UR GREAT- NTS, HUH?
THEY SEEM TO REGARD ME AS A LIVING DRESS-UP DOLL.
IT'S HORRIBLE. THEY'RE *STRONGER* THAN ME. IF NOT FOR THE HAIR GEL THEY SLATHERED ME WITH, I'D NEVER HAVE SLIPPED FREE.
NIXON 7
ARE *YOU* ALL RIGHT?
PFFT. JUST TIRED.
I WAS NEVER A WEEPER TILL I STARTED HANGING OUT WITH ANGEL. IT'S LIKE AN ANGST CONTACT HIGH.
I, AH...I DO APOLOGIZE. FOR ANY INAPPROPRIATE... *STARING* ON MY PART.
IT AIN'T YOUR FAULT. YOU'RE A TWELVE-YEAR-OLD BOY.
BUT I'M *NOT!*
I'M A *GROWN MAN,* DAMN IT ALL! I WEAR SAVILE ROW CLOTHES AND DRINK DARJEELING TEA AND APPRECIATE THE NUANCES OF DOSTOYEVSKY IN THE *ORIGINAL RUSSIAN!*
I AM NOT SOME FLIGHTY, HORMONAL *CHILD* WHO BELIEVES THE WORLD REVOLVES AROUND HIM AND THROWS TANTRUMS WHEN HE DOESN'T GET HIS WAY!
UM.
THAT WOULD HAVE SOUNDED BETTER IF MY VOICE HADN'T CRACKED.

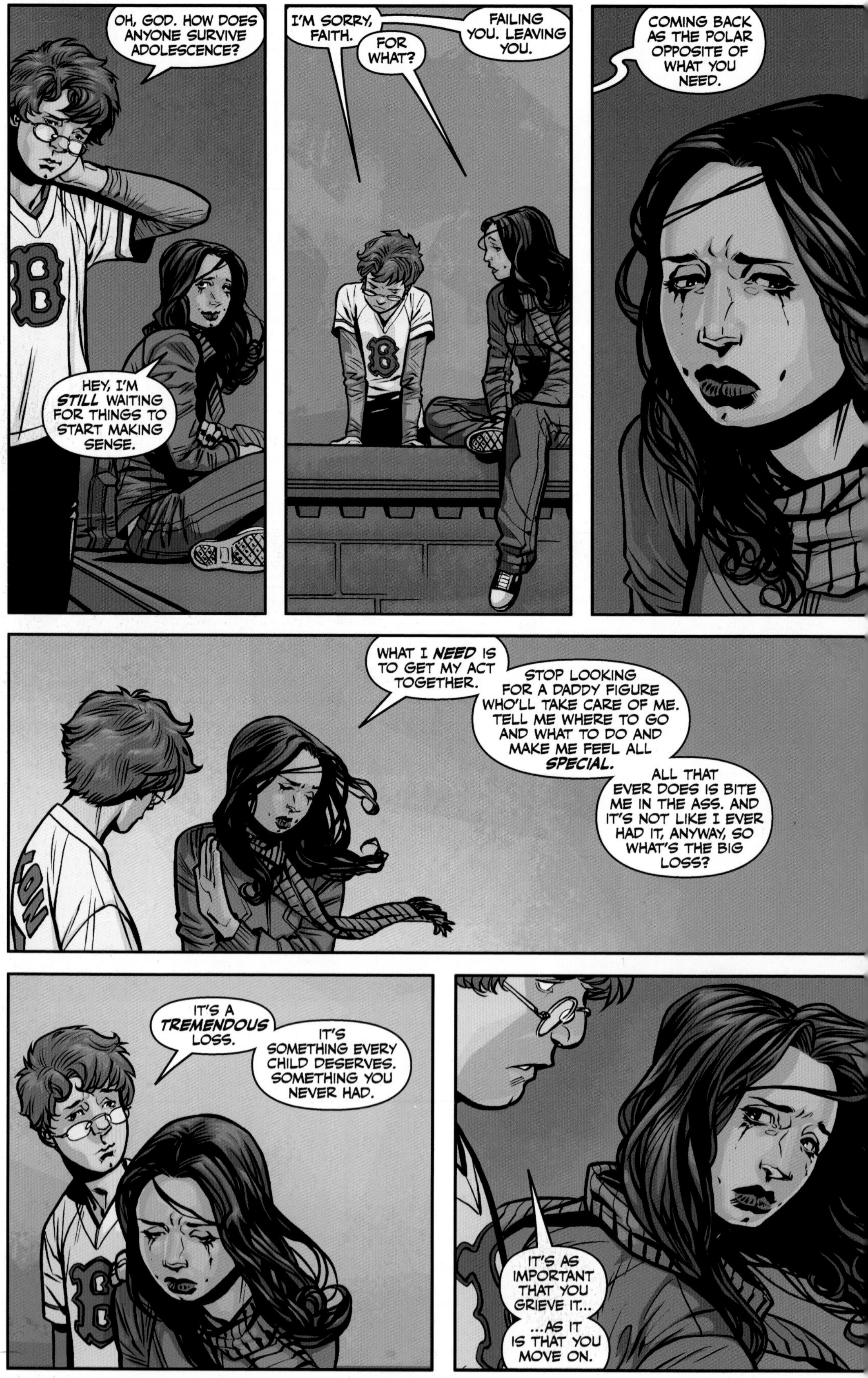
OH, GOD. HOW DOES ANYONE SURVIVE ADOLESCENCE?
HEY, I'M *STILL* WAITING FOR THINGS TO START MAKING SENSE.
I'M SORRY, FAITH.
FOR WHAT?
FAILING YOU. LEAVING YOU.
COMING BACK AS THE POLAR OPPOSITE OF WHAT YOU NEED.
WHAT I *NEED* IS TO GET MY ACT TOGETHER.
STOP LOOKING FOR A DADDY FIGURE WHO'LL TAKE CARE OF ME. TELL ME WHERE TO GO AND WHAT TO DO AND MAKE ME FEEL ALL *SPECIAL.*
ALL THAT EVER DOES IS BITE ME IN THE ASS. AND IT'S NOT LIKE I EVER HAD IT, ANYWAY, SO WHAT'S THE BIG LOSS?
IT'S A *TREMENDOUS* LOSS.
IT'S SOMETHING EVERY CHILD DESERVES. SOMETHING YOU NEVER HAD.
IT'S AS IMPORTANT THAT YOU GRIEVE IT...
...AS IT IS THAT YOU MOVE ON.

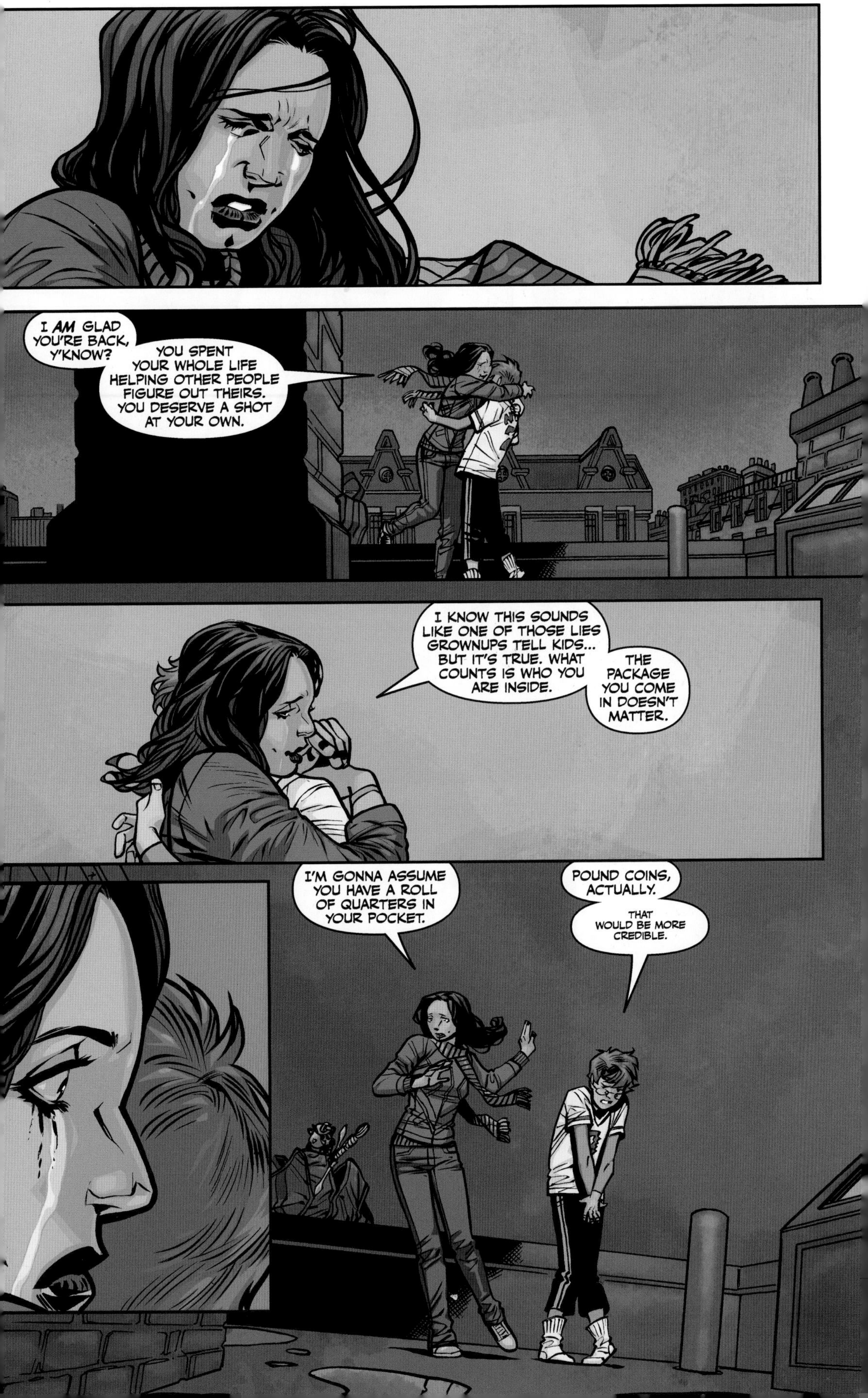
I *AM* GLAD YOU'RE BACK, Y'KNOW?
YOU SPENT YOUR WHOLE LIFE HELPING OTHER PEOPLE FIGURE OUT THEIRS. YOU DESERVE A SHOT AT YOUR OWN.
I KNOW THIS SOUNDS LIKE ONE OF THOSE LIES GROWNUPS TELL KIDS... BUT IT'S TRUE. WHAT COUNTS IS WHO YOU ARE INSIDE.
THE PACKAGE YOU COME IN DOESN'T MATTER.
I'M GONNA ASSUME YOU HAVE A ROLL OF QUARTERS IN YOUR POCKET.
POUND COINS, ACTUALLY.
THAT WOULD BE MORE CREDIBLE.

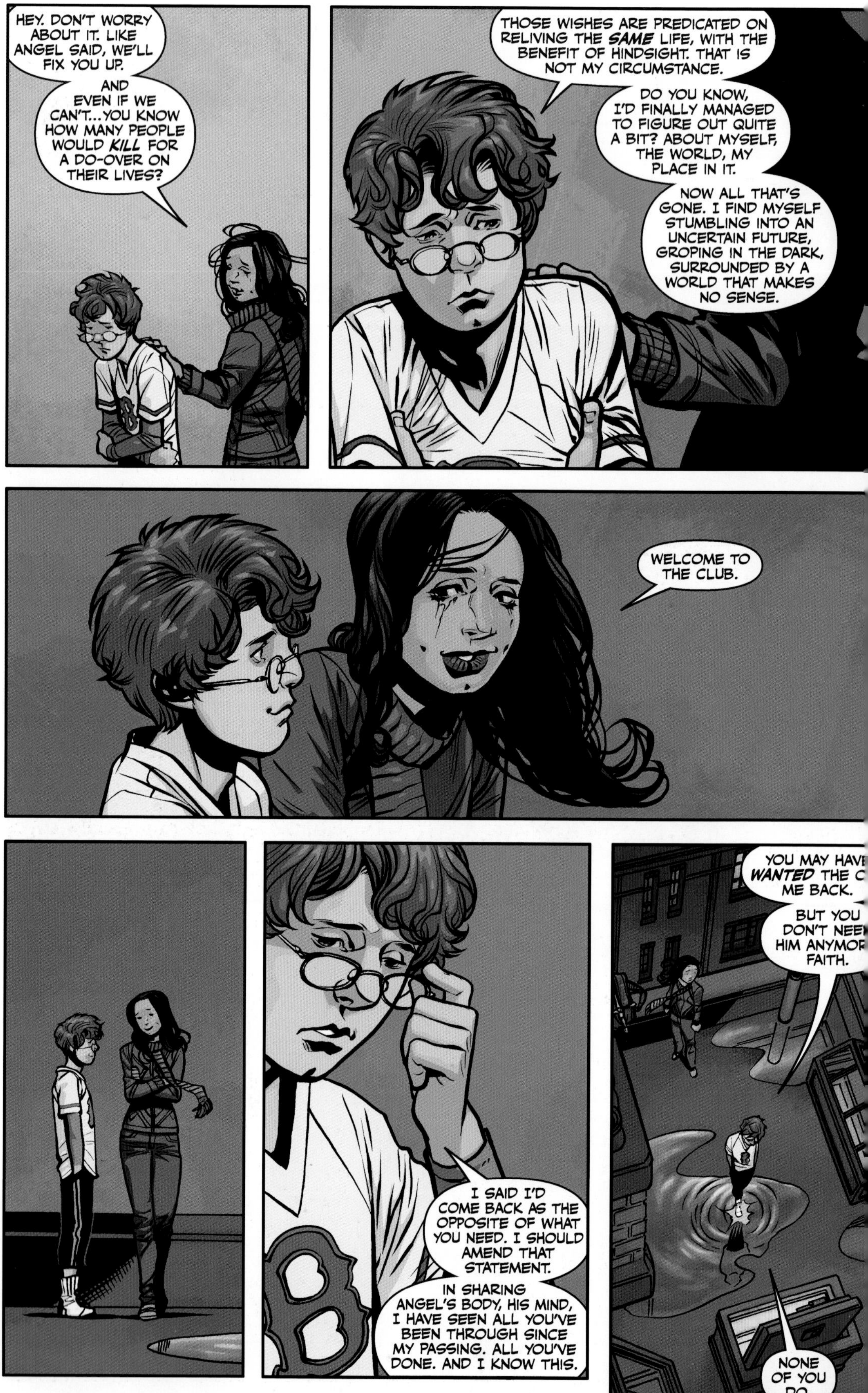

HEY. DON'T WORRY ABOUT IT. LIKE ANGEL SAID, WE'LL FIX YOU UP.
AND EVEN IF WE CAN'T...YOU KNOW HOW MANY PEOPLE WOULD *KILL* FOR A DO-OVER ON THEIR LIVES?
THOSE WISHES ARE PREDICATED ON RELIVING THE *SAME* LIFE, WITH THE BENEFIT OF HINDSIGHT. THAT IS NOT MY CIRCUMSTANCE.
DO YOU KNOW, I'D FINALLY MANAGED TO FIGURE OUT QUITE A BIT? ABOUT MYSELF, THE WORLD, MY PLACE IN IT.
NOW ALL THAT'S GONE. I FIND MYSELF STUMBLING INTO AN UNCERTAIN FUTURE, GROPING IN THE DARK, SURROUNDED BY A WORLD THAT MAKES NO SENSE.
WELCOME TO THE CLUB.
I SAID I'D COME BACK AS THE OPPOSITE OF WHAT YOU NEED. I SHOULD AMEND THAT STATEMENT.
IN SHARING ANGEL'S BODY, HIS MIND, I HAVE SEEN ALL YOU'VE BEEN THROUGH SINCE MY PASSING. ALL YOU'VE DONE. AND I KNOW THIS.
YOU MAY HAVE *WANTED* THE C ME BACK.
BUT YOU DON'T NEE HIM ANYMOR FAITH.
NONE OF YOU DO.

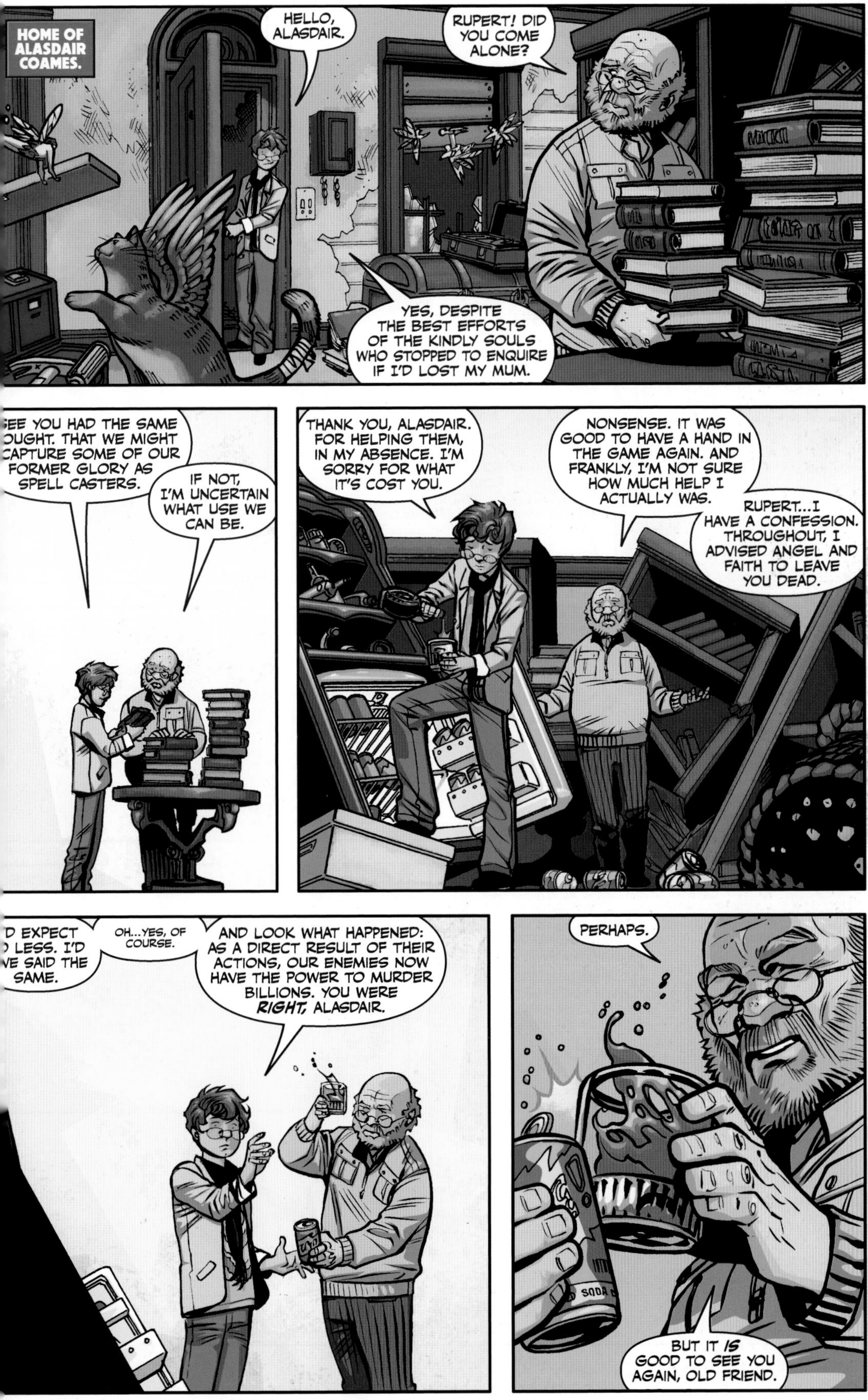
HOME OF ALASDAIR COAMES.
HELLO, ALASDAIR.
RUPERT! DID YOU COME ALONE?
YES, DESPITE THE BEST EFFORTS OF THE KINDLY SOULS WHO STOPPED TO ENQUIRE IF I'D LOST MY MUM.
EE YOU HAD THE SAME OUGHT. THAT WE MIGHT CAPTURE SOME OF OUR FORMER GLORY AS SPELL CASTERS.
IF NOT, I'M UNCERTAIN WHAT USE WE CAN BE.
THANK YOU, ALASDAIR. FOR HELPING THEM, IN MY ABSENCE. I'M SORRY FOR WHAT IT'S COST YOU.
NONSENSE. IT WAS GOOD TO HAVE A HAND IN THE GAME AGAIN. AND FRANKLY, I'M NOT SURE HOW MUCH HELP I ACTUALLY WAS.
RUPERT...I HAVE A CONFESSION. THROUGHOUT, I ADVISED ANGEL AND FAITH TO LEAVE YOU DEAD.
D EXPECT D LESS. I'D VE SAID THE SAME.
OH...YES, OF COURSE.
AND LOOK WHAT HAPPENED: AS A DIRECT RESULT OF THEIR ACTIONS, OUR ENEMIES NOW HAVE THE POWER TO MURDER BILLIONS. YOU WERE *RIGHT,* ALASDAIR.
PERHAPS.
SODA
BUT IT *IS* GOOD TO SEE YOU AGAIN, OLD FRIEND.

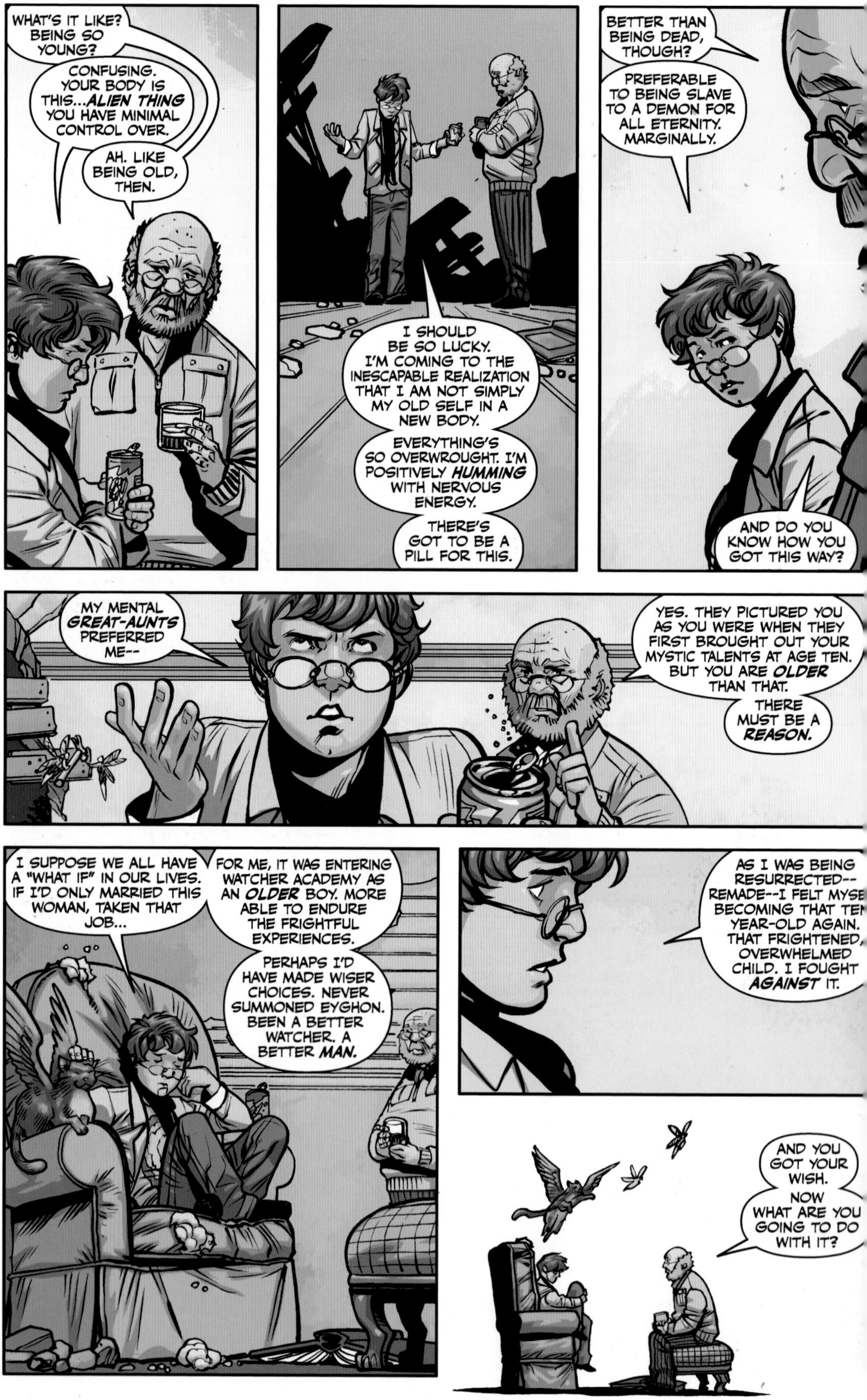
WHAT'S IT LIKE? BEING SO YOUNG?
CONFUSING. YOUR BODY IS THIS...ALIEN THING YOU HAVE MINIMAL CONTROL OVER.
AH. LIKE BEING OLD, THEN.
I SHOULD BE SO LUCKY. I'M COMING TO THE INESCAPABLE REALIZATION THAT I AM NOT SIMPLY MY OLD SELF IN A NEW BODY.
EVERYTHING'S SO OVERWROUGHT. I'M POSITIVELY HUMMING WITH NERVOUS ENERGY.
THERE'S GOT TO BE A PILL FOR THIS.
BETTER THAN BEING DEAD, THOUGH?
PREFERABLE TO BEING SLAVE TO A DEMON FOR ALL ETERNITY. MARGINALLY.
AND DO YOU KNOW HOW YOU GOT THIS WAY?
MY MENTAL GREAT-AUNTS PREFERRED ME--
YES. THEY PICTURED YOU AS YOU WERE WHEN THEY FIRST BROUGHT OUT YOUR MYSTIC TALENTS AT AGE TEN. BUT YOU ARE OLDER THAN THAT.
THERE MUST BE A REASON.
I SUPPOSE WE ALL HAVE A "WHAT IF" IN OUR LIVES. IF I'D ONLY MARRIED THIS WOMAN, TAKEN THAT JOB...
FOR ME, IT WAS ENTERING WATCHER ACADEMY AS AN OLDER BOY. MORE ABLE TO ENDURE THE FRIGHTFUL EXPERIENCES.
PERHAPS I'D HAVE MADE WISER CHOICES. NEVER SUMMONED EYGHON. BEEN A BETTER WATCHER. A BETTER MAN.
AS I WAS BEING RESURRECTED--REMADE--I FELT MYSE BECOMING THAT TE YEAR-OLD AGAIN. THAT FRIGHTENED, OVERWHELMED CHILD. I FOUGHT AGAINST IT.
AND YOU GOT YOUR WISH.
NOW WHAT ARE YOU GOING TO DO WITH IT?

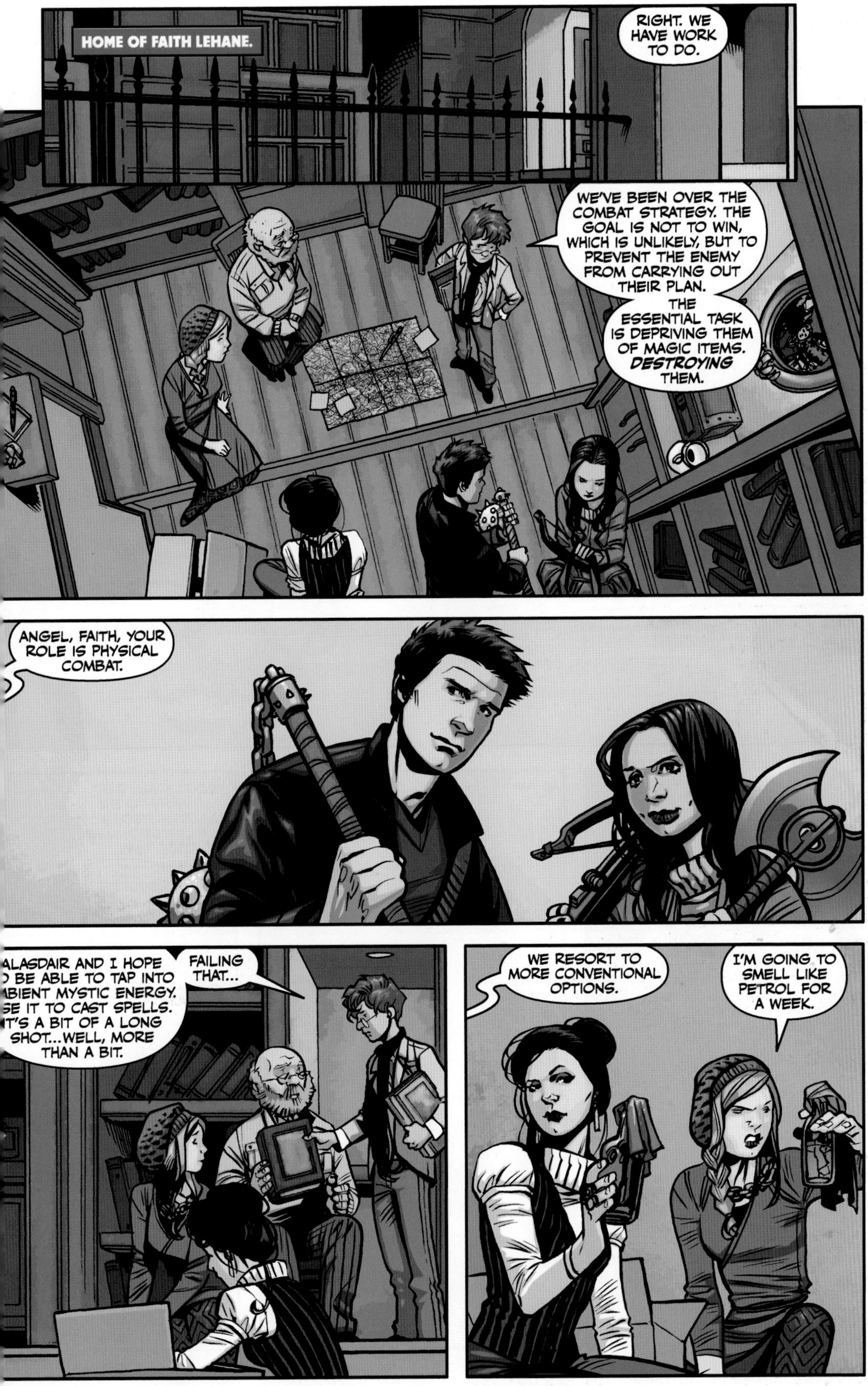

HOME OF FAITH LEHANE.
RIGHT. WE HAVE WORK TO DO.
WE'VE BEEN OVER THE COMBAT STRATEGY. THE GOAL IS NOT TO WIN, WHICH IS UNLIKELY, BUT TO PREVENT THE ENEMY FROM CARRYING OUT THEIR PLAN.
THE ESSENTIAL TASK IS DEPRIVING THEM OF MAGIC ITEMS. *DESTROYING* THEM.
ANGEL, FAITH, YOUR ROLE IS PHYSICAL COMBAT.
ALASDAIR AND I HOPE D BE ABLE TO TAP INTO MBIENT MYSTIC ENERGY. SE IT TO CAST SPELLS. T'S A BIT OF A LONG SHOT...WELL, MORE THAN A BIT.
FAILING THAT...
WE RESORT TO MORE CONVENTIONAL OPTIONS.
I'M GOING TO SMELL LIKE PETROL FOR A WEEK.

LISTEN...THIS IS PRACTICALLY A SUICIDE MISSION. WHISTLER COULD KILL US ALL HIMSELF. I WISH YOU'D LET ME--

WHY DO YOU EVEN BOTHER SAYING CRAP LIKE THAT?

ANGEL DOES RAISE A POINT I WISH TO ADDRESS. OUR ADVERSARIES MUST BE STOPPED. YOU'VE LEFT MESSAGES FOR BUFFY, WILLOW, AND OTHERS.

I'D FEEL BETTER IF WE'D ACTUALLY REACHED SOME OF THEM, BUT WE'VE DONE ALL WE CAN TO ENSURE THE FIGHT WILL GO ON, SHOULD WE FALL.

IF SOME OF US DO--INCLUDING MYSELF--I WANT YOUR WORD THAT YOUR ENERGIES WILL REMAIN FOCUSED ON THE TASK AT HAND.

I AM... GRATEFUL FOR WHAT YOU'VE DONE FOR ME. TO KNOW THAT ONE IS MISSED... VALUED...

FORGIVE ME. I HAD NO INTENTION OF--WELL.

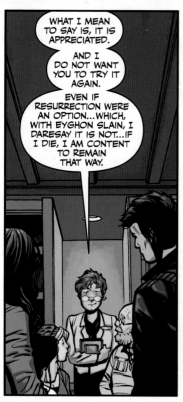

WHAT I MEAN TO SAY IS, IT IS APPRECIATED.

AND I DO NOT WANT YOU TO TRY IT AGAIN.

EVEN IF RESURRECTION WERE AN OPTION...WHICH, WITH EYGHON SLAIN, I DARESAY IT IS NOT...IF I DIE, I AM CONTENT TO REMAIN THAT WAY.

AS AM I.

I SHOULD'VE DIED THREE CENTURIES AGO.

NEVER FIGURED I'D LAST THIS LONG.

YOU'RE ALL DAFT. I WANT TO BE RESURRECTED. WITH A TIGHTER TUMMY THIS TIME.

I'LL RESURRECT YOU.

YOU'RE A LOVE

DULY NOTED. NOW THAT'S OUT OF THE WAY, ALL THAT REMAINS IS TO LOCATE OUR TARGETS.

ANGEL, YOU OBTAINED SOMETHING APPROPRIATE?

ENCHANTED LODESTONE. USED TO BE A DIME A DOZEN. GETTING HARDER TO COME BY, BUT THEY CAN STILL BE HAD FOR THE RIGHT PRICE.

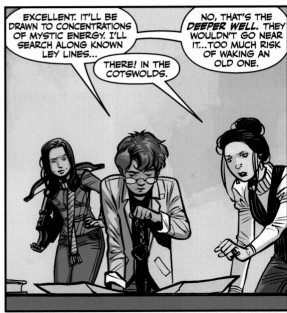

EXCELLENT. IT'LL BE DRAWN TO CONCENTRATIONS OF MYSTIC ENERGY. I'LL SEARCH ALONG KNOWN LEY LINES...

THERE! IN THE COTSWOLDS.

NO, THAT'S THE *DEEPER WELL.* THEY WOULDN'T GO NEAR IT...TOO MUCH RISK OF WAKING AN OLD ONE.

UT THAT'S QUITE A FLARE OF ENERGY, FOR A PLACE WHERE EVERYONE'S DORMANT. IT BEARS INVESTIGATING, IF--

HANG ON. THERE'S SOMETHING CLOSER... BUILDING INTENSITY BY THE MOMENT--

BRAKCH

OH.

OH DEAR.

WHAT?

THEY'RE IN HACKNEY. NEVER EVEN LEFT LONDON. WHICH CAN MEAN ONLY ONE THING.

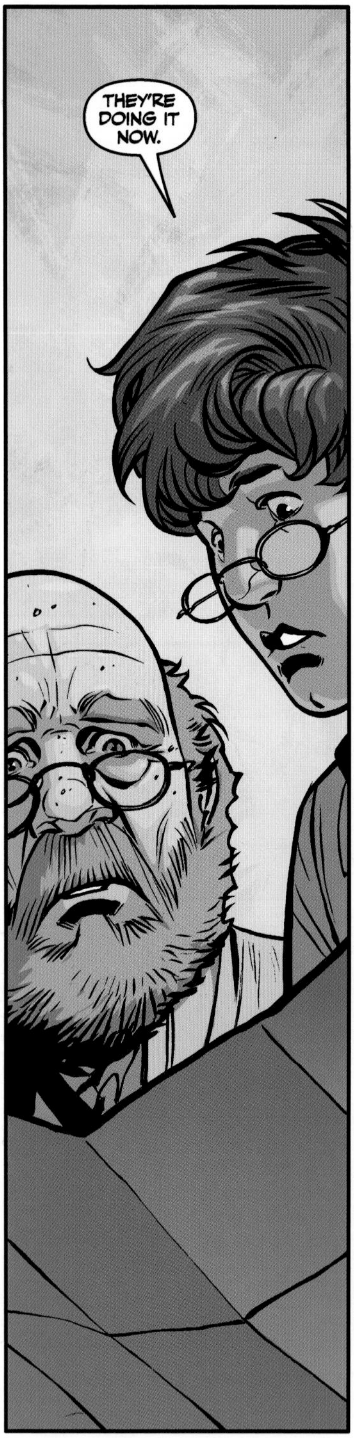
THEY'RE DOING IT NOW.

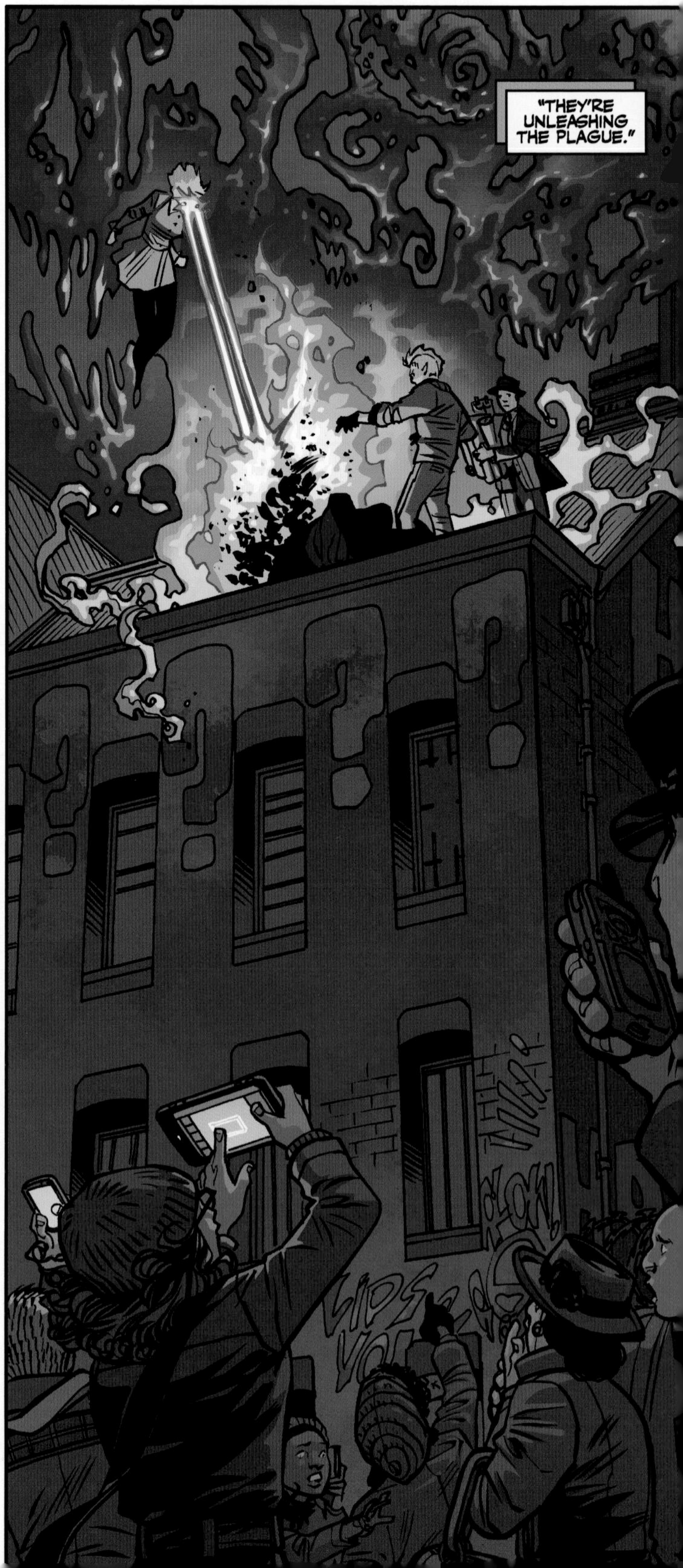
"THEY'RE UNLEASHING THE PLAGUE."

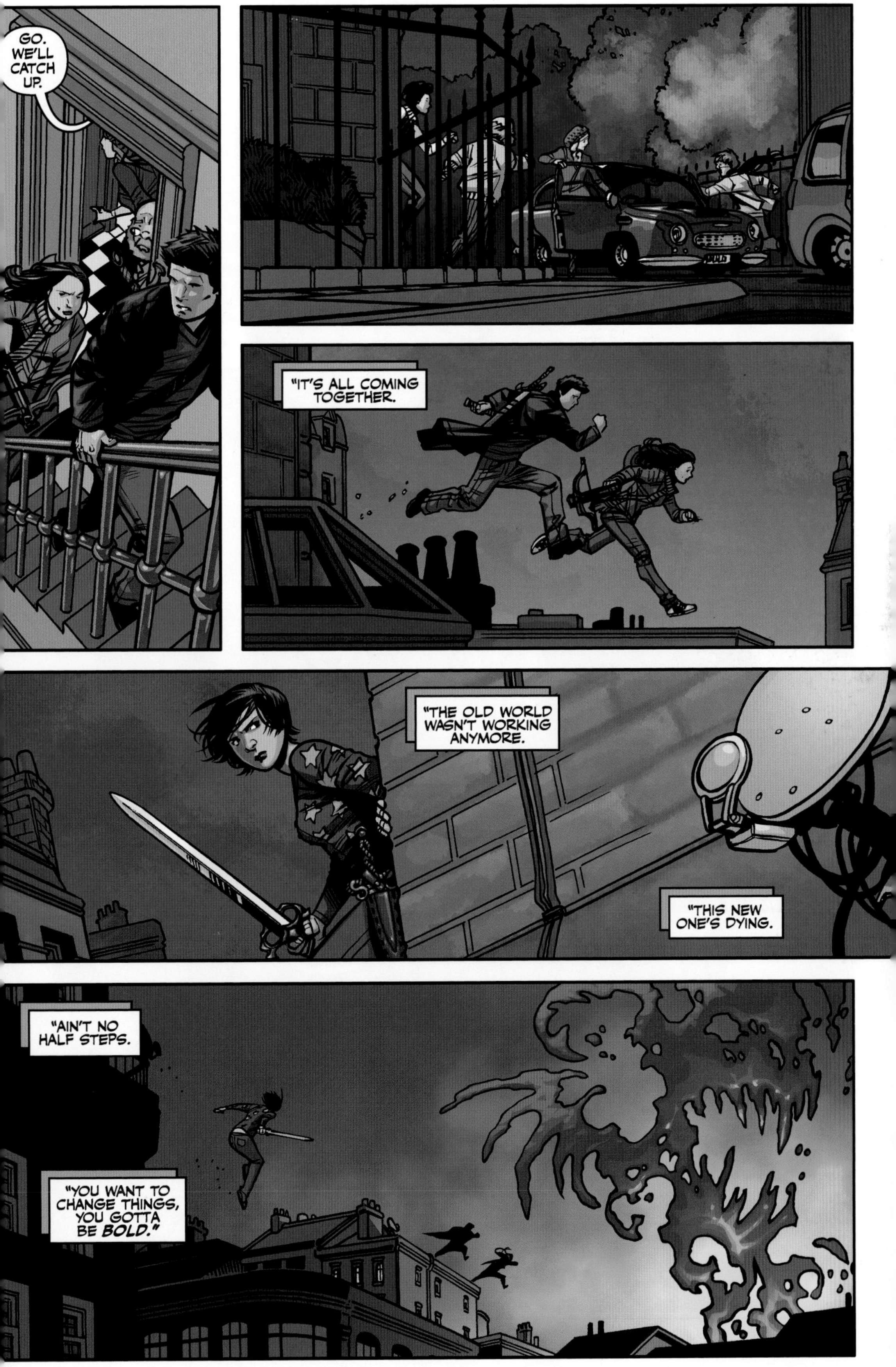

GO. WE'LL CATCH UP.
"IT'S ALL COMING TOGETHER.
"THE OLD WORLD WASN'T WORKING ANYMORE.
"THIS NEW ONE'S DYING.
"AIN'T NO HALF STEPS.
"YOU WANT TO CHANGE THINGS, YOU GOTTA BE *BOLD.*"

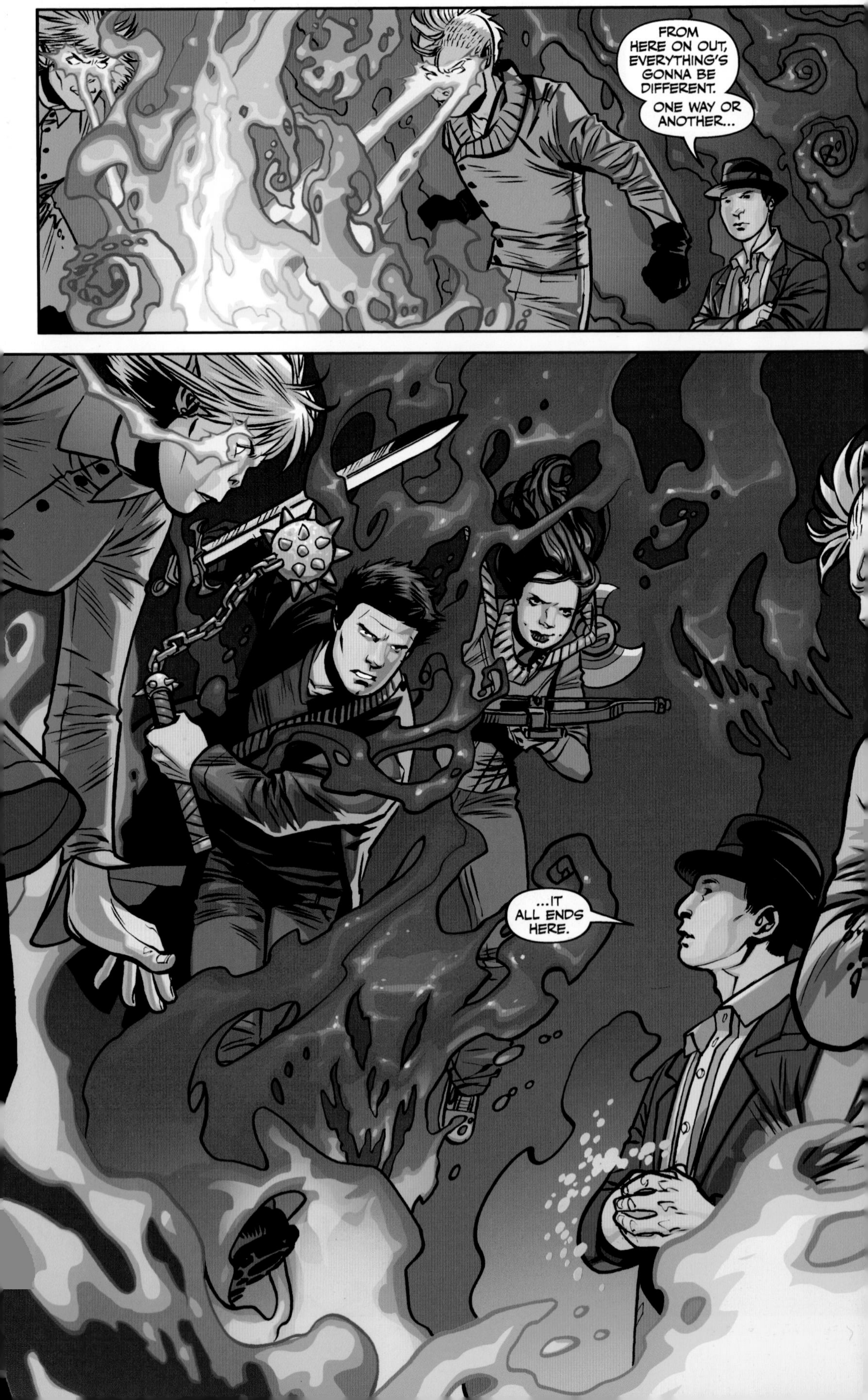
FROM HERE ON OUT, EVERYTHING'S GONNA BE DIFFERENT.
ONE WAY OR ANOTHER...
...IT ALL ENDS HERE.

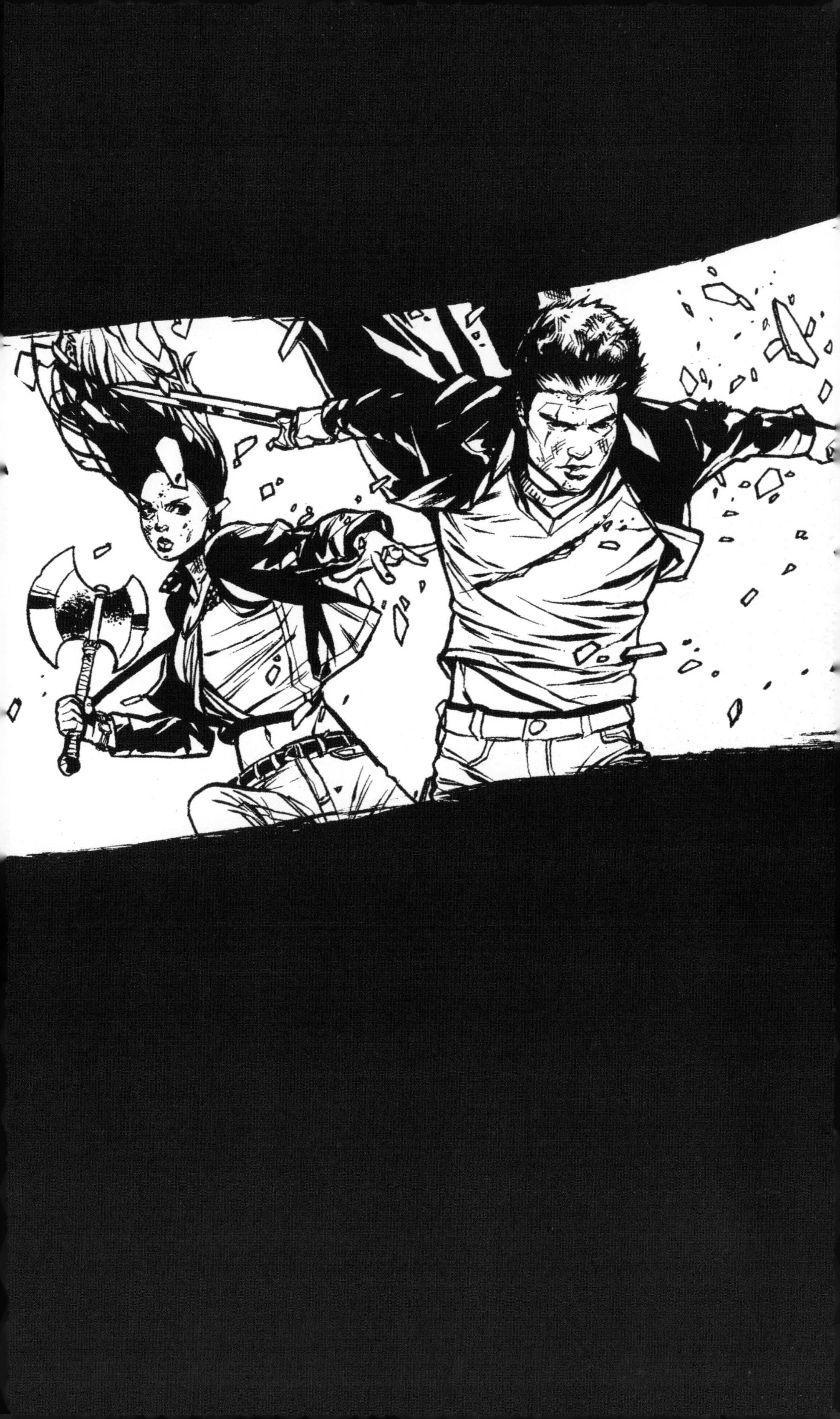

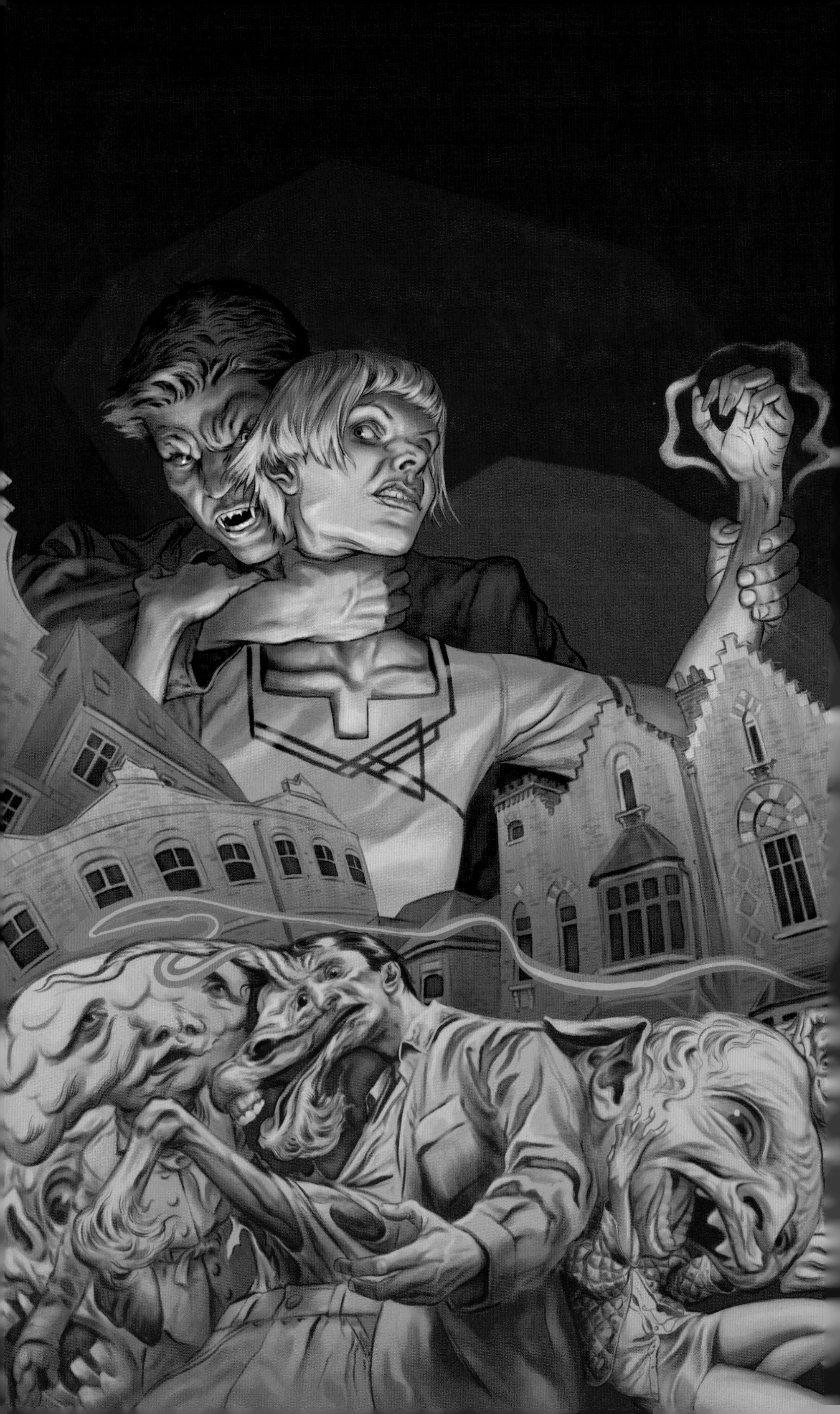

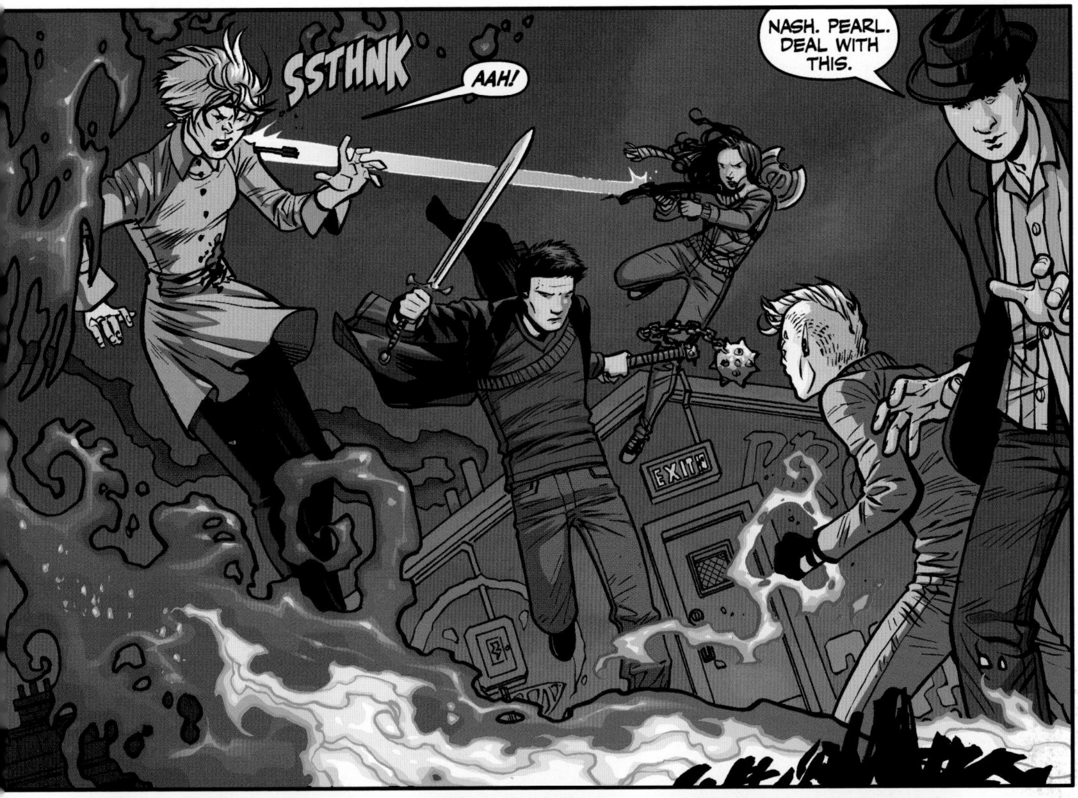
SSTHNK
AAH!
NASH. PEARL. DEAL WITH THIS.

WHAT YOU WANT, NOT WHAT YOU NEED

PART 3

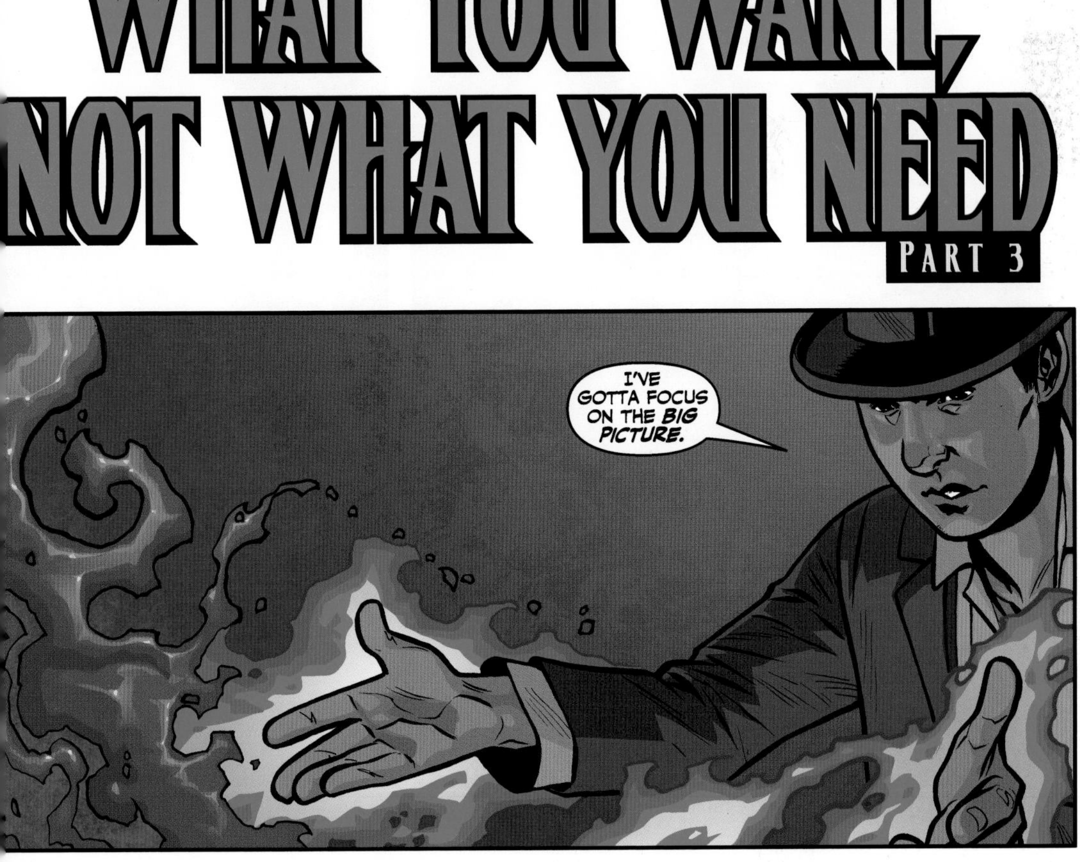
I'VE GOTTA FOCUS ON THE *BIG PICTURE.*

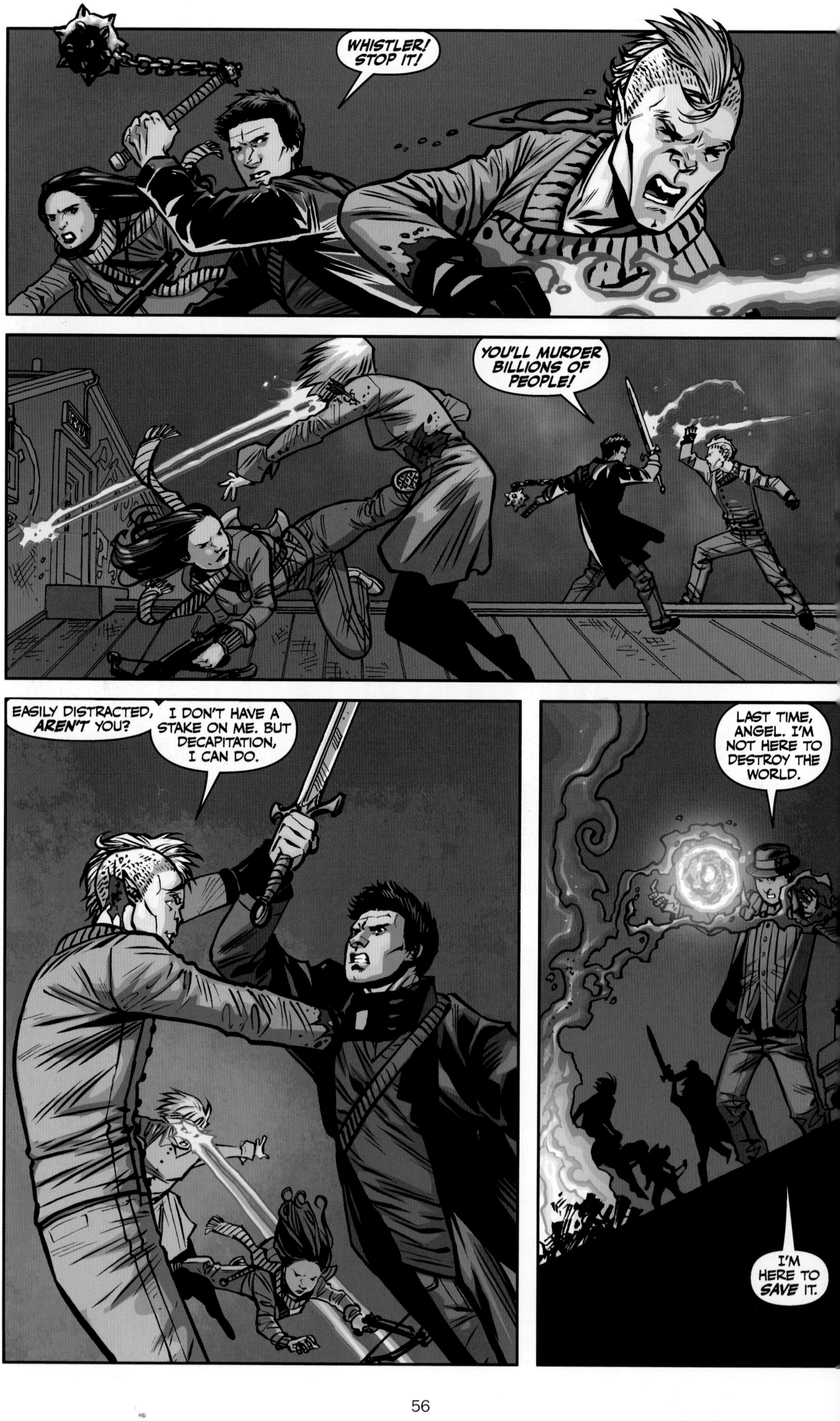
WHISTLER! STOP IT!
YOU'LL MURDER BILLIONS OF PEOPLE!
EASILY DISTRACTED, *AREN'T* YOU?
I DON'T HAVE A STAKE ON ME. BUT DECAPITATION, I CAN DO.
LAST TIME, ANGEL. I'M NOT HERE TO DESTROY THE WORLD.
I'M HERE TO *SAVE* IT.

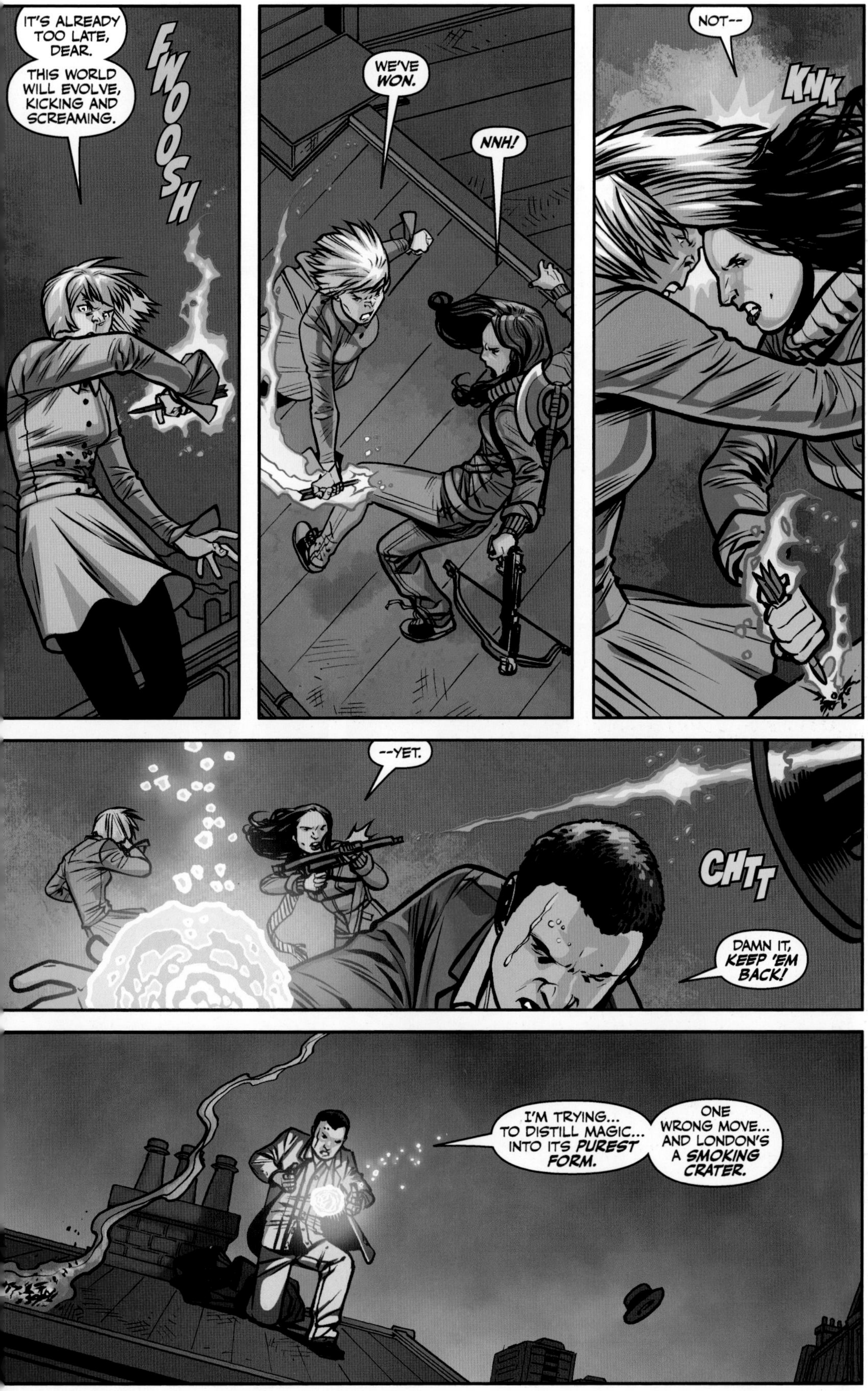
IT'S ALREADY TOO LATE, DEAR.
THIS WORLD WILL EVOLVE, KICKING AND SCREAMING.
FWOOSH
WE'VE WON.
NNH!
NOT--
KNK
--YET.
CHTT
DAMN IT, KEEP 'EM BACK!
I'M TRYING... TO DISTILL MAGIC... INTO ITS PUREST FORM.
ONE WRONG MOVE... AND LONDON'S A SMOKING CRATER.

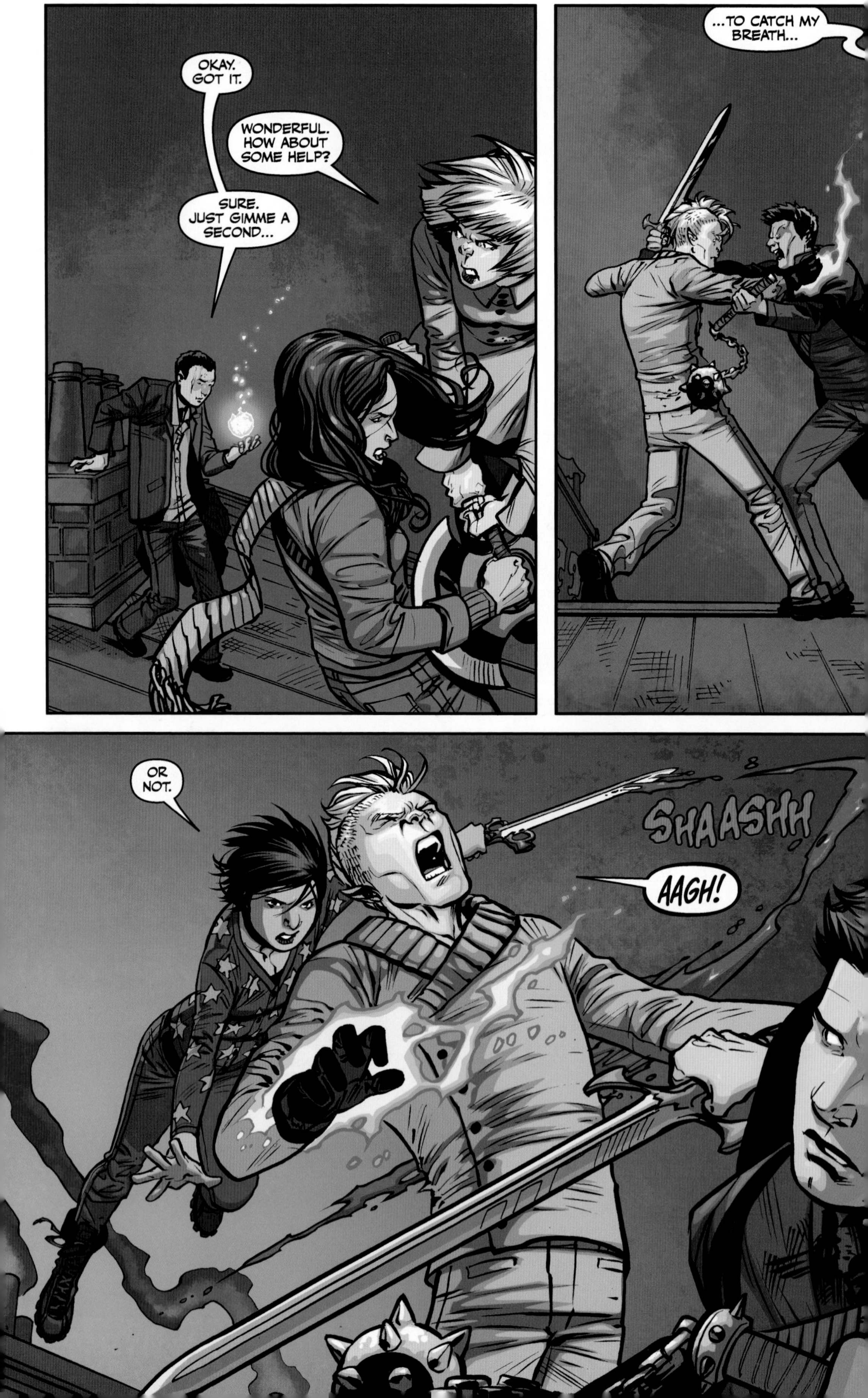
OKAY. GOT IT.
WONDERFUL. HOW ABOUT SOME HELP?
SURE. JUST GIMME A SECOND...
...TO CATCH MY BREATH...
OR NOT.
SHAASHH
AAGH!

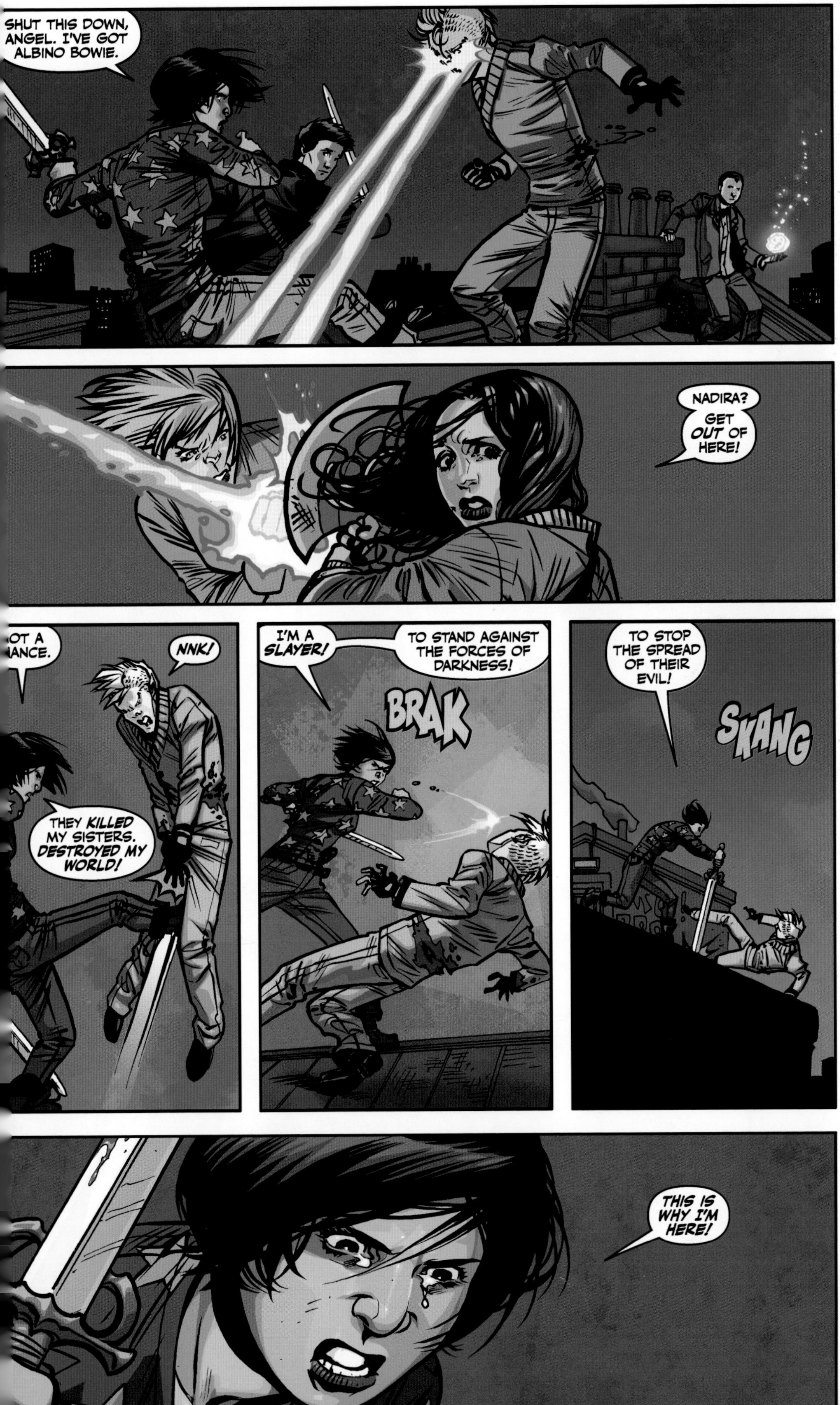
SHUT THIS DOWN, ANGEL. I'VE GOT ALBINO BOWIE.
NADIRA? GET OUT OF HERE!
NNK!
THEY KILLED MY SISTERS. DESTROYED MY WORLD!
I'M A SLAYER!
TO STAND AGAINST THE FORCES OF DARKNESS!
BRAK
TO STOP THE SPREAD OF THEIR EVIL!
SKANG
THIS IS WHY I'M HERE!

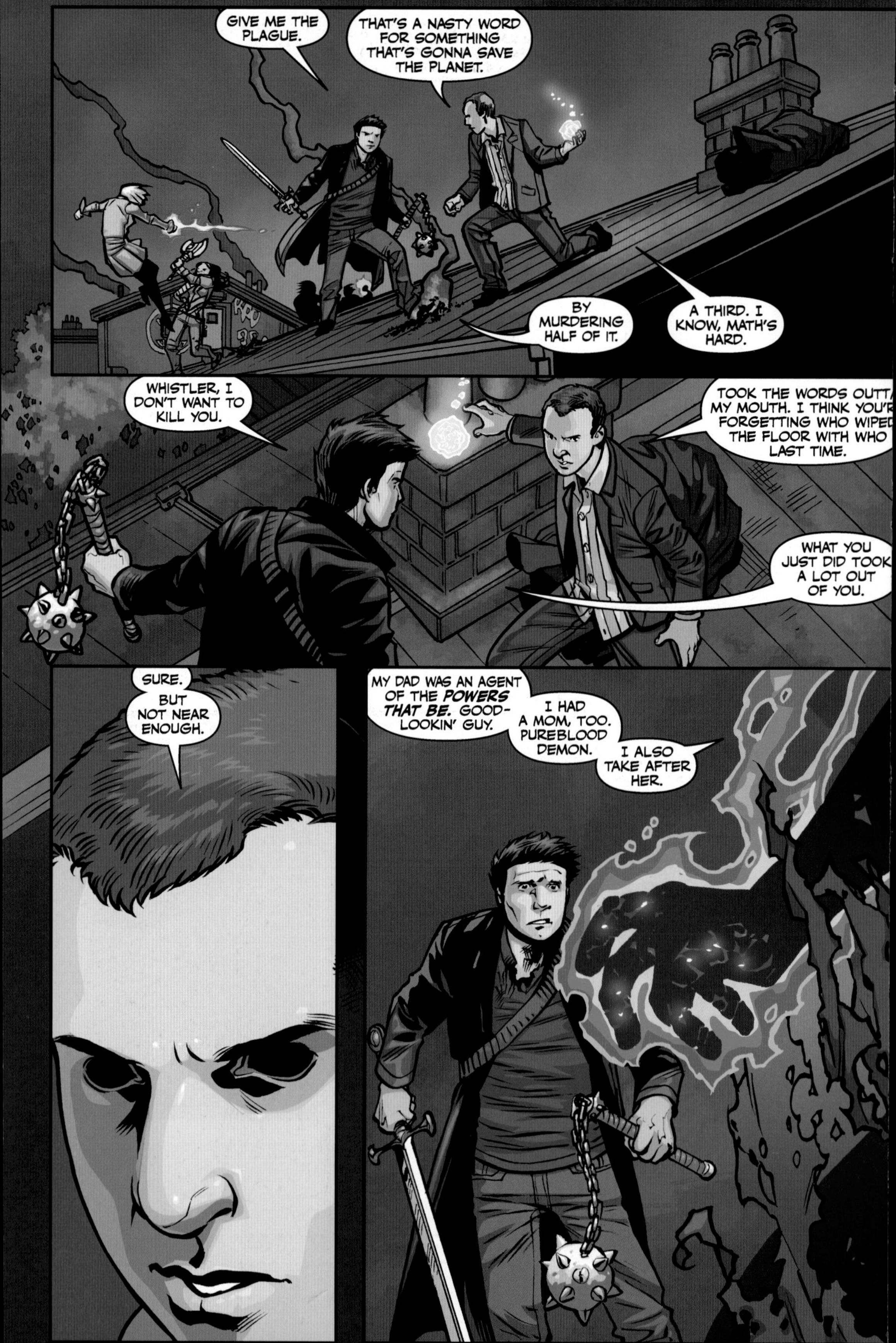
GIVE ME THE PLAGUE.
THAT'S A NASTY WORD FOR SOMETHING THAT'S GONNA SAVE THE PLANET.
BY MURDERING HALF OF IT.
A THIRD. I KNOW, MATH'S HARD.
WHISTLER, I DON'T WANT TO KILL YOU.
TOOK THE WORDS OUTTA MY MOUTH. I THINK YOU'RE FORGETTING WHO WIPED THE FLOOR WITH WHO LAST TIME.
WHAT YOU JUST DID TOOK A LOT OUT OF YOU.
SURE.
BUT NOT NEAR ENOUGH.
MY DAD WAS AN AGENT OF THE POWERS THAT BE. GOOD-LOOKIN' GUY.
I HAD A MOM, TOO. PUREBLOOD DEMON.
I ALSO TAKE AFTER HER.

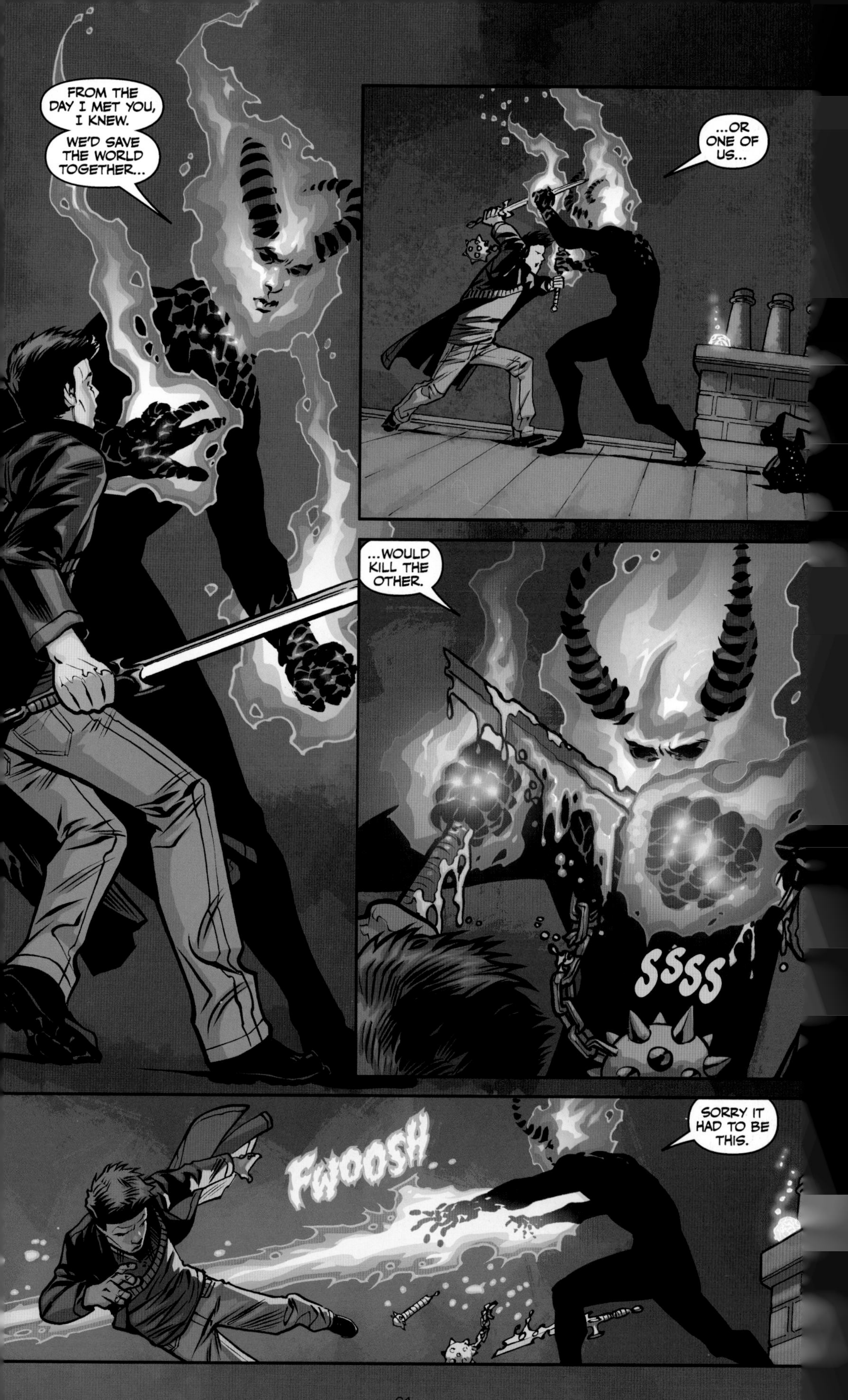
FROM THE DAY I MET YOU, I KNEW.
WE'D SAVE THE WORLD TOGETHER...
...OR ONE OF US...
...WOULD KILL THE OTHER.
SSSS
FWOOSH
SORRY IT HAD TO BE THIS.

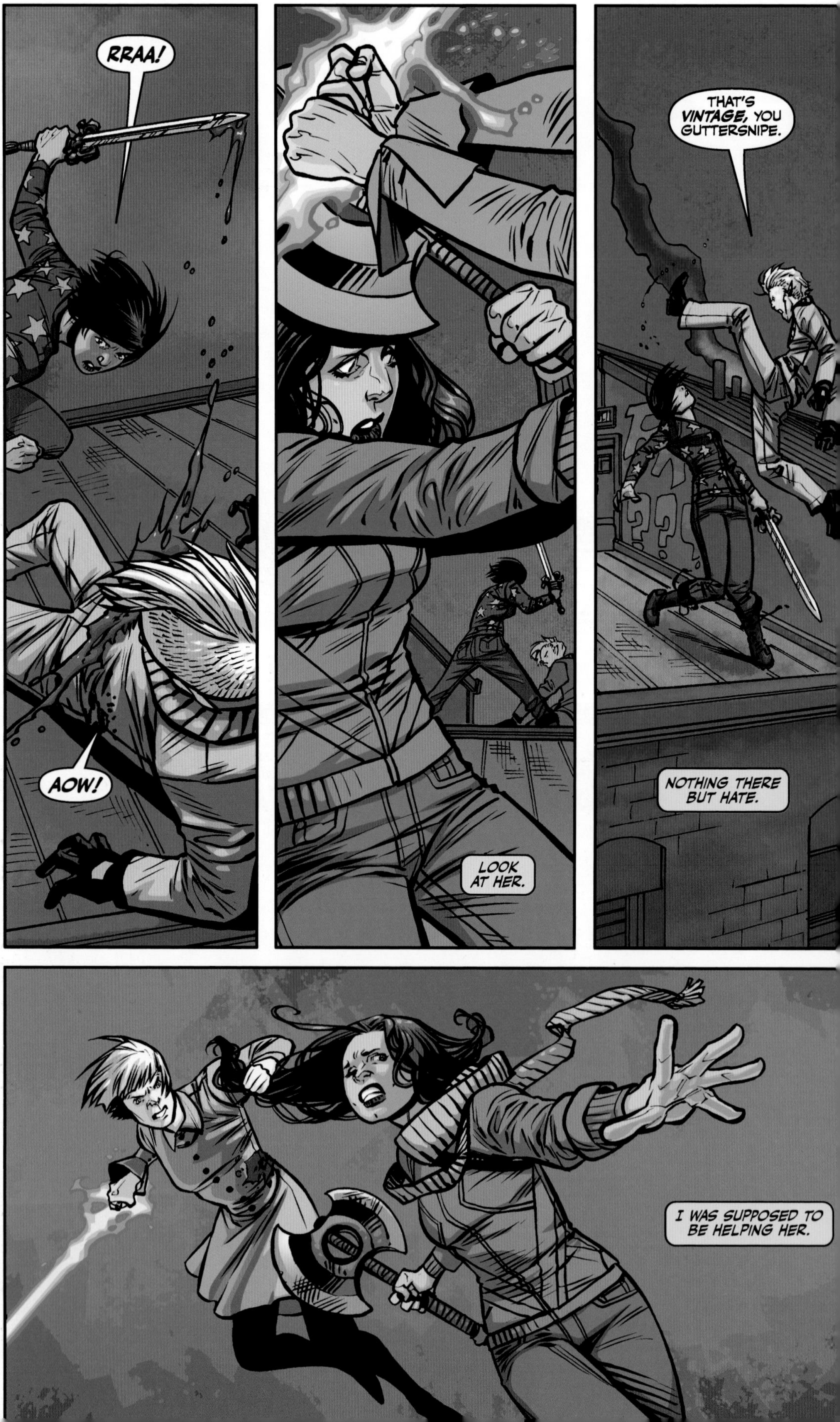
RRAA!
AOW!
LOOK AT HER.
THAT'S VINTAGE, YOU GUTTERSNIPE.
NOTHING THERE BUT HATE.
I WAS SUPPOSED TO BE HELPING HER.

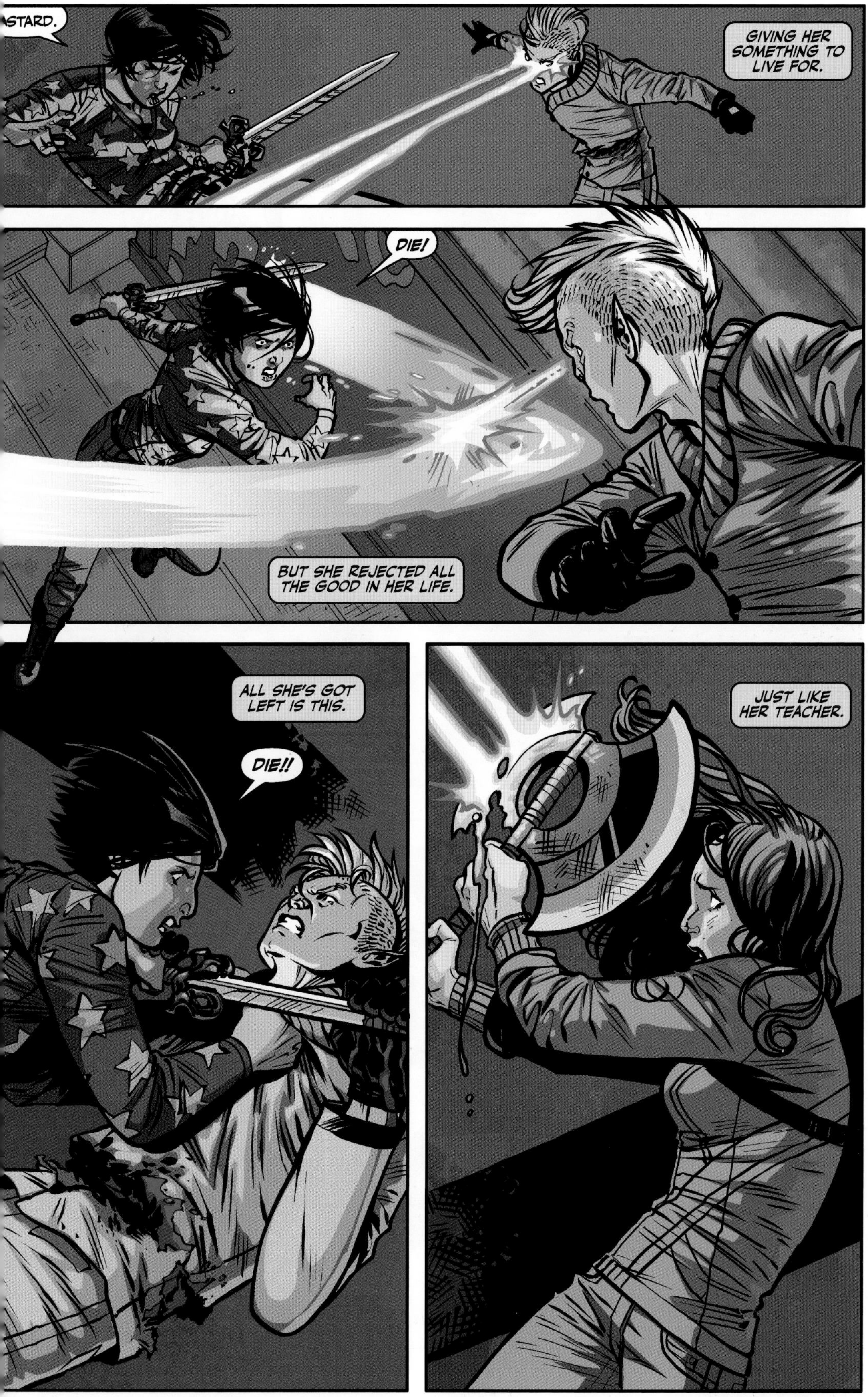

STARD.
GIVING HER SOMETHING TO LIVE FOR.
DIE!
BUT SHE REJECTED ALL THE GOOD IN HER LIFE.
ALL SHE'S GOT LEFT IS THIS.
DIE!!
JUST LIKE HER TEACHER.

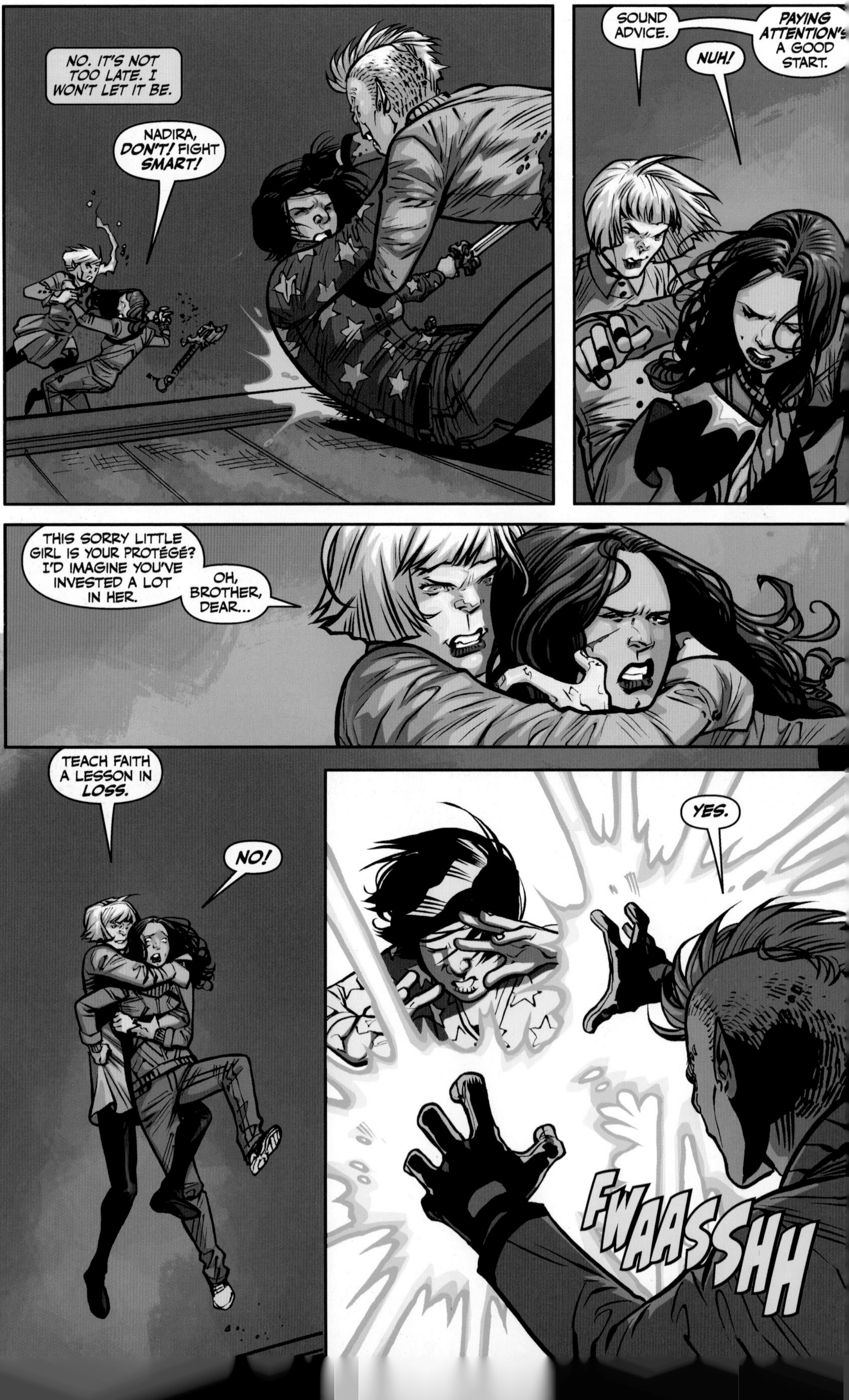
NO. IT'S NOT TOO LATE. I WON'T LET IT BE.
NADIRA, DON'T! FIGHT SMART!
SOUND ADVICE.
PAYING ATTENTION'S A GOOD START.
NUH!
THIS SORRY LITTLE GIRL IS YOUR PROTÉGÉ? I'D IMAGINE YOU'VE INVESTED A LOT IN HER.
OH, BROTHER, DEAR...
TEACH FAITH A LESSON IN LOSS.
NO!
YES.
FWAASSHH

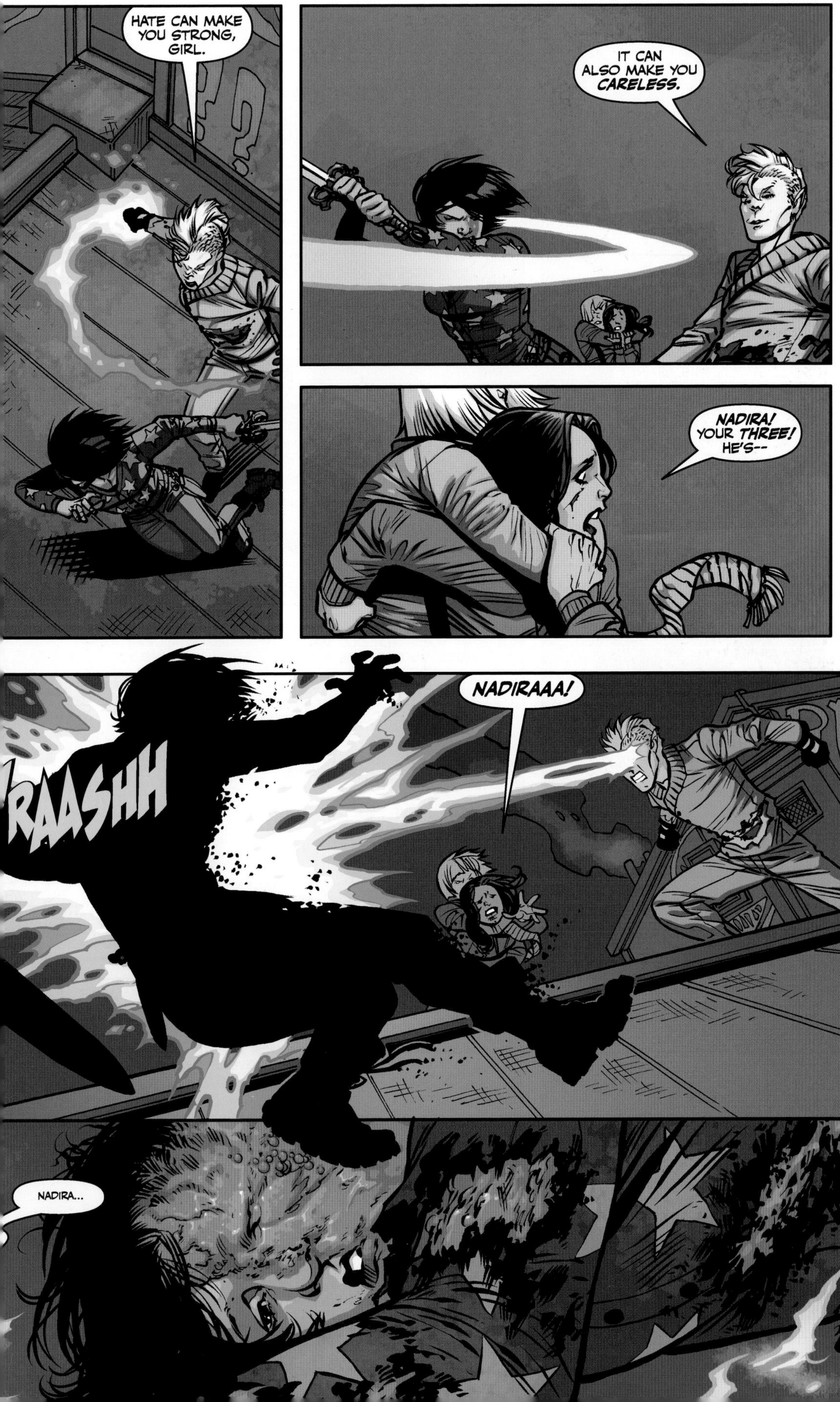
HATE CAN MAKE YOU STRONG, GIRL.
IT CAN ALSO MAKE YOU CARELESS.
NADIRA! YOUR THREE! HE'S--
RAASHH
NADIRAAA!
NADIRA...

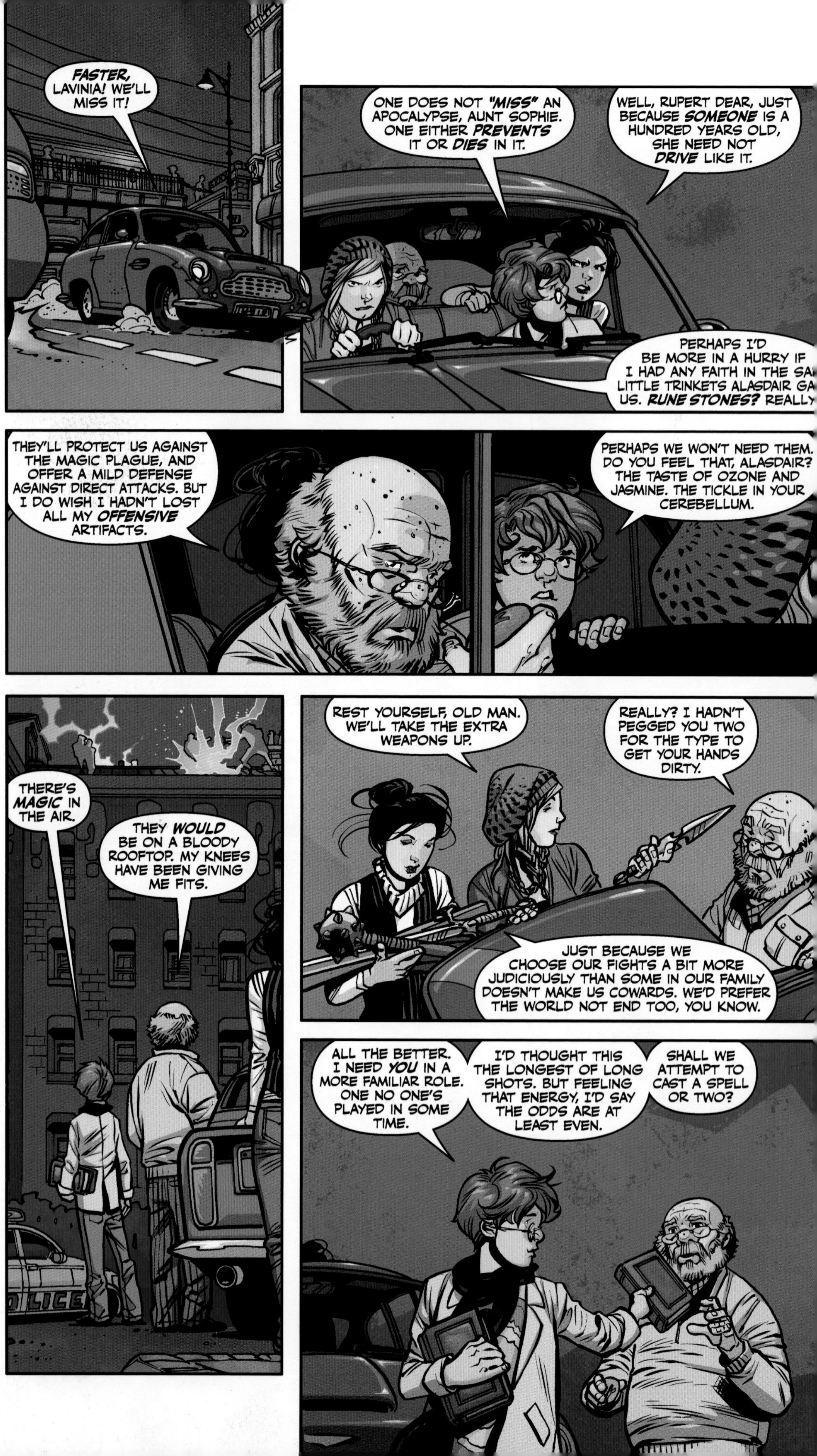
FASTER, LAVINIA! WE'LL MISS IT!
ONE DOES NOT "MISS" AN APOCALYPSE, AUNT SOPHIE. ONE EITHER PREVENTS IT OR DIES IN IT.
WELL, RUPERT DEAR, JUST BECAUSE SOMEONE IS A HUNDRED YEARS OLD, SHE NEED NOT DRIVE LIKE IT.
PERHAPS I'D BE MORE IN A HURRY IF I HAD ANY FAITH IN THE SA LITTLE TRINKETS ALASDAIR GA US. RUNE STONES? REALLY
THEY'LL PROTECT US AGAINST THE MAGIC PLAGUE, AND OFFER A MILD DEFENSE AGAINST DIRECT ATTACKS. BUT I DO WISH I HADN'T LOST ALL MY OFFENSIVE ARTIFACTS.
PERHAPS WE WON'T NEED THEM. DO YOU FEEL THAT, ALASDAIR? THE TASTE OF OZONE AND JASMINE. THE TICKLE IN YOUR CEREBELLUM.
THERE'S MAGIC IN THE AIR.
THEY WOULD BE ON A BLOODY ROOFTOP. MY KNEES HAVE BEEN GIVING ME FITS.
POLICE
REST YOURSELF, OLD MAN. WE'LL TAKE THE EXTRA WEAPONS UP.
REALLY? I HADN'T PEGGED YOU TWO FOR THE TYPE TO GET YOUR HANDS DIRTY.
JUST BECAUSE WE CHOOSE OUR FIGHTS A BIT MORE JUDICIOUSLY THAN SOME IN OUR FAMILY DOESN'T MAKE US COWARDS. WE'D PREFER THE WORLD NOT END TOO, YOU KNOW.
ALL THE BETTER. I NEED YOU IN A MORE FAMILIAR ROLE. ONE NO ONE'S PLAYED IN SOME TIME.
I'D THOUGHT THIS THE LONGEST OF LONG SHOTS. BUT FEELING THAT ENERGY, I'D SAY THE ODDS ARE AT LEAST EVEN.
SHALL WE ATTEMPT TO CAST A SPELL OR TWO?

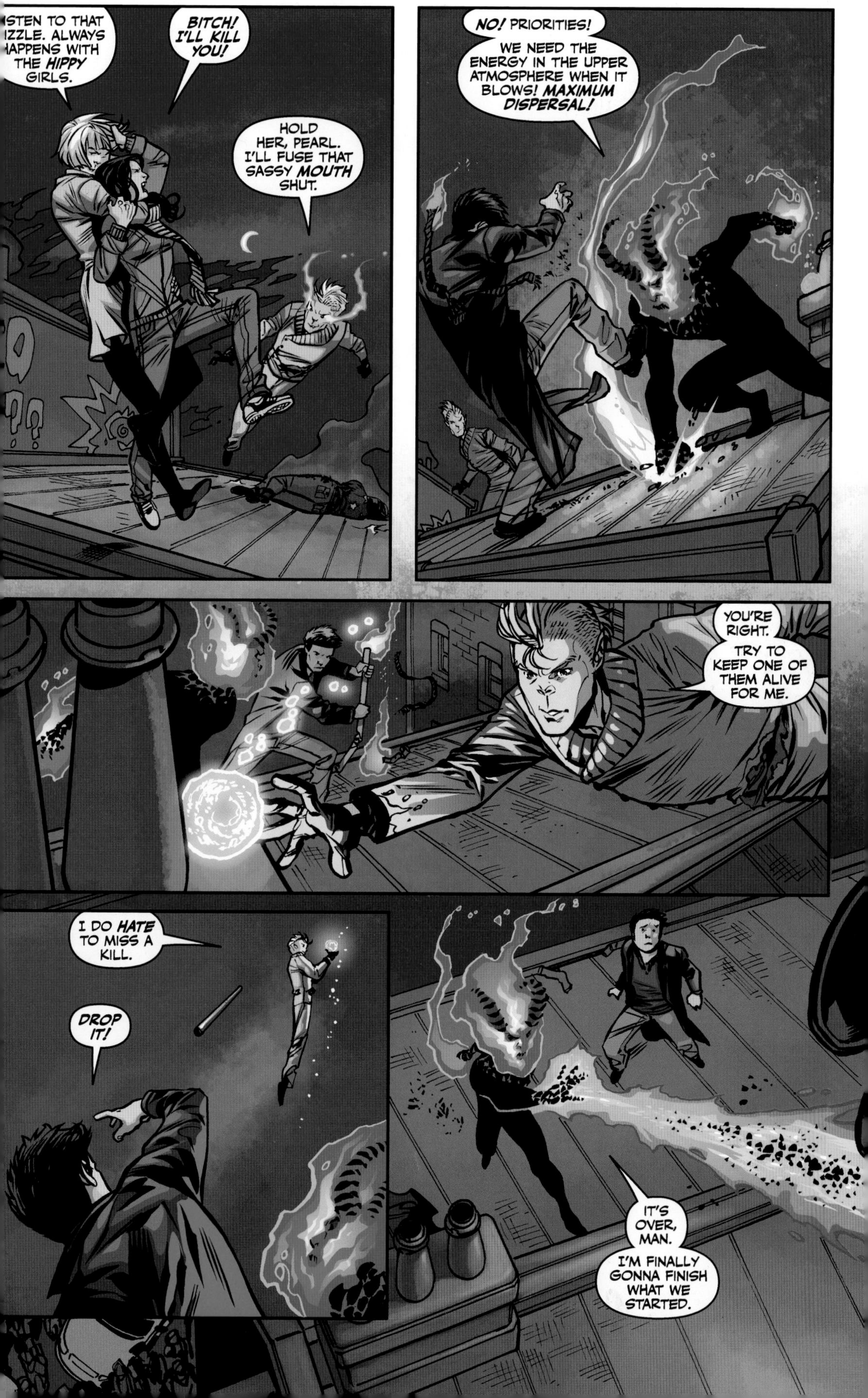
STEN TO THAT
IZZLE. ALWAYS
HAPPENS WITH
THE *HIPPY*
GIRLS.
BITCH! I'LL KILL YOU!
HOLD HER, PEARL. I'LL FUSE THAT SASSY *MOUTH* SHUT.
NO! PRIORITIES!
WE NEED THE ENERGY IN THE UPPER ATMOSPHERE WHEN IT BLOWS! *MAXIMUM DISPERSAL!*
YOU'RE RIGHT.
TRY TO KEEP ONE OF THEM ALIVE FOR ME.
I DO *HATE* TO MISS A KILL.
DROP IT!
IT'S OVER, MAN.
I'M FINALLY GONNA FINISH WHAT WE STARTED.

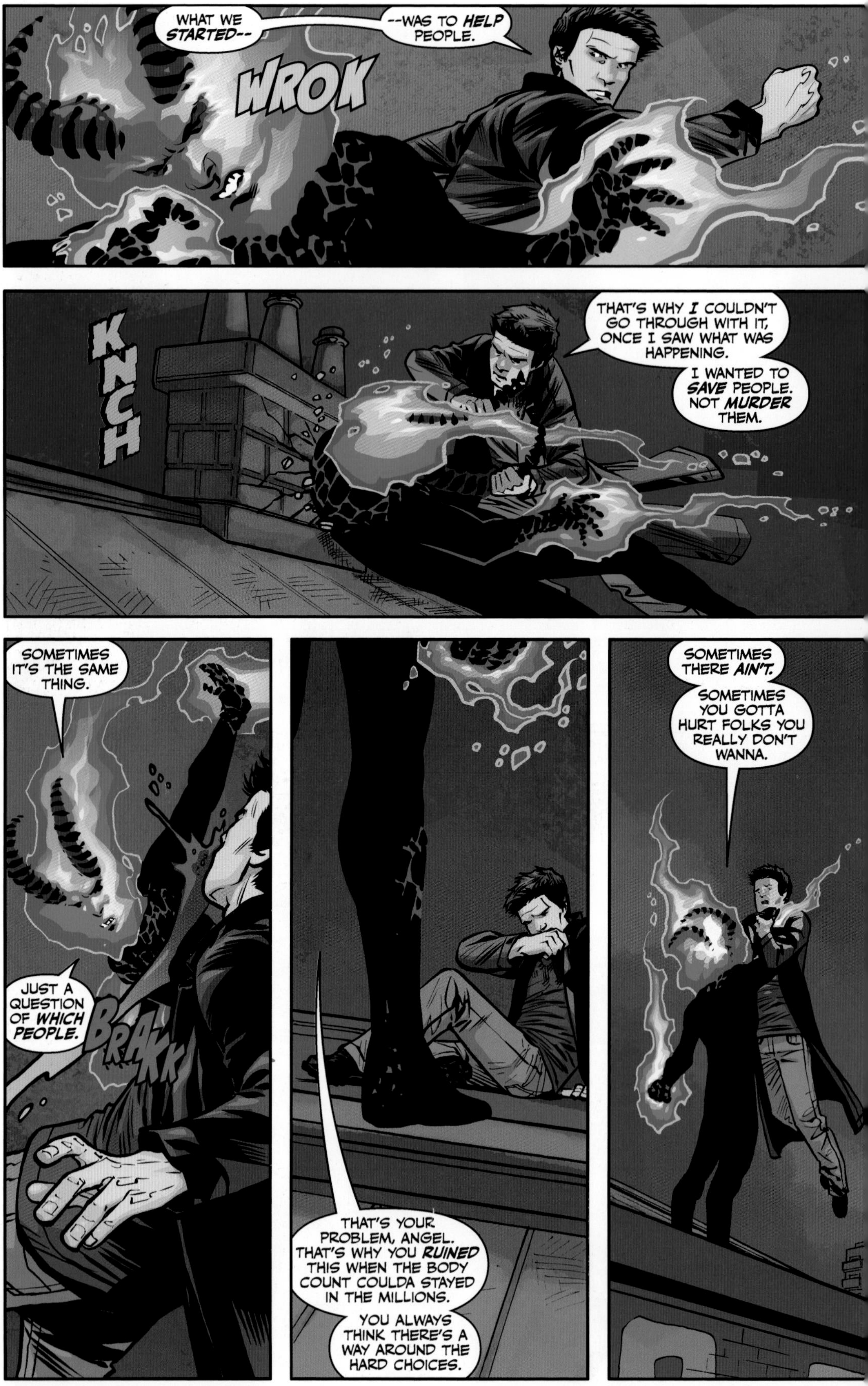

WHAT WE STARTED--
--WAS TO HELP PEOPLE.
WROK
KNCH
THAT'S WHY I COULDN'T GO THROUGH WITH IT, ONCE I SAW WHAT WAS HAPPENING.
I WANTED TO SAVE PEOPLE. NOT MURDER THEM.
SOMETIMES IT'S THE SAME THING.
JUST A QUESTION OF WHICH PEOPLE.
BRAKK
THAT'S YOUR PROBLEM, ANGEL. THAT'S WHY YOU RUINED THIS WHEN THE BODY COUNT COULDA STAYED IN THE MILLIONS.
YOU ALWAYS THINK THERE'S A WAY AROUND THE HARD CHOICES.
SOMETIMES THERE AIN'T.
SOMETIMES YOU GOTTA HURT FOLKS YOU REALLY DON'T WANNA.

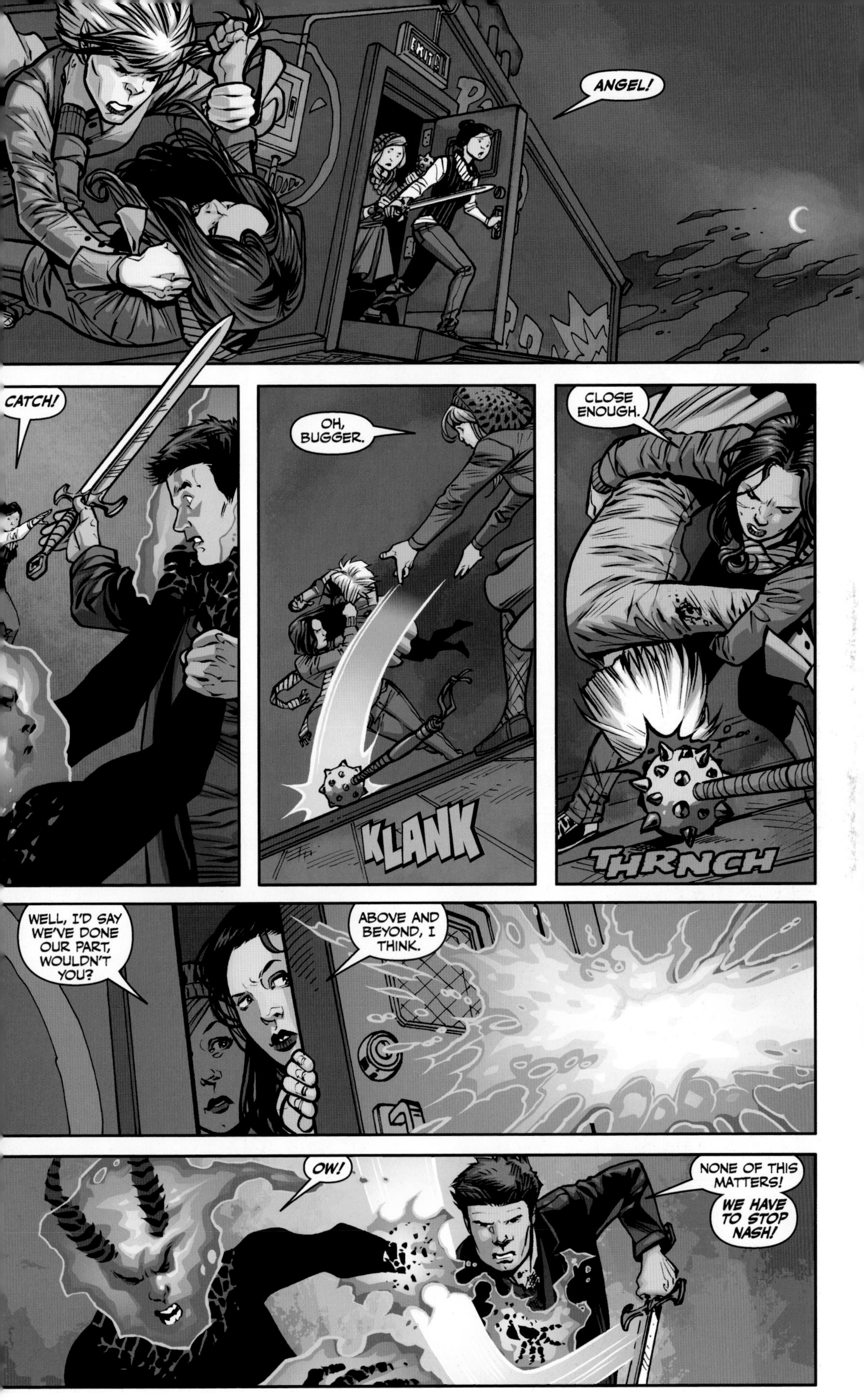
ANGEL!
CATCH!
OH, BUGGER.
KLANK
CLOSE ENOUGH.
THRNCH
WELL, I'D SAY WE'VE DONE OUR PART, WOULDN'T YOU?
ABOVE AND BEYOND, I THINK.
OW!
NONE OF THIS MATTERS!
WE HAVE TO STOP NASH!

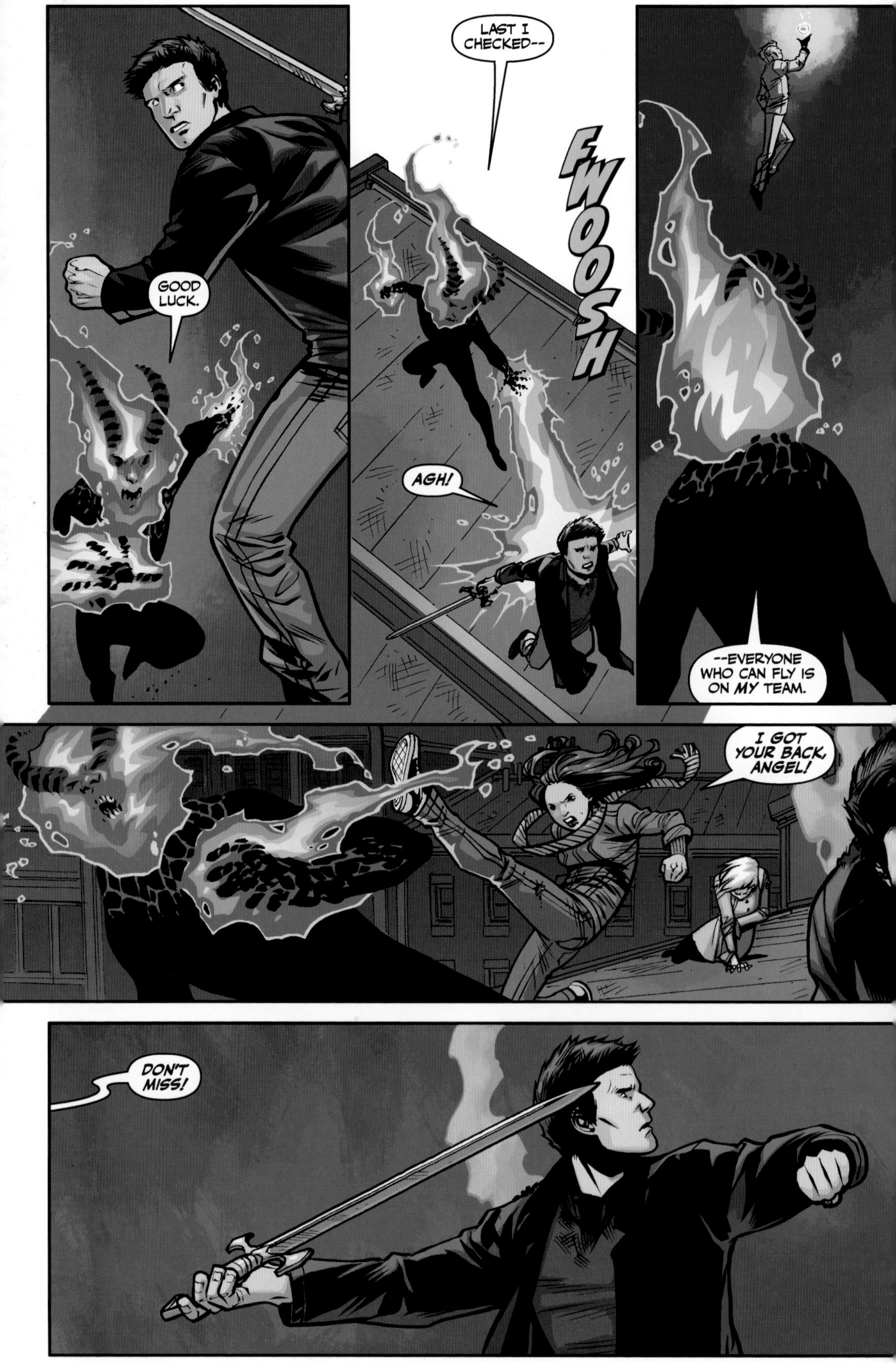
GOOD LUCK.
LAST I CHECKED--
FWOOSH
AGH!
--EVERYONE WHO CAN FLY IS ON MY TEAM.
I GOT YOUR BACK, ANGEL!
DON'T MISS!

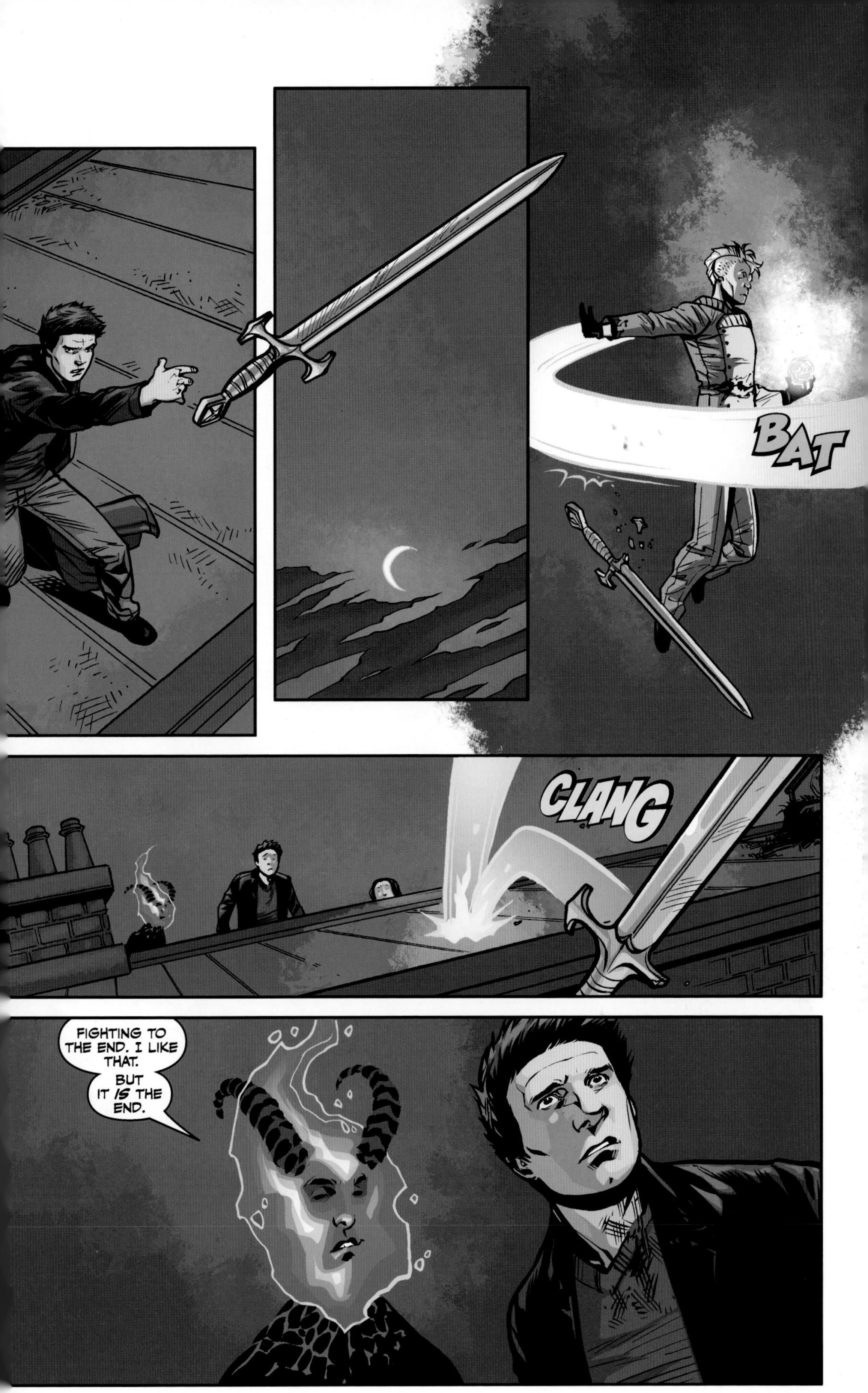
BAT
CLANG
FIGHTING TO THE END. I LIKE THAT.
BUT IT *IS* THE END.

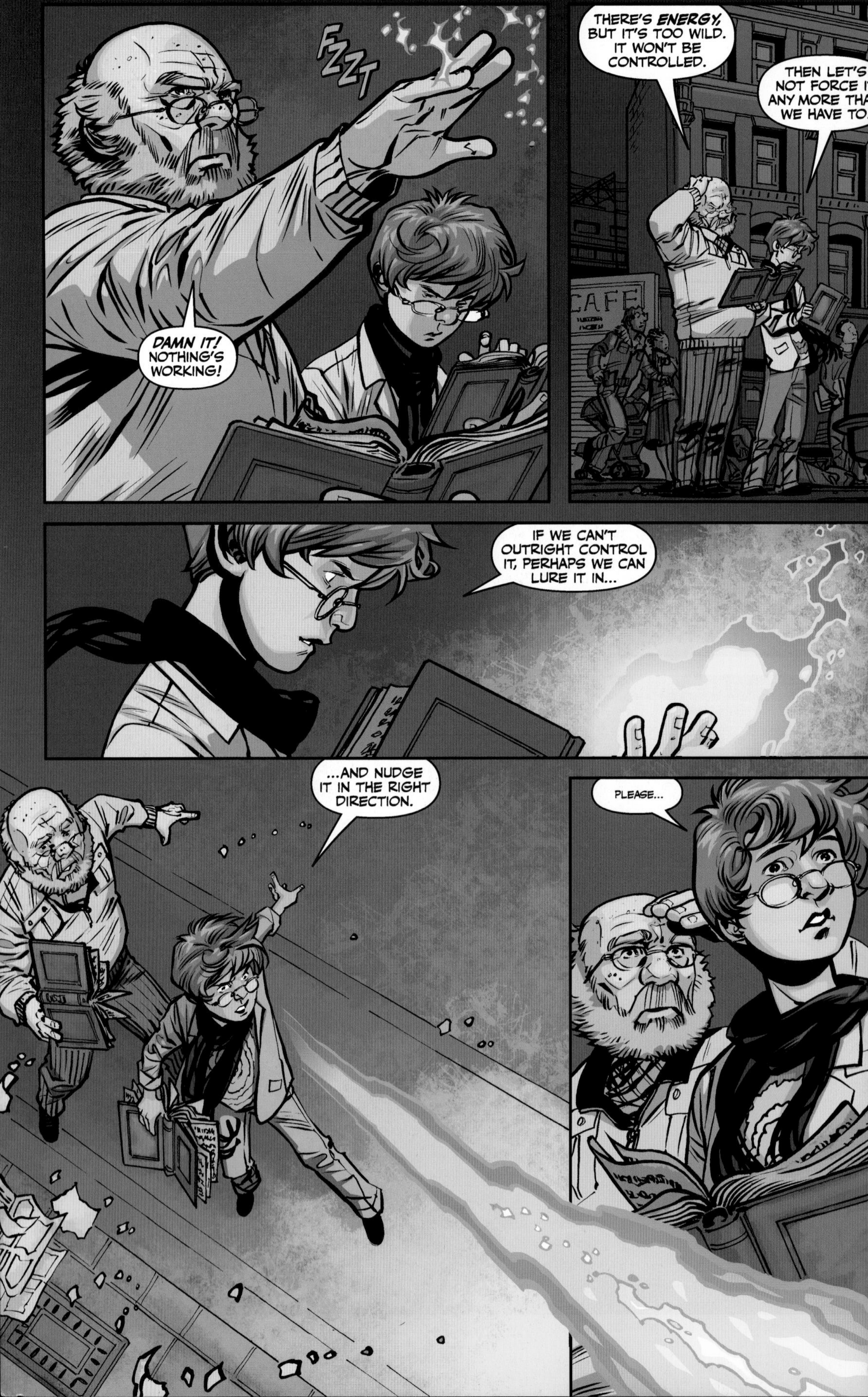
FZZT
DAMN IT! NOTHING'S WORKING!
THERE'S ENERGY, BUT IT'S TOO WILD. IT WON'T BE CONTROLLED.
THEN LET'S NOT FORCE IT ANY MORE THA WE HAVE TO.
CAFE
IF WE CAN'T OUTRIGHT CONTROL IT, PERHAPS WE CAN LURE IT IN...
...AND NUDGE IT IN THE RIGHT DIRECTION.
PLEASE...

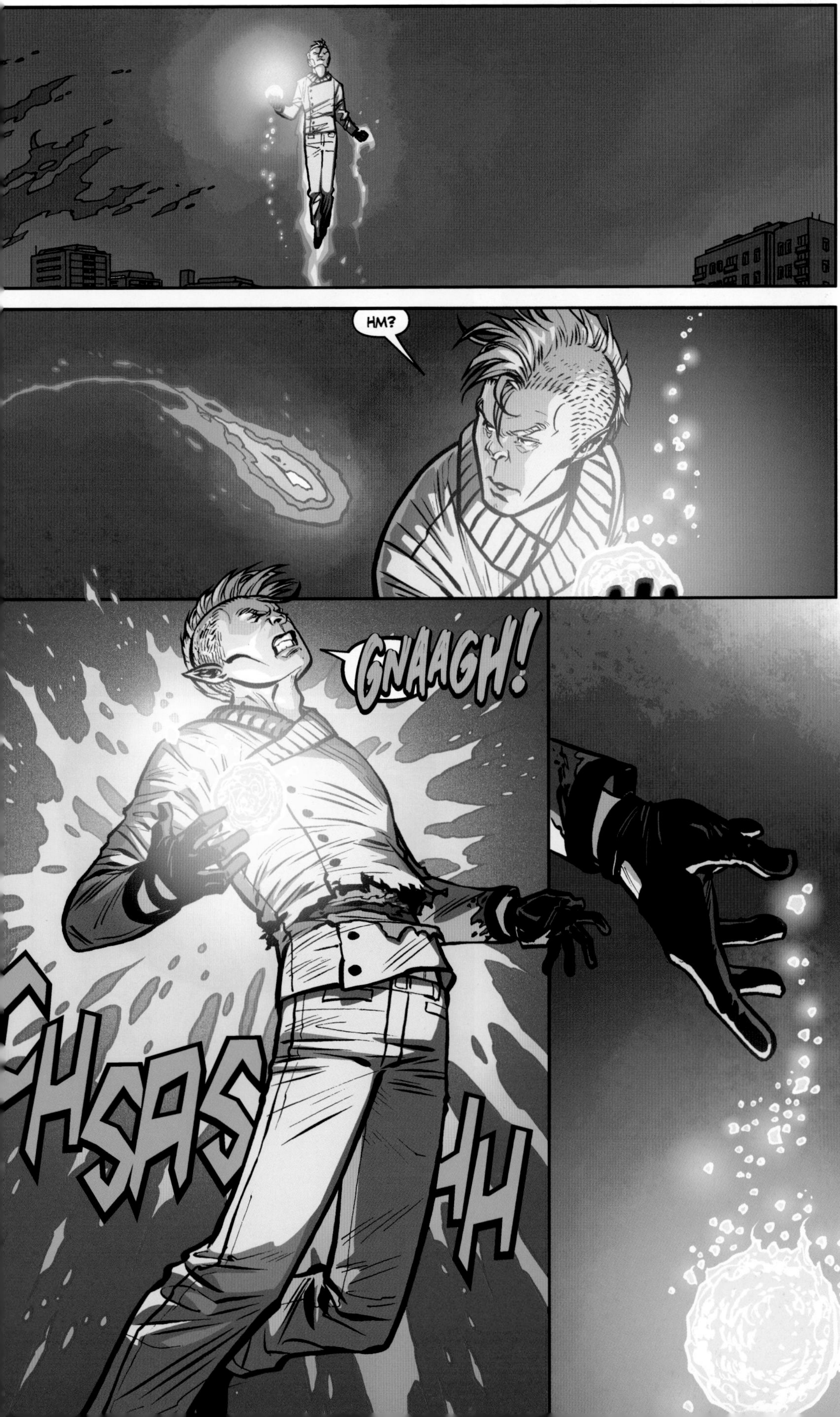
HM?
GNAAGH!
CHSASHH

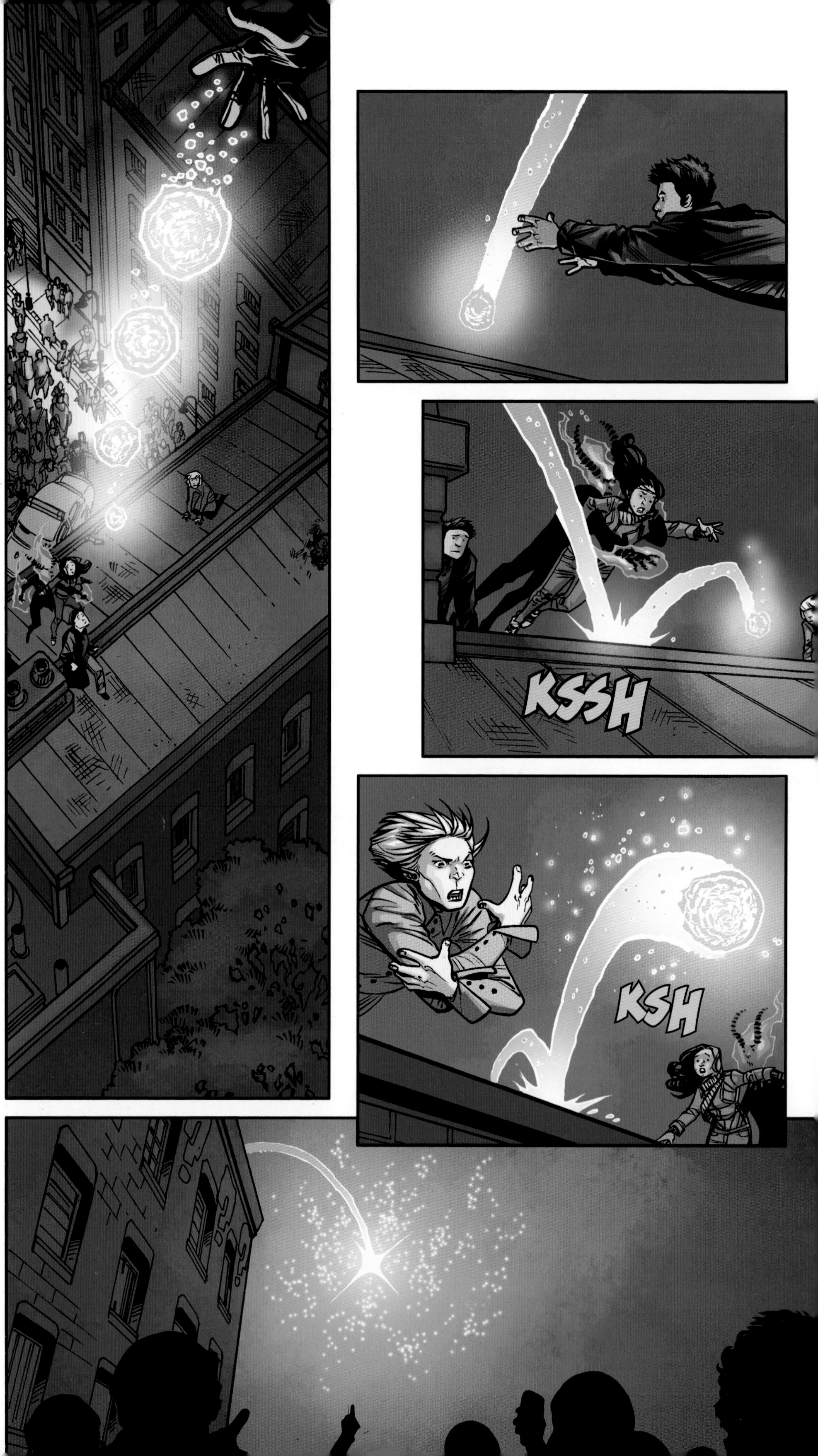
KSSH
KSH

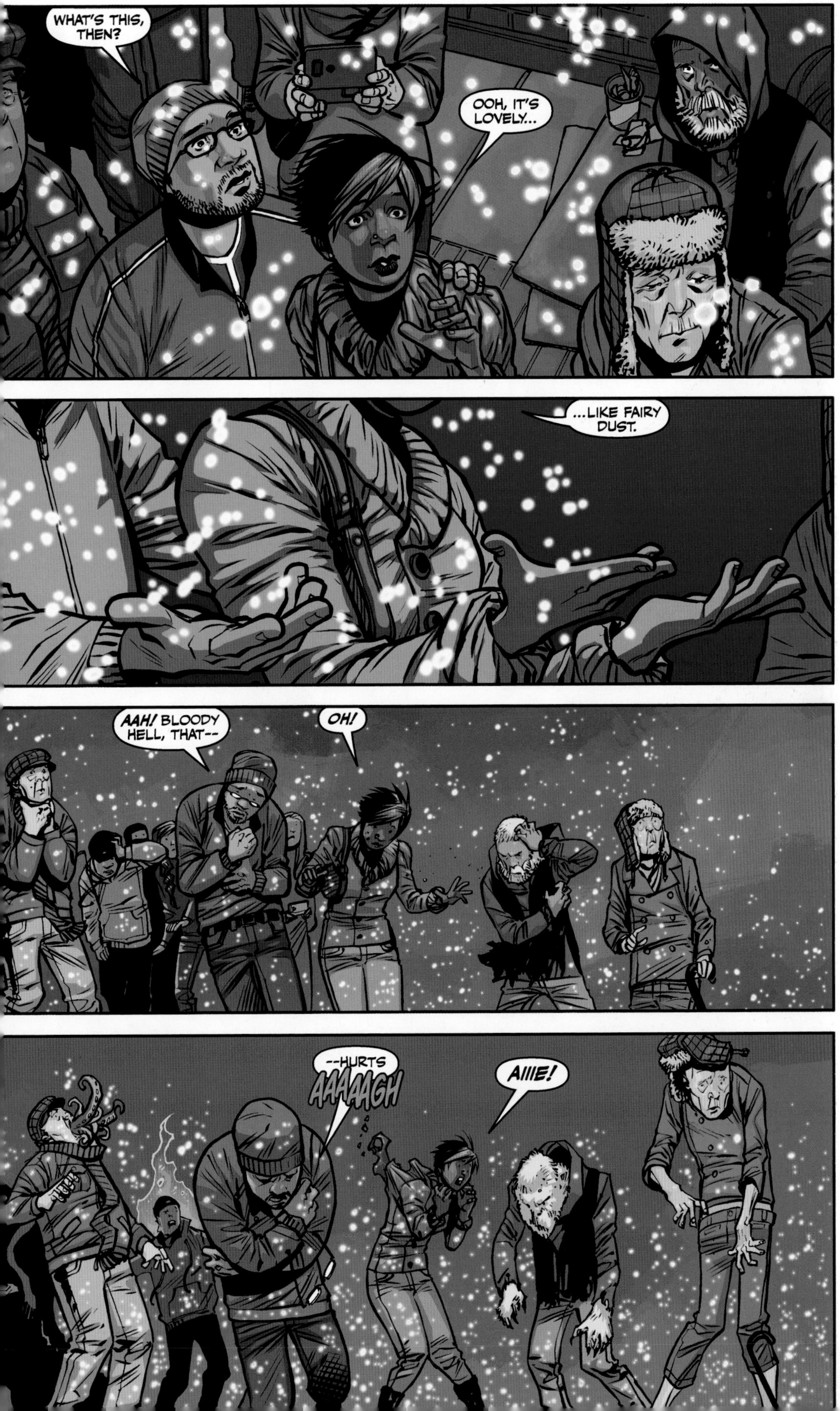
WHAT'S THIS, THEN?
OOH, IT'S LOVELY...
...LIKE FAIRY DUST.
AAH! BLOODY HELL, THAT--
OH!
--HURTS
AAAAAGH
AIIIE!

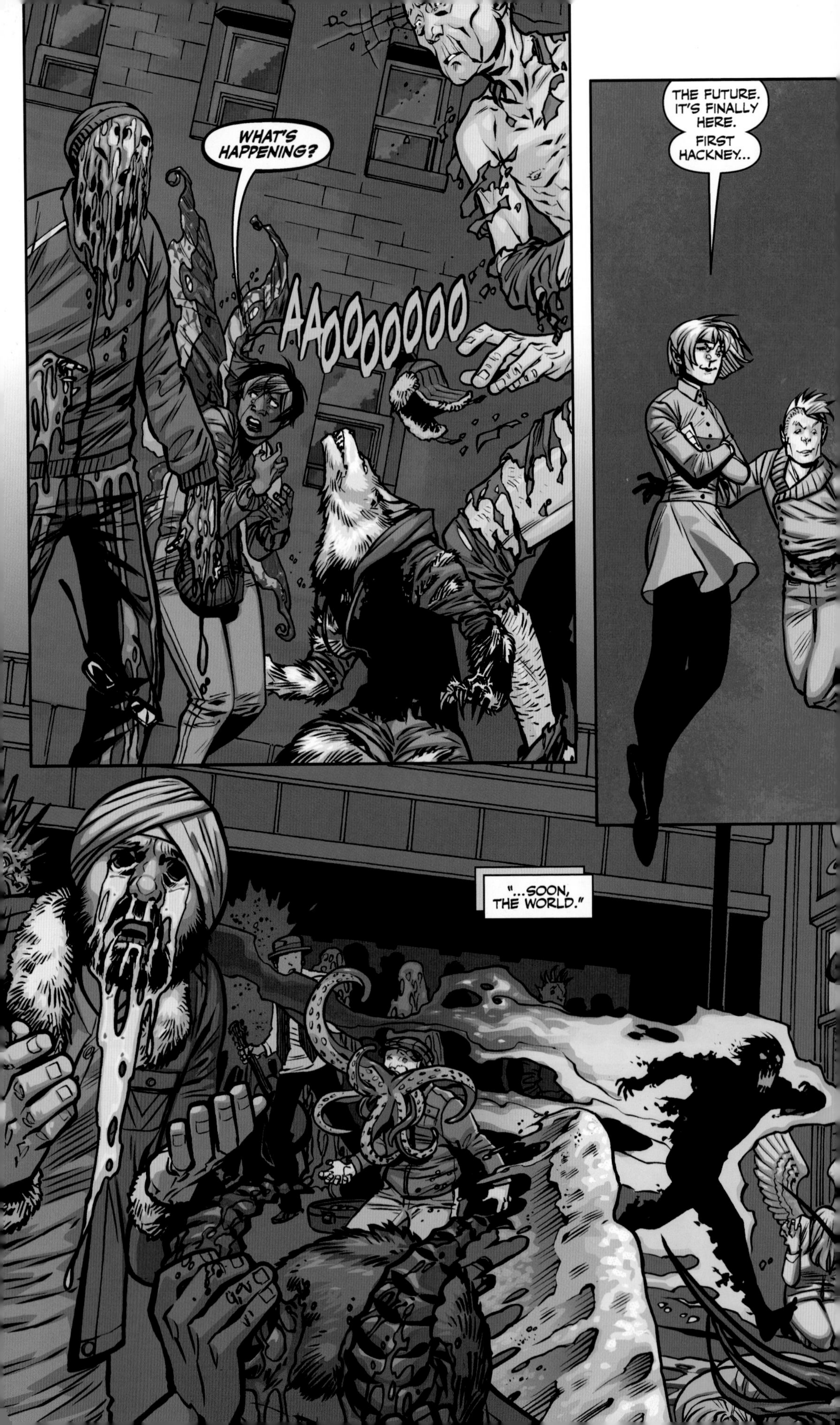
WHAT'S HAPPENING?
AAOOOOOOO
THE FUTURE. IT'S FINALLY HERE. FIRST HACKNEY...
"...SOON, THE WORLD."

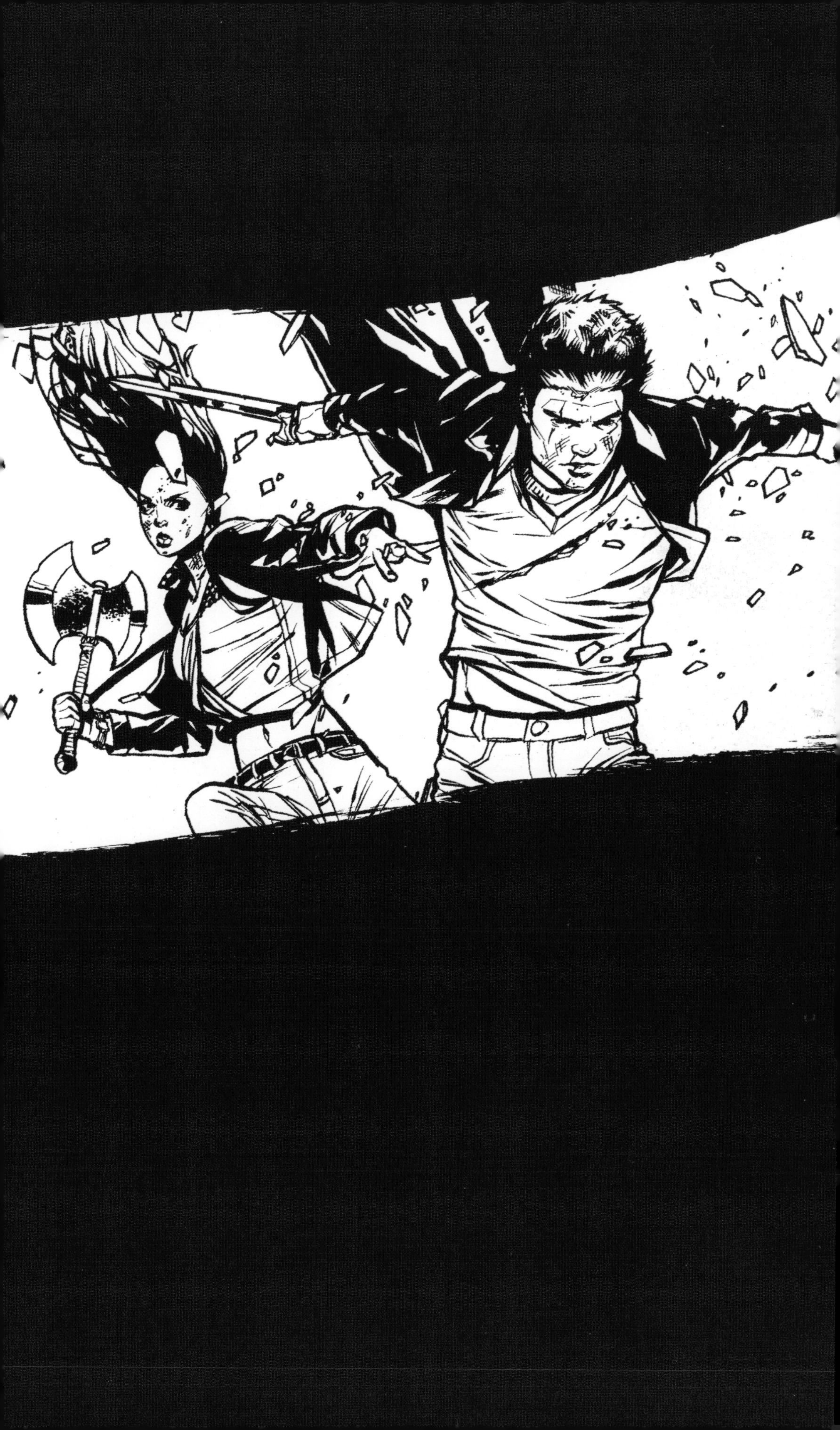

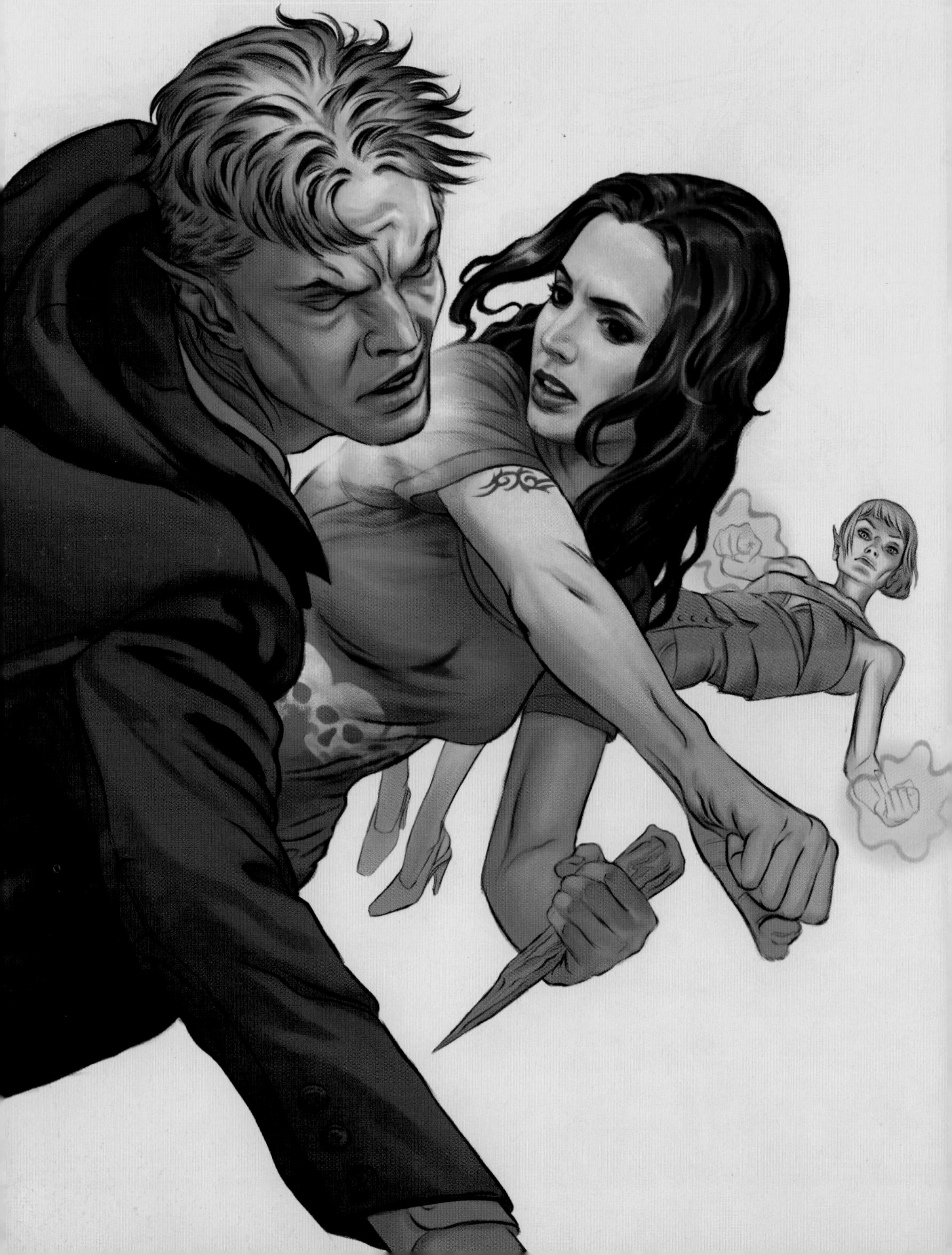

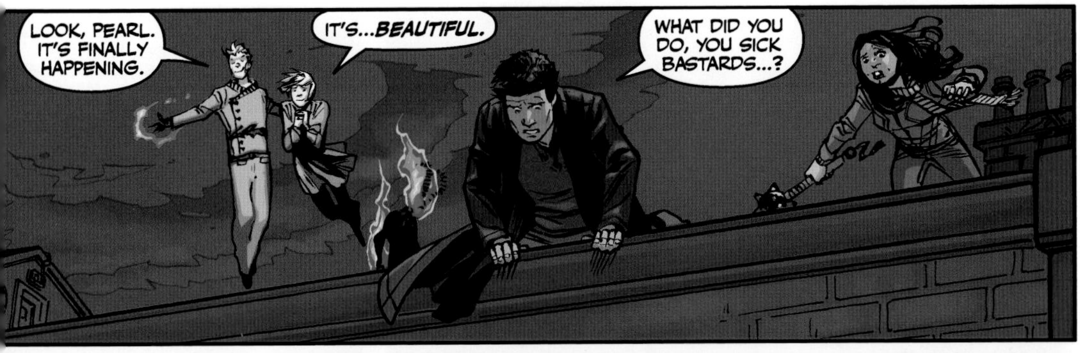
LOOK, PEARL. IT'S FINALLY HAPPENING.
IT'S...BEAUTIFUL.
WHAT DID YOU DO, YOU SICK BASTARDS...?

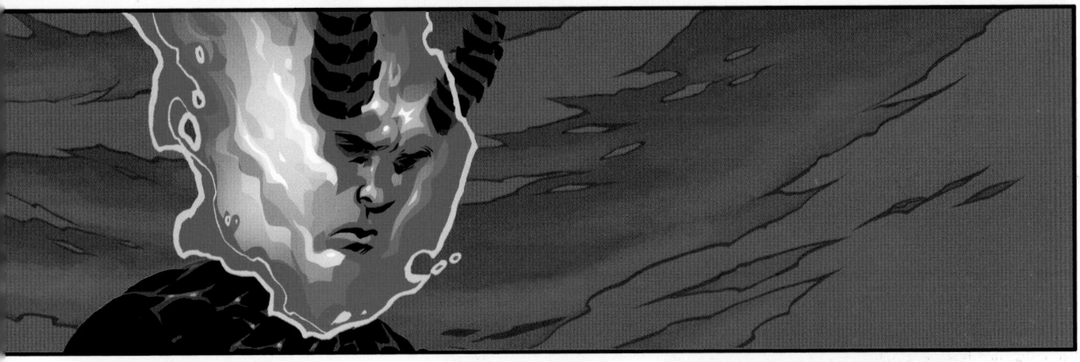

WHAT YOU WANT, NOT WHAT YOU NEED

PART 4

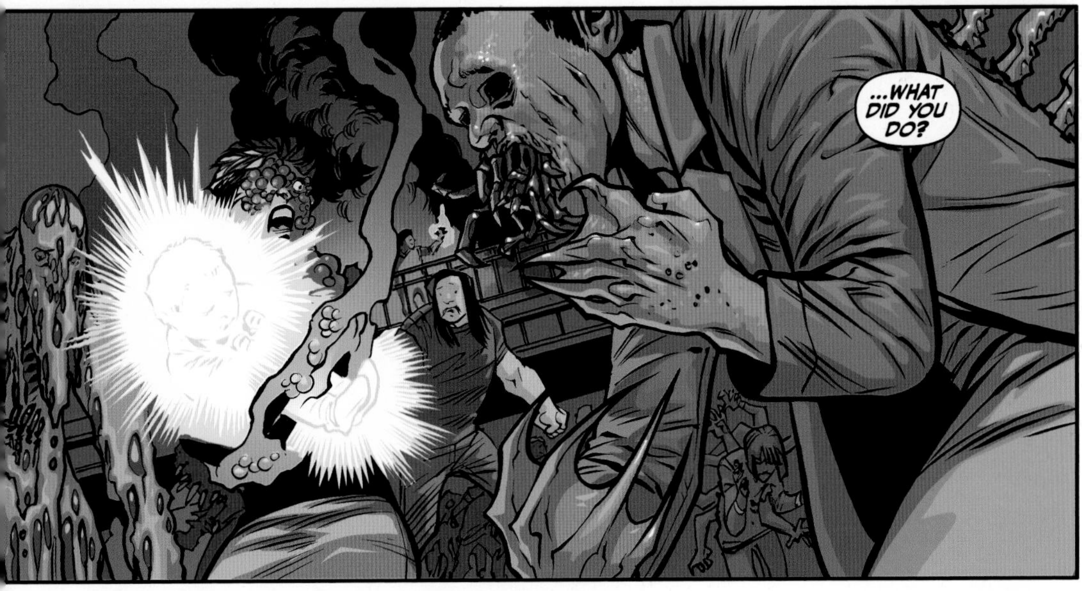
...WHAT DID YOU DO?

ANGEL, *DOWN!*

NASH. PEARL. GET THE ORB.

"IT'S DOWN THERE SOMEWHERE. BUILDING TO CRITICAL MASS."

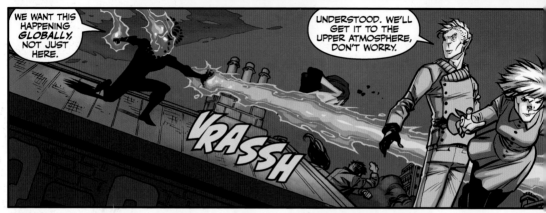

WE WANT THIS HAPPENING *GLOBALLY,* NOT JUST HERE.

UNDERSTOOD. WE'LL GET IT TO THE UPPER ATMOSPHERE, DON'T WORRY.

VRASSH

FAITH, I'LL TAKE WHISTLER. YOU NEED TO GET THE ORB.

HE'LL KILL YOU.

IF THAT THING EXPLODES, WE ALL DIE. I'LL COVER YOU.

GO!

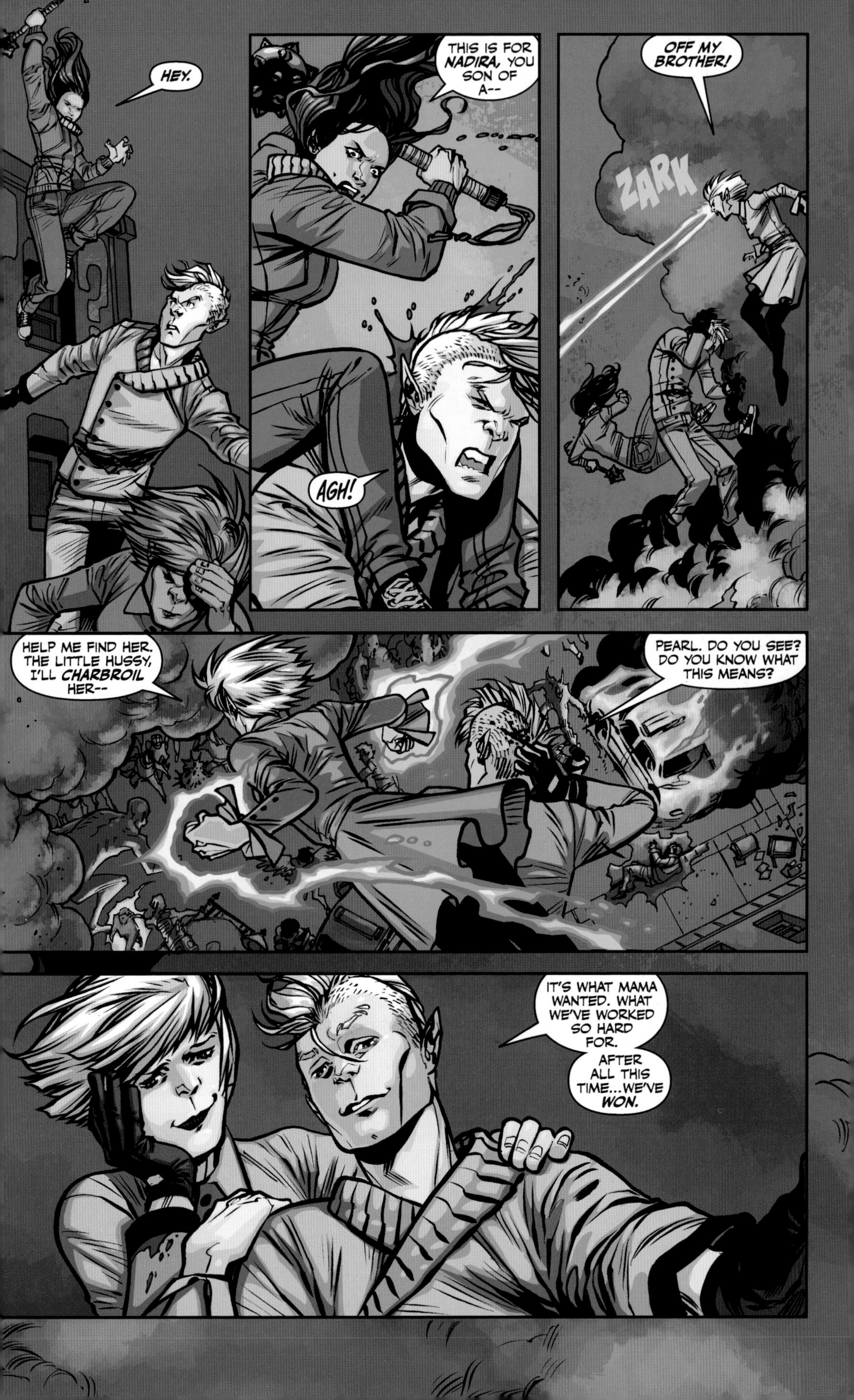
HEY.
THIS IS FOR NADIRA, YOU SON OF A--
AGH!
OFF MY BROTHER!
ZARK
HELP ME FIND HER. THE LITTLE HUSSY, I'LL CHARBROIL HER--
PEARL. DO YOU SEE? DO YOU KNOW WHAT THIS MEANS?
IT'S WHAT MAMA WANTED. WHAT WE'VE WORKED SO HARD FOR.
AFTER ALL THIS TIME...WE'VE WON.

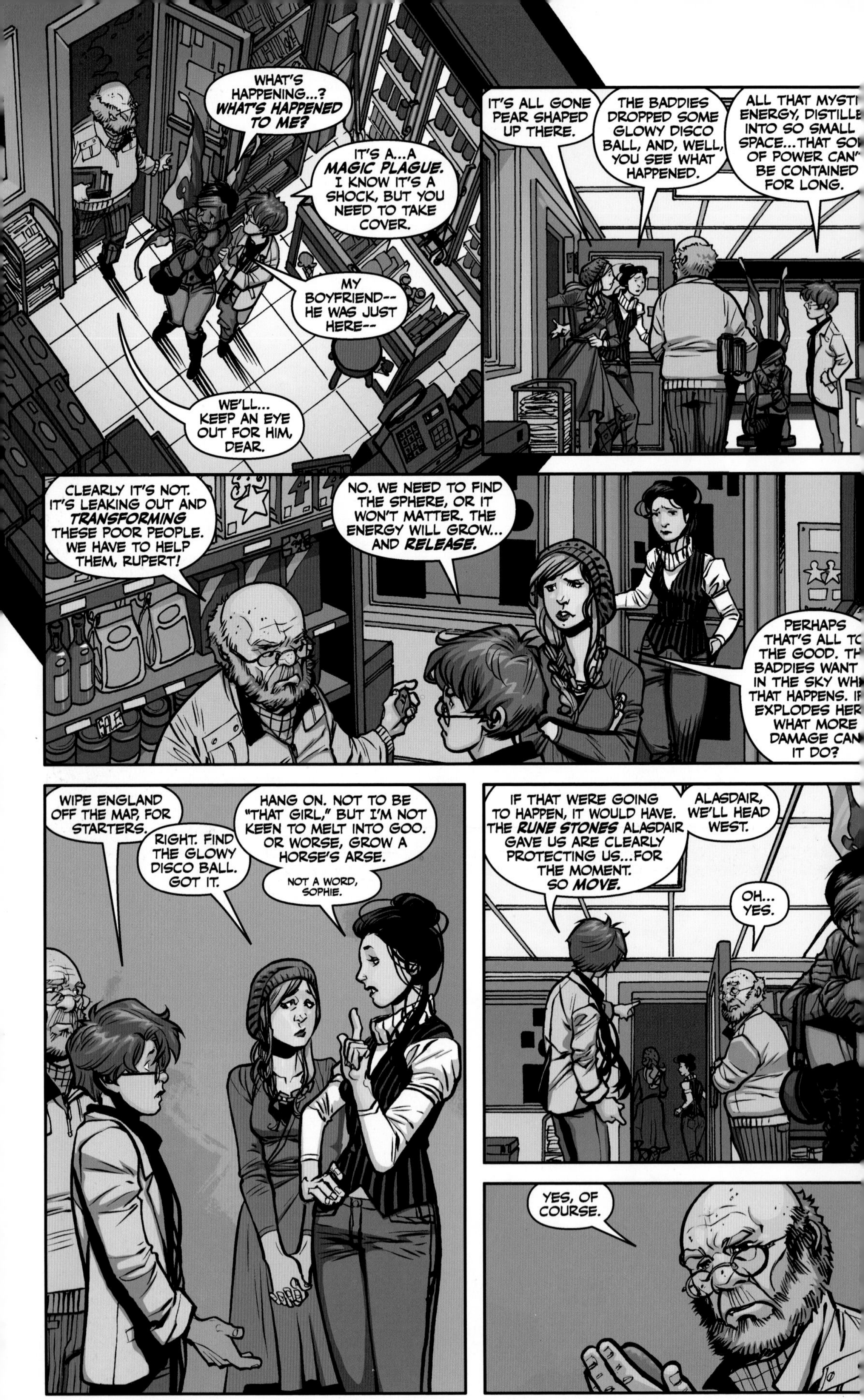
WHAT'S HAPPENING...? WHAT'S HAPPENED TO ME?
IT'S A...A MAGIC PLAGUE. I KNOW IT'S A SHOCK, BUT YOU NEED TO TAKE COVER.
MY BOYFRIEND-- HE WAS JUST HERE--
WE'LL... KEEP AN EYE OUT FOR HIM, DEAR.
IT'S ALL GONE PEAR SHAPED UP THERE.
THE BADDIES DROPPED SOME GLOWY DISCO BALL, AND, WELL, YOU SEE WHAT HAPPENED.
ALL THAT MYSTI ENERGY, DISTILLE INTO SO SMALL SPACE...THAT SO OF POWER CAN' BE CONTAINED FOR LONG.
CLEARLY IT'S NOT. IT'S LEAKING OUT AND TRANSFORMING THESE POOR PEOPLE. WE HAVE TO HELP THEM, RUPERT!
NO. WE NEED TO FIND THE SPHERE, OR IT WON'T MATTER. THE ENERGY WILL GROW... AND RELEASE.
PERHAPS THAT'S ALL TO THE GOOD. TH BADDIES WANT IN THE SKY WH THAT HAPPENS. IF EXPLODES HER WHAT MORE DAMAGE CAN IT DO?
WIPE ENGLAND OFF THE MAP, FOR STARTERS.
RIGHT. FIND THE GLOWY DISCO BALL. GOT IT.
HANG ON. NOT TO BE "THAT GIRL," BUT I'M NOT KEEN TO MELT INTO GOO. OR WORSE, GROW A HORSE'S ARSE.
NOT A WORD, SOPHIE.
IF THAT WERE GOING TO HAPPEN, IT WOULD HAVE. THE RUNE STONES ALASDAIR GAVE US ARE CLEARLY PROTECTING US...FOR THE MOMENT. SO MOVE.
ALASDAIR, WE'LL HEAD WEST.
OH... YES.
YES, OF COURSE.

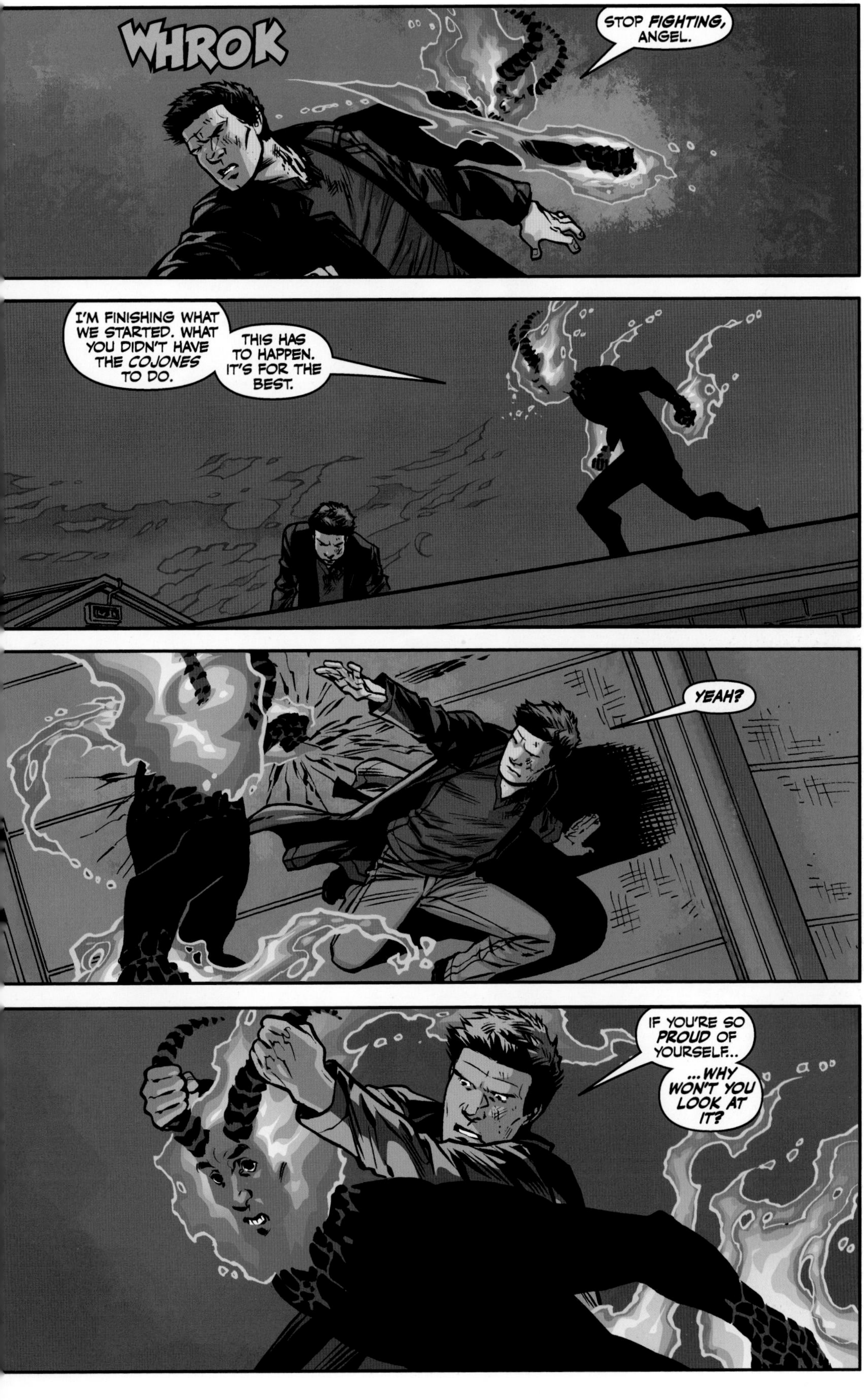
WHROK
STOP FIGHTING, ANGEL.
I'M FINISHING WHAT WE STARTED. WHAT YOU DIDN'T HAVE THE COJONES TO DO.
THIS HAS TO HAPPEN. IT'S FOR THE BEST.
YEAH?
IF YOU'RE SO PROUD OF YOURSELF...
...WHY WON'T YOU LOOK AT IT?

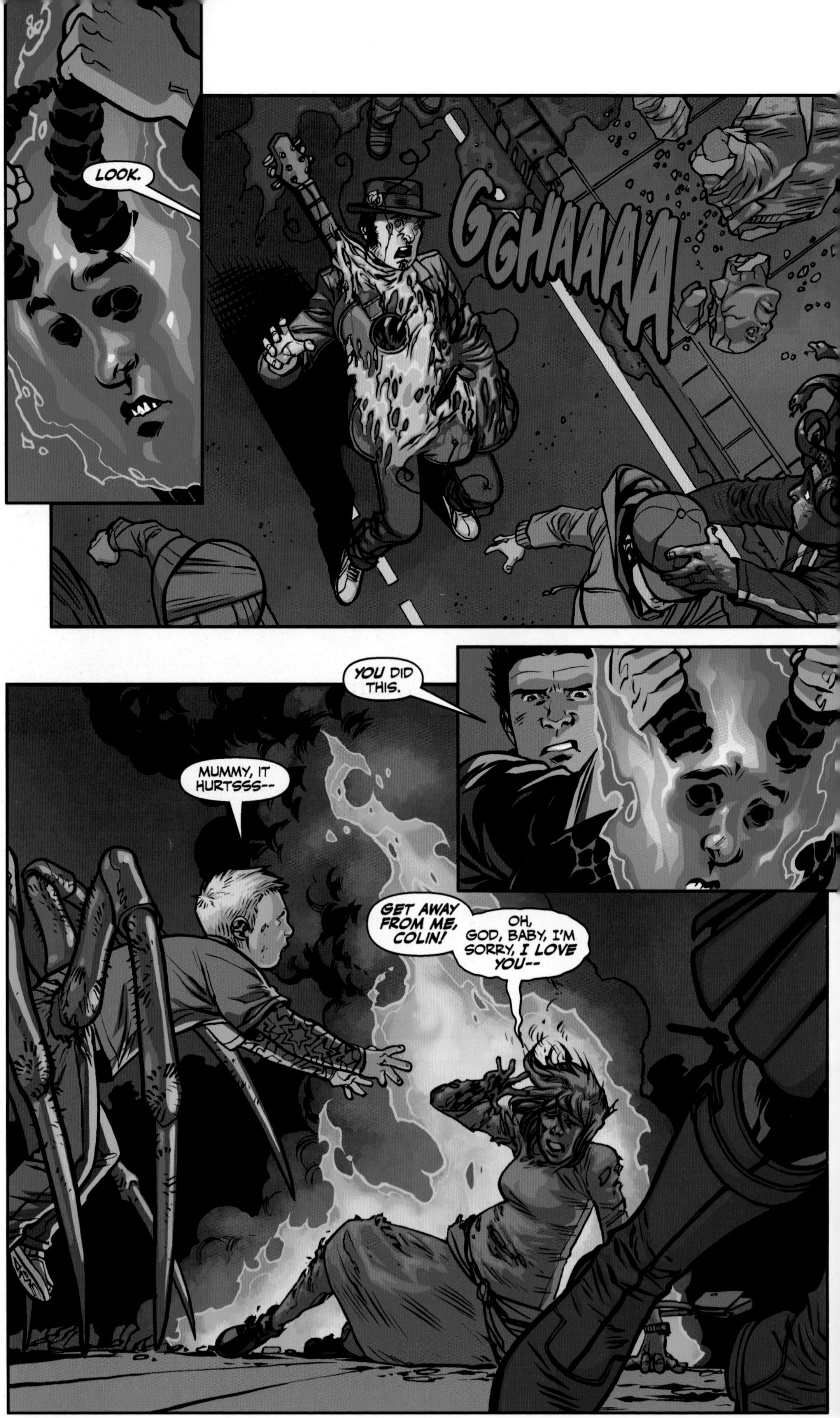
LOOK.
GGHAAAAA
YOU DID THIS.
MUMMY, IT HURTSSS--
GET AWAY FROM ME, COLIN!
OH, GOD, BABY, I'M SORRY, I LOVE YOU--

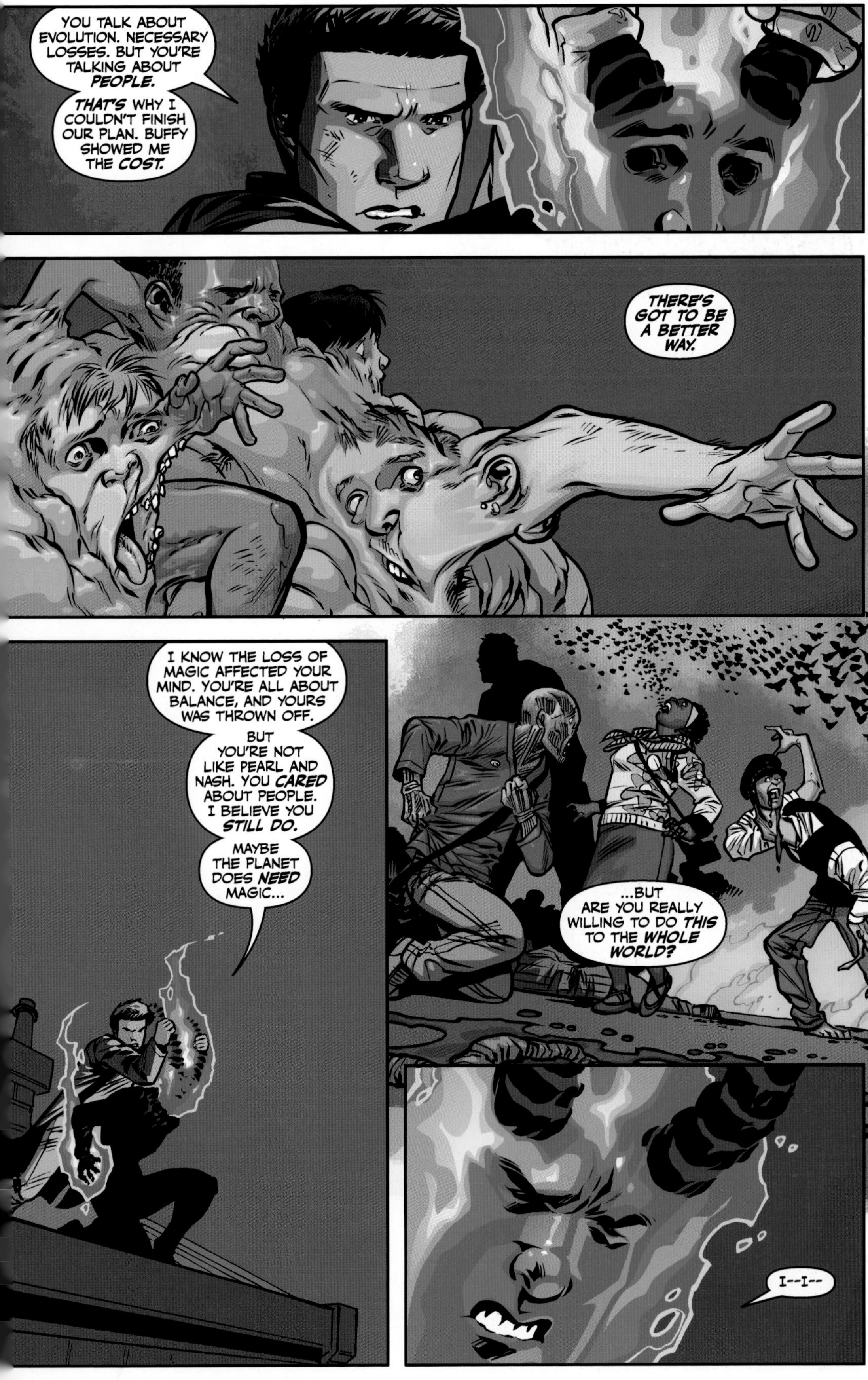
YOU TALK ABOUT EVOLUTION. NECESSARY LOSSES. BUT YOU'RE TALKING ABOUT PEOPLE.
THAT'S WHY I COULDN'T FINISH OUR PLAN. BUFFY SHOWED ME THE COST.
THERE'S GOT TO BE A BETTER WAY.
I KNOW THE LOSS OF MAGIC AFFECTED YOUR MIND. YOU'RE ALL ABOUT BALANCE, AND YOURS WAS THROWN OFF.
BUT YOU'RE NOT LIKE PEARL AND NASH. YOU CARED ABOUT PEOPLE. I BELIEVE YOU STILL DO.
MAYBE THE PLANET DOES NEED MAGIC...
...BUT ARE YOU REALLY WILLING TO DO THIS TO THE WHOLE WORLD?
I--I--

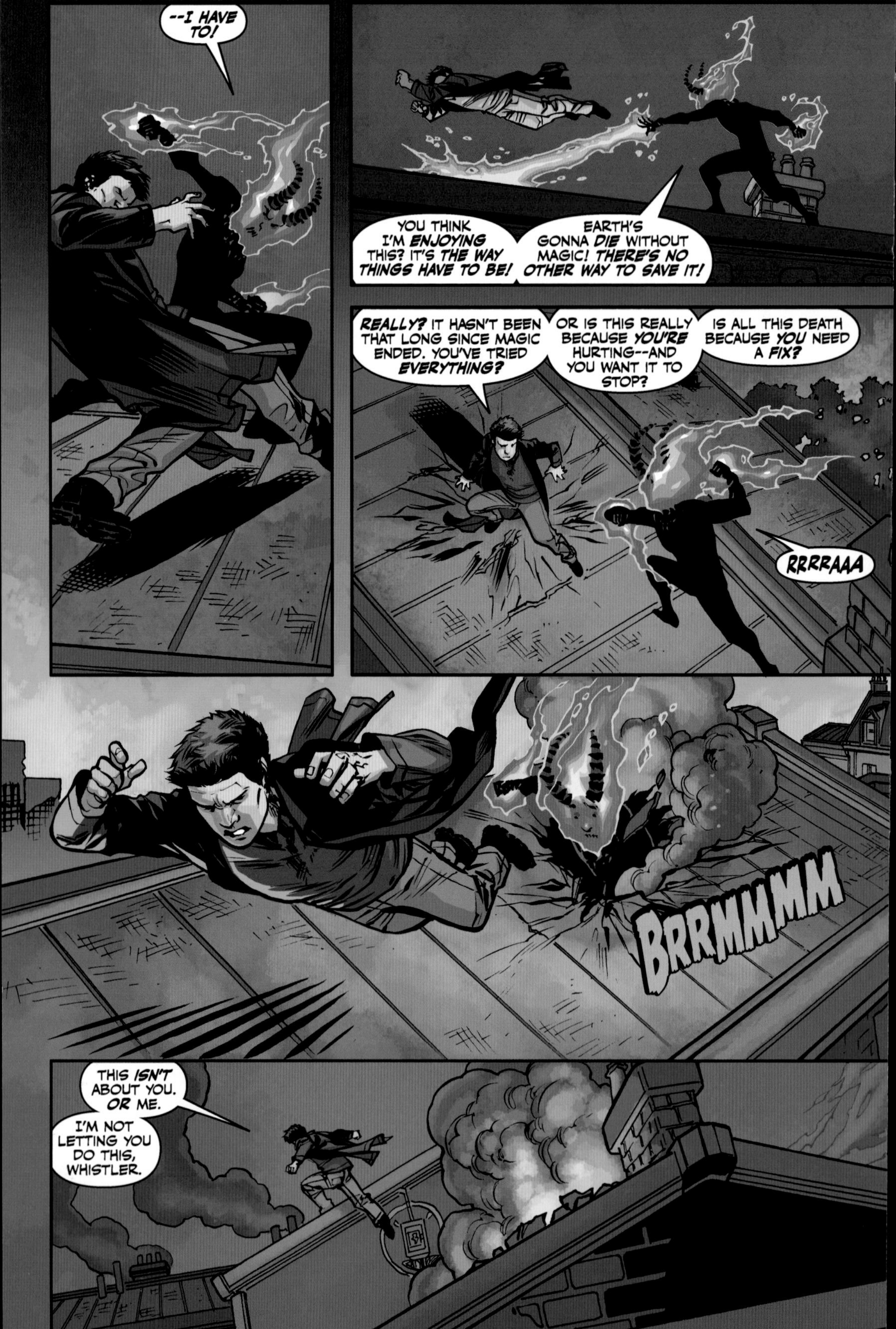
--I HAVE TO!
YOU THINK I'M ENJOYING THIS? IT'S THE WAY THINGS HAVE TO BE!
EARTH'S GONNA DIE WITHOUT MAGIC! THERE'S NO OTHER WAY TO SAVE IT!
REALLY? IT HASN'T BEEN THAT LONG SINCE MAGIC ENDED. YOU'VE TRIED EVERYTHING?
OR IS THIS REALLY BECAUSE YOU'RE HURTING--AND YOU WANT IT TO STOP?
IS ALL THIS DEATH BECAUSE YOU NEED A FIX?
RRRRAAA
BRRMMMM
THIS ISN'T ABOUT YOU. OR ME.
I'M NOT LETTING YOU DO THIS, WHISTLER.

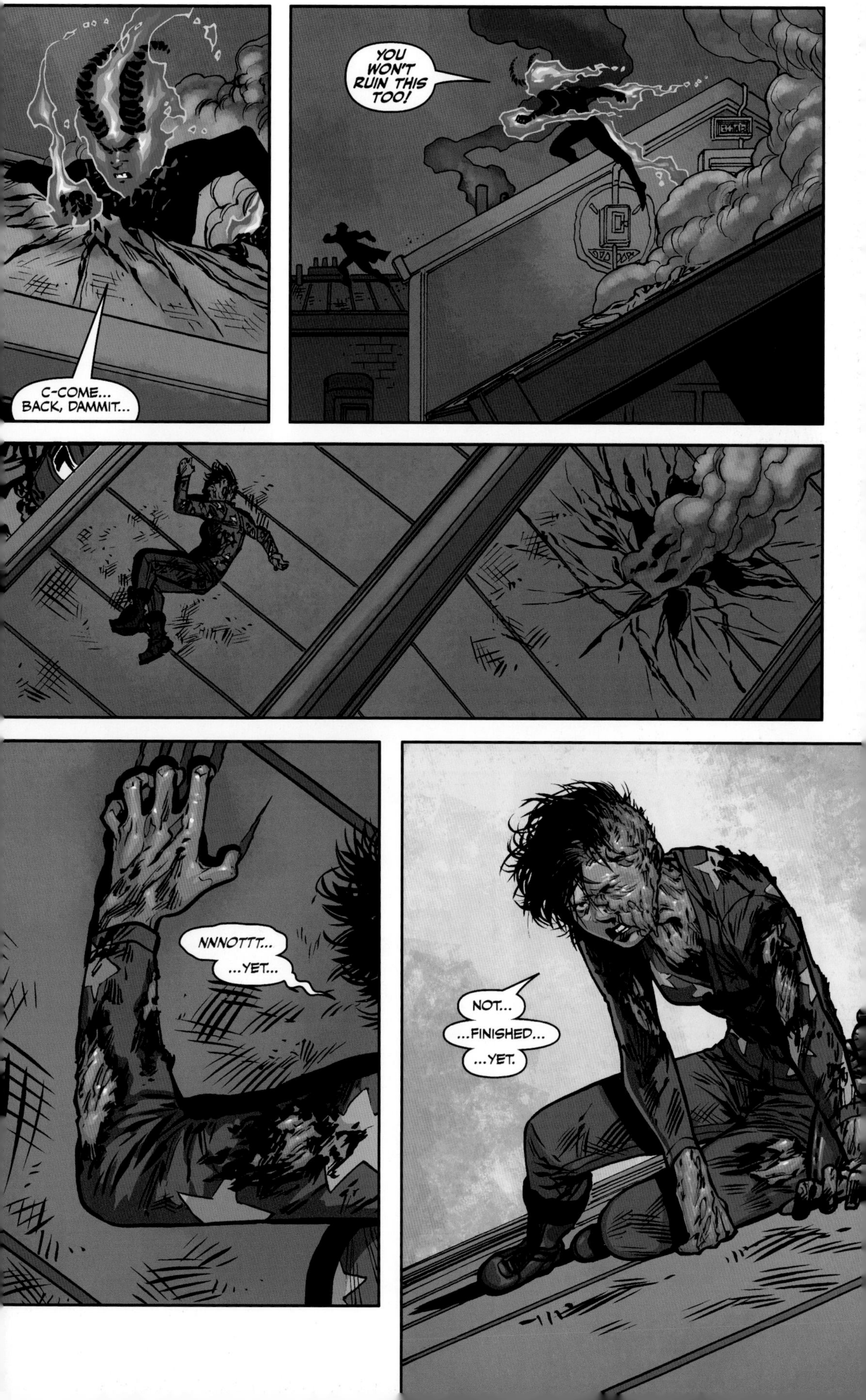

C-COME... BACK, DAMMIT...
YOU WON'T RUIN THIS TOO!
NNNOTTT... ...YET...
NOT... ...FINISHED... ...YET.

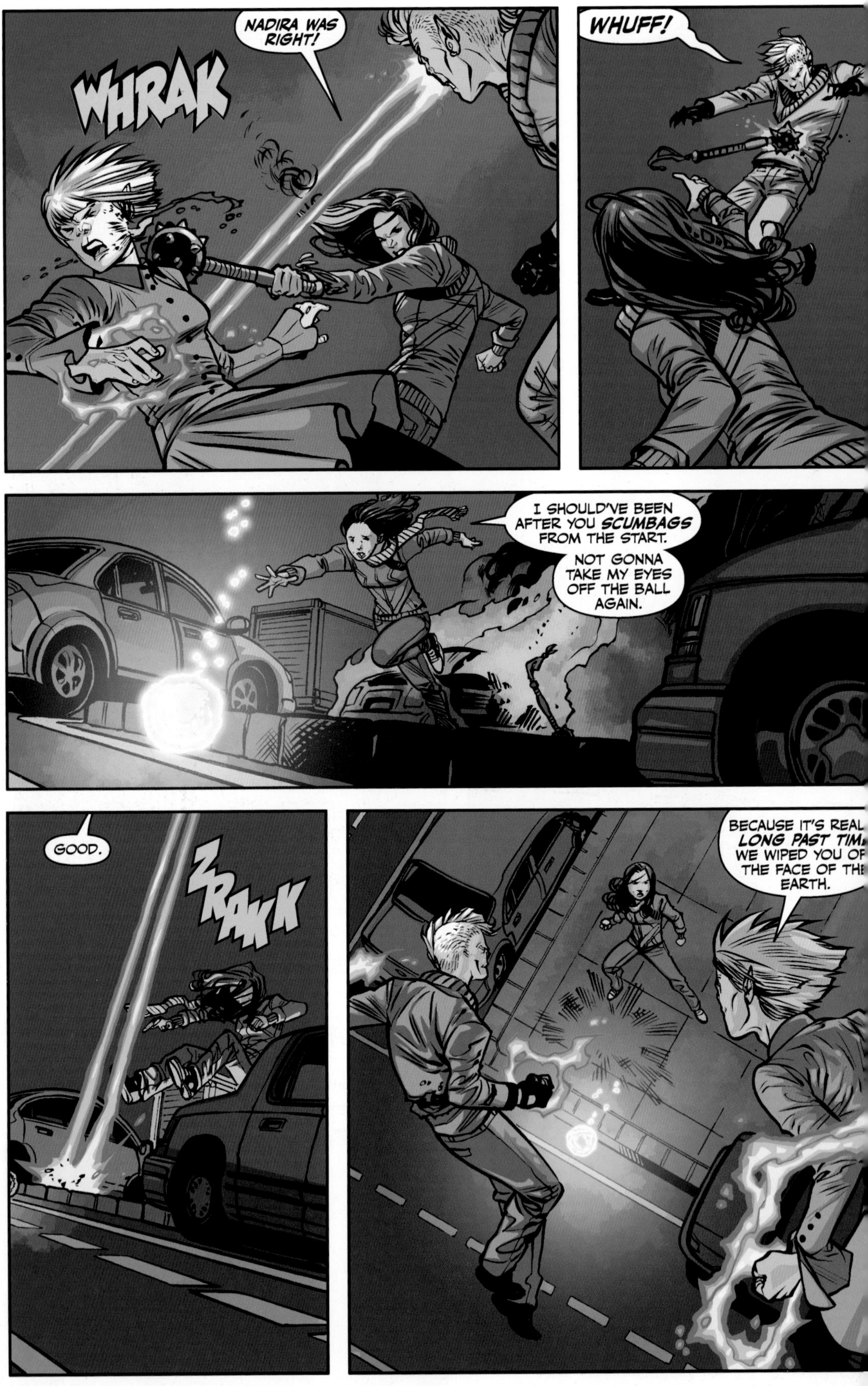
NADIRA WAS RIGHT!
WHRAK
WHUFF!
I SHOULD'VE BEEN AFTER YOU SCUMBAGS FROM THE START.
NOT GONNA TAKE MY EYES OFF THE BALL AGAIN.
GOOD.
ZRAKK
BECAUSE IT'S REAL LONG PAST TIM WE WIPED YOU OF THE FACE OF TH EARTH.

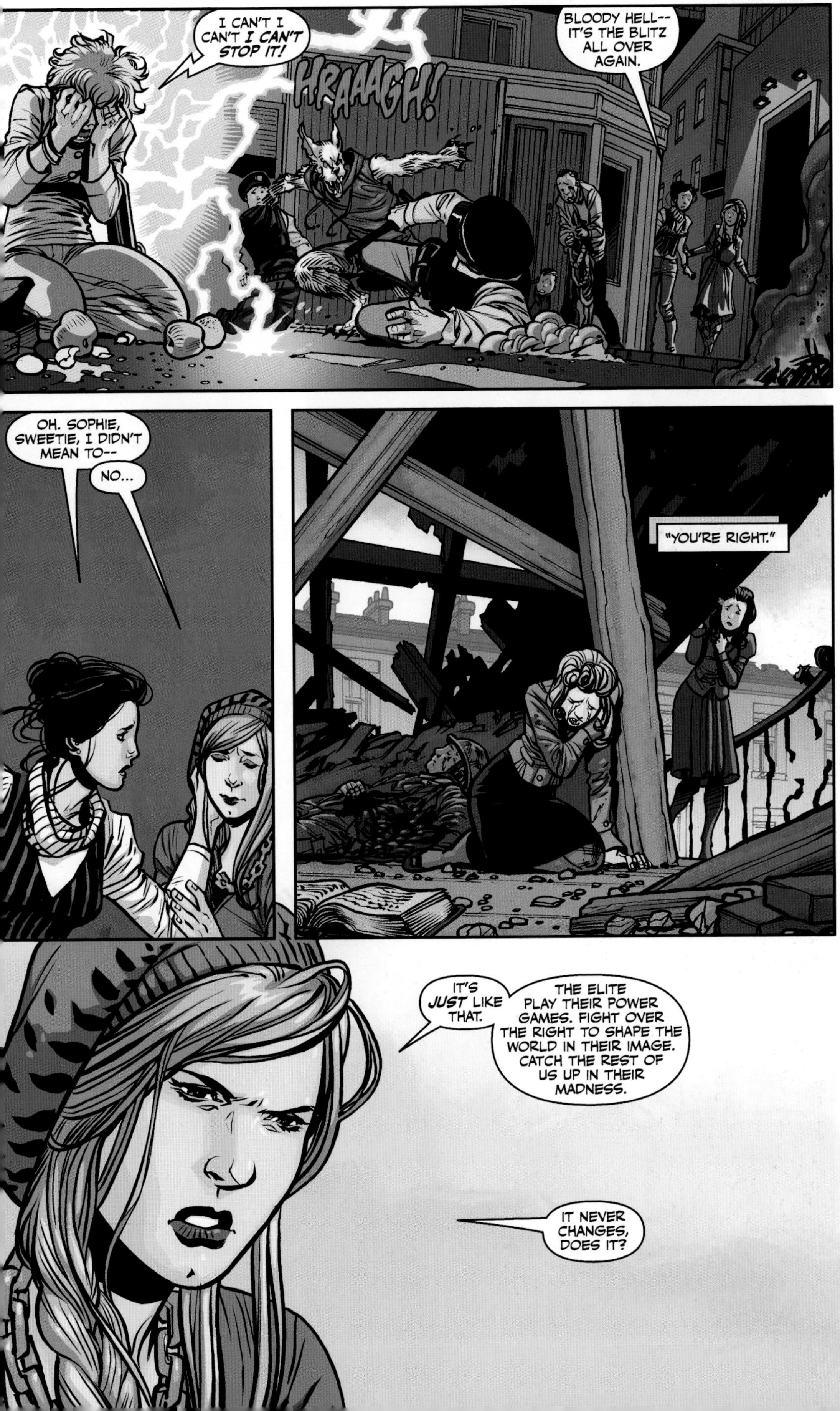
I CAN'T I CAN'T *I CAN'T STOP IT!*
HRAAAGH!
BLOODY HELL-- IT'S THE BLITZ ALL OVER AGAIN.
OH. SOPHIE, SWEETIE, I DIDN'T MEAN TO--
NO...
"YOU'RE RIGHT."
IT'S *JUST* LIKE THAT.
THE ELITE PLAY THEIR POWER GAMES. FIGHT OVER THE RIGHT TO SHAPE THE WORLD IN THEIR IMAGE. CATCH THE REST OF US UP IN THEIR MADNESS.
IT NEVER CHANGES, DOES IT?

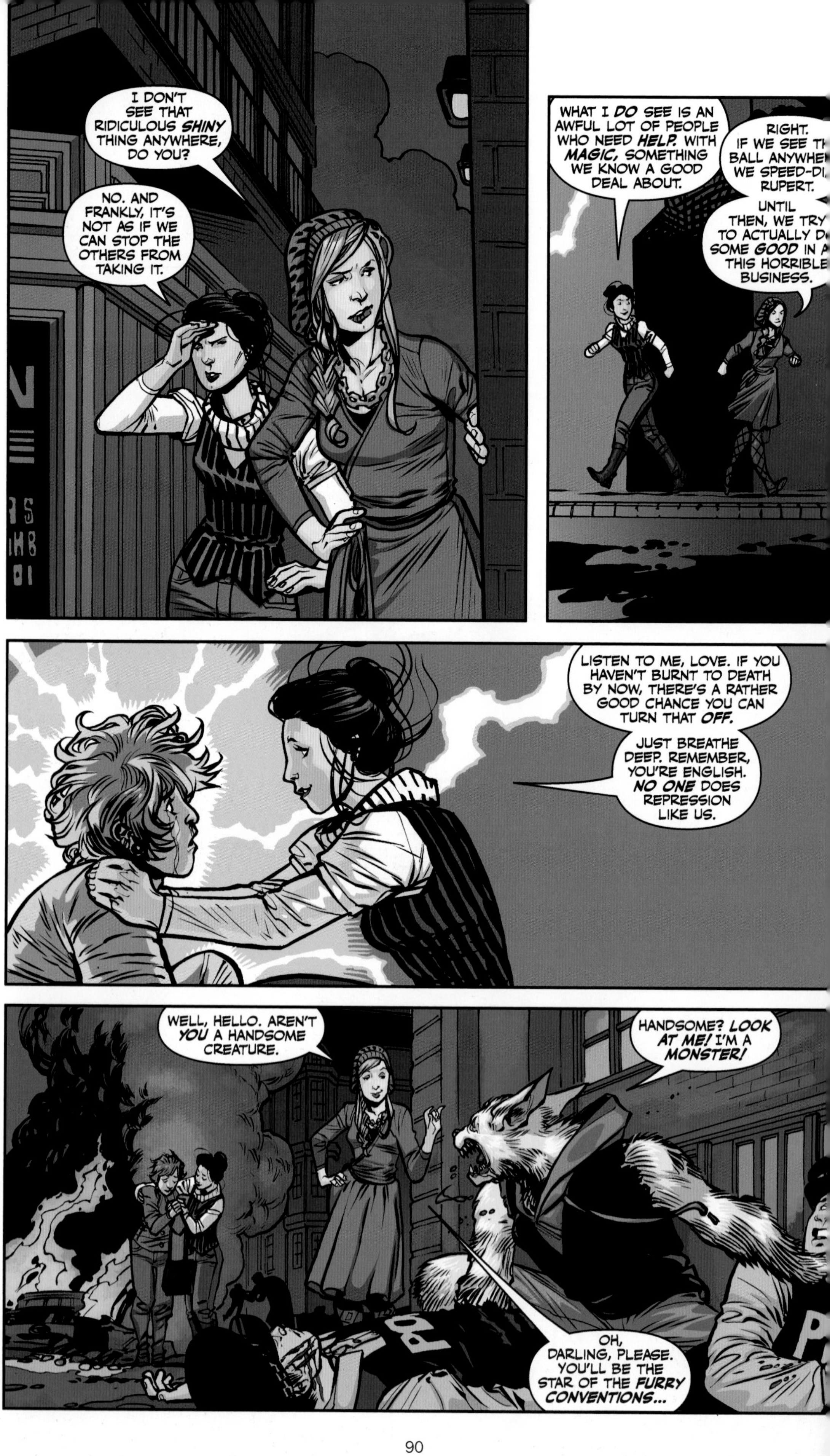
I DON'T SEE THAT RIDICULOUS *SHINY* THING ANYWHERE, DO YOU?
NO. AND FRANKLY, IT'S NOT AS IF WE CAN STOP THE OTHERS FROM TAKING IT.
WHAT I *DO* SEE IS AN AWFUL LOT OF PEOPLE WHO NEED *HELP.* WITH *MAGIC,* SOMETHING WE KNOW A GOOD DEAL ABOUT.
RIGHT. IF WE SEE T BALL ANYWHE WE SPEED-DI RUPERT.
UNTIL THEN, WE TRY TO ACTUALLY D SOME *GOOD* IN A THIS HORRIBLE BUSINESS.
LISTEN TO ME, LOVE. IF YOU HAVEN'T BURNT TO DEATH BY NOW, THERE'S A RATHER GOOD CHANCE YOU CAN TURN THAT *OFF.*
JUST BREATHE DEEP. REMEMBER, YOU'RE ENGLISH. *NO ONE* DOES REPRESSION LIKE US.
WELL, HELLO. AREN'T *YOU* A HANDSOME CREATURE.
HANDSOME? *LOOK AT ME!* I'M A *MONSTER!*
OH, DARLING, PLEASE. YOU'LL BE THE STAR OF THE *FURRY CONVENTIONS...*

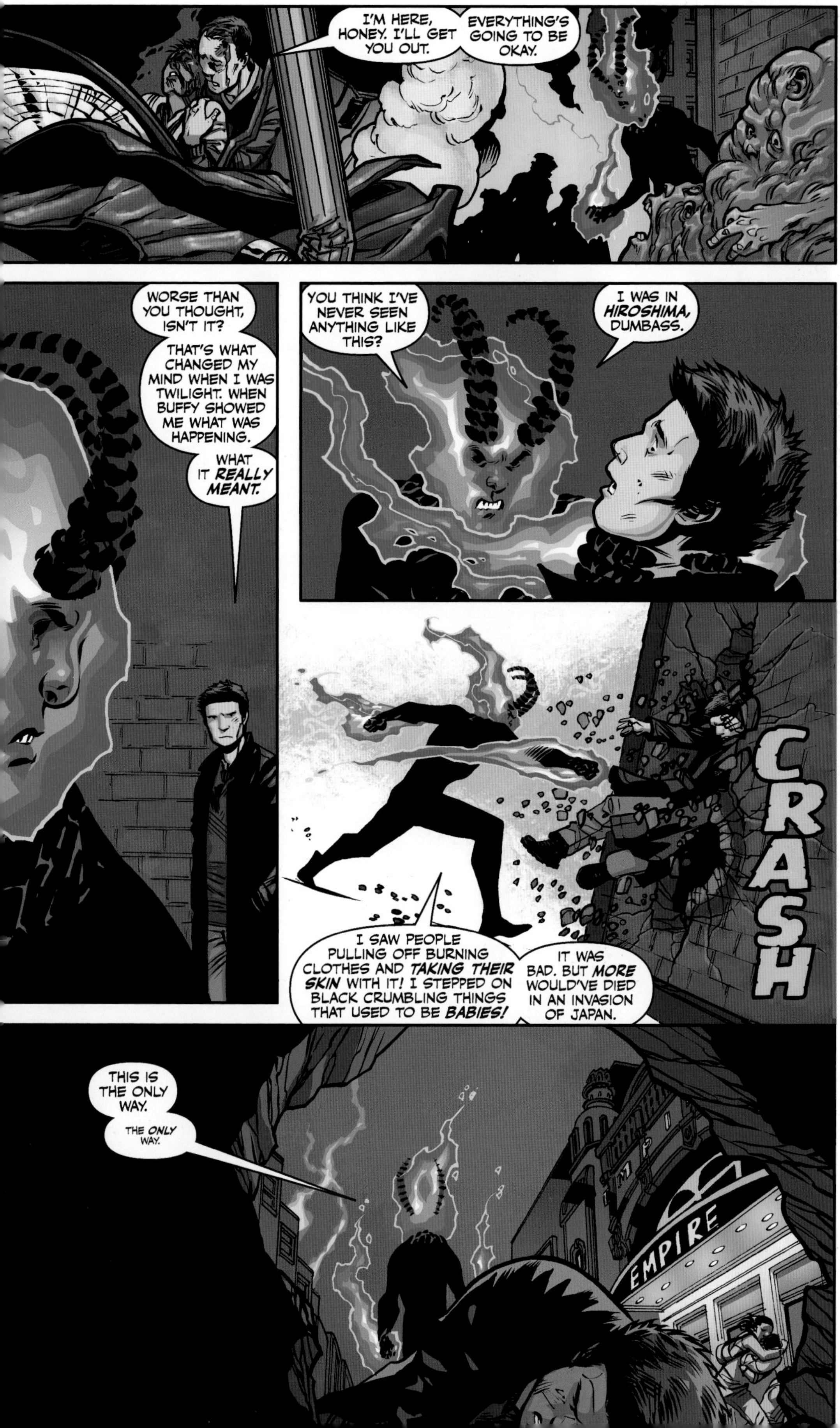
I'M HERE, HONEY. I'LL GET YOU OUT.
EVERYTHING'S GOING TO BE OKAY.
WORSE THAN YOU THOUGHT, ISN'T IT?
THAT'S WHAT CHANGED MY MIND WHEN I WAS TWILIGHT. WHEN BUFFY SHOWED ME WHAT WAS HAPPENING.
WHAT IT *REALLY MEANT.*
YOU THINK I'VE NEVER SEEN ANYTHING LIKE THIS?
I WAS IN *HIROSHIMA,* DUMBASS.
CRASH
I SAW PEOPLE PULLING OFF BURNING CLOTHES AND *TAKING THEIR SKIN* WITH IT! I STEPPED ON BLACK CRUMBLING THINGS THAT USED TO BE *BABIES!*
IT WAS BAD. BUT *MORE* WOULD'VE DIED IN AN INVASION OF JAPAN.
THIS IS THE ONLY WAY.
THE *ONLY* WAY.
EMPIRE

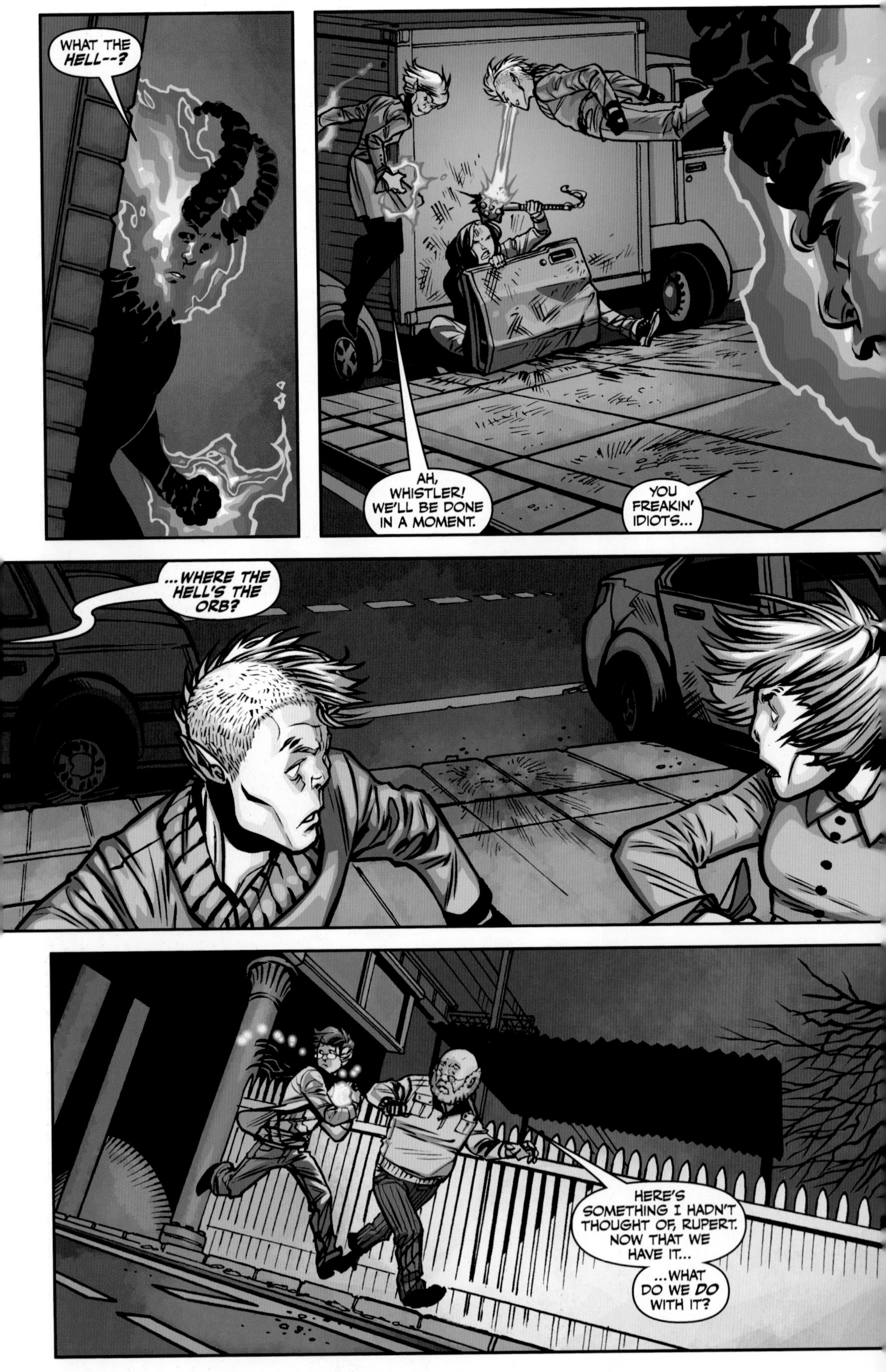
WHAT THE HELL--?
AH, WHISTLER! WE'LL BE DONE IN A MOMENT.
YOU FREAKIN' IDIOTS...
...WHERE THE HELL'S THE ORB?
HERE'S SOMETHING I HADN'T THOUGHT OF, RUPERT. NOW THAT WE HAVE IT...
...WHAT DO WE DO WITH IT?

ITS ENERGY MUST BE RELEASED...IN *CONTROLLED* FASHION.

EVEN GIVEN OUR EXPERIENCE WITH MAGIC, AND THE PROTECTIVE RUNE STONES, THERE'S GREAT RISK, MANIPULATING SUCH FORCES. YOU SHOULD TAKE COVER, ALASDAIR.

LET *ME*, RUPERT. YOU'VE JUST BEEN RESURRECTED. YOU HAVE AN ENTIRE LIFE AHEAD OF YOU. I'M OLD. I'VE LIVED LONGER THAN I EVER EXPECTED.

YOU'RE NOT MUCH OLDER THAN ME. DON'T FEEL YOU HAVE TO--

WE'RE AFTER THE SAME THING, AREN'T WE...?

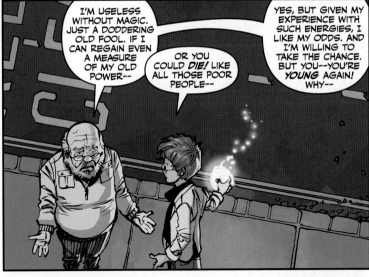

I'M USELESS WITHOUT MAGIC. JUST A DODDERING OLD FOOL. IF I CAN REGAIN EVEN A MEASURE OF MY OLD POWER--

OR YOU COULD *DIE!* LIKE ALL THOSE POOR PEOPLE--

YES, BUT GIVEN MY EXPERIENCE WITH SUCH ENERGIES, I LIKE MY ODDS. AND I'M WILLING TO TAKE THE CHANCE. BUT YOU--YOU'RE *YOUNG* AGAIN! WHY--

WHY? *LOOK* AT ME!

AT LEAST YOUR *LIFE*, YOUR *LEGACY*, IS STILL YOUR OWN. I'M NO GOOD TO *ANYONE* LIKE THIS!

I *FEEL* LIKE I'M GOING *MAD!*

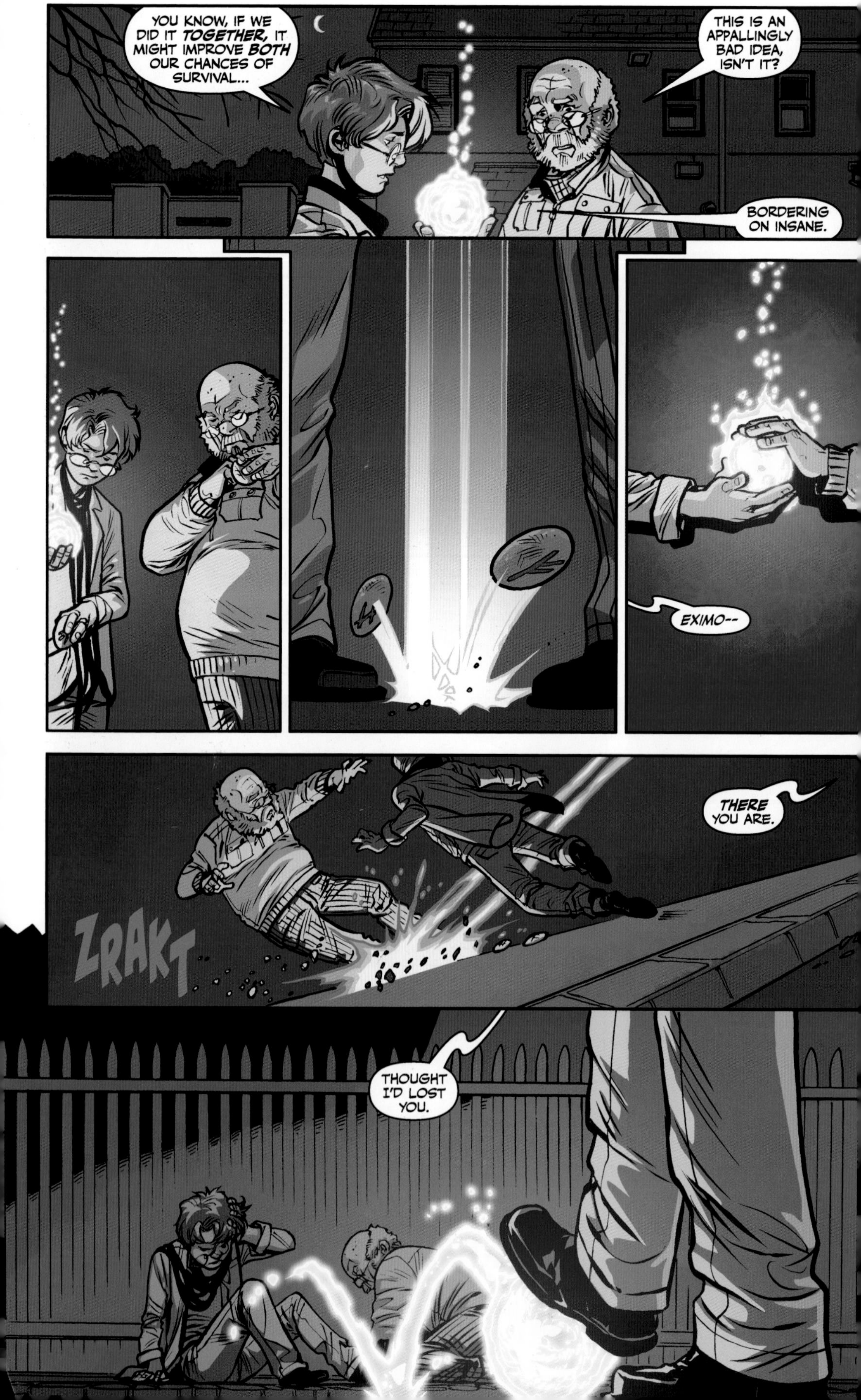
YOU KNOW, IF WE DID IT TOGETHER, IT MIGHT IMPROVE BOTH OUR CHANCES OF SURVIVAL...
THIS IS AN APPALLINGLY BAD IDEA, ISN'T IT?
BORDERING ON INSANE.
EXIMO--
THERE YOU ARE.
ZRAKT
THOUGHT I'D LOST YOU.

CKY FOR ME YOU
STOOD AROUND
NATTERING.

TEENAGERS AND OLD PEOPLE.

YOU DO LOVE THE SOUND OF YOUR OWN VOICE.

NO!

DAMN IT! FAITH, CAN YOU--

I'M TRYING!

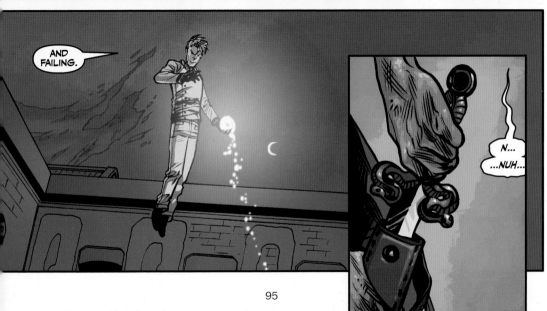

AND FAILING.

N...
...NUH...

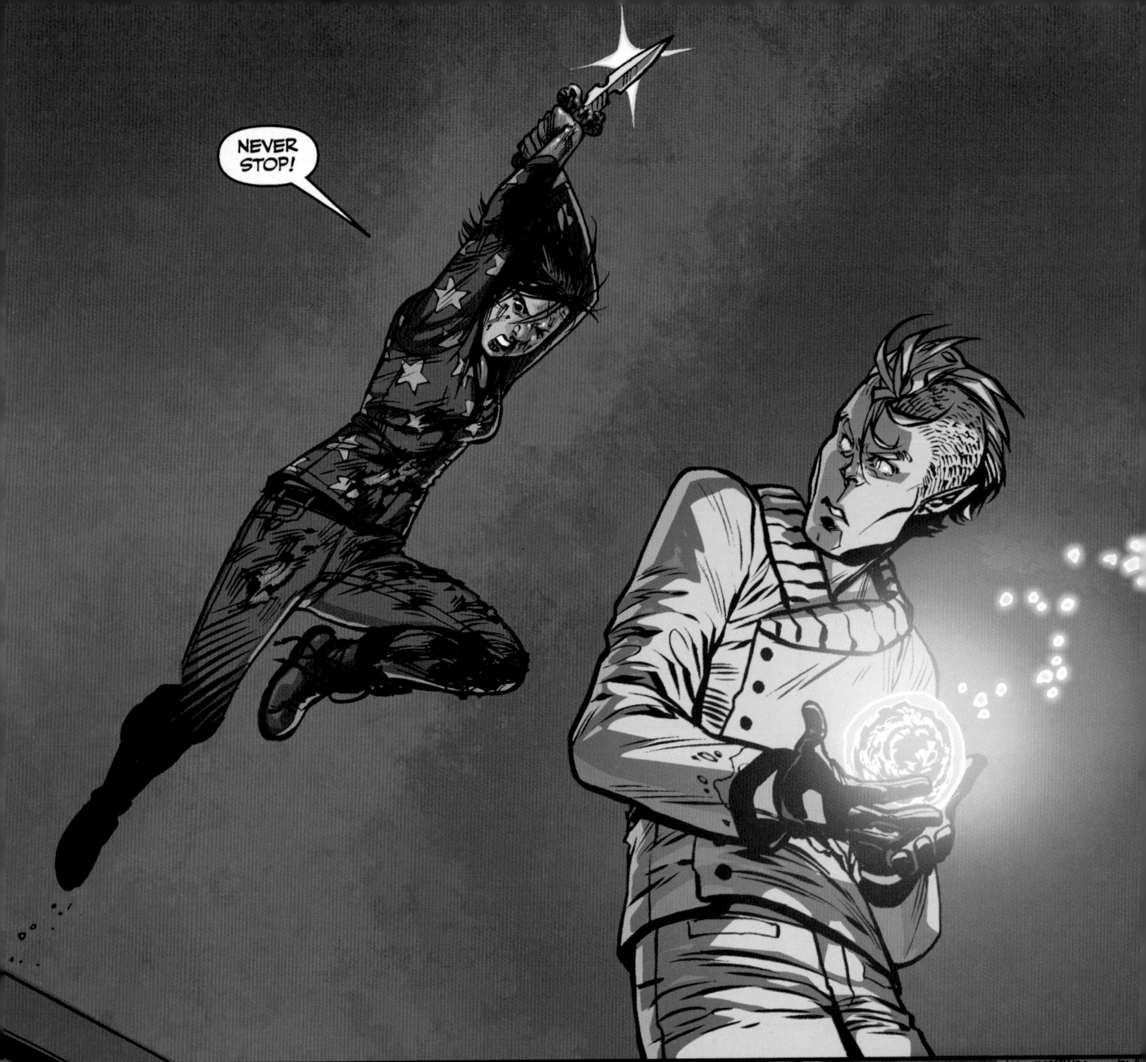
NEVER STOP!

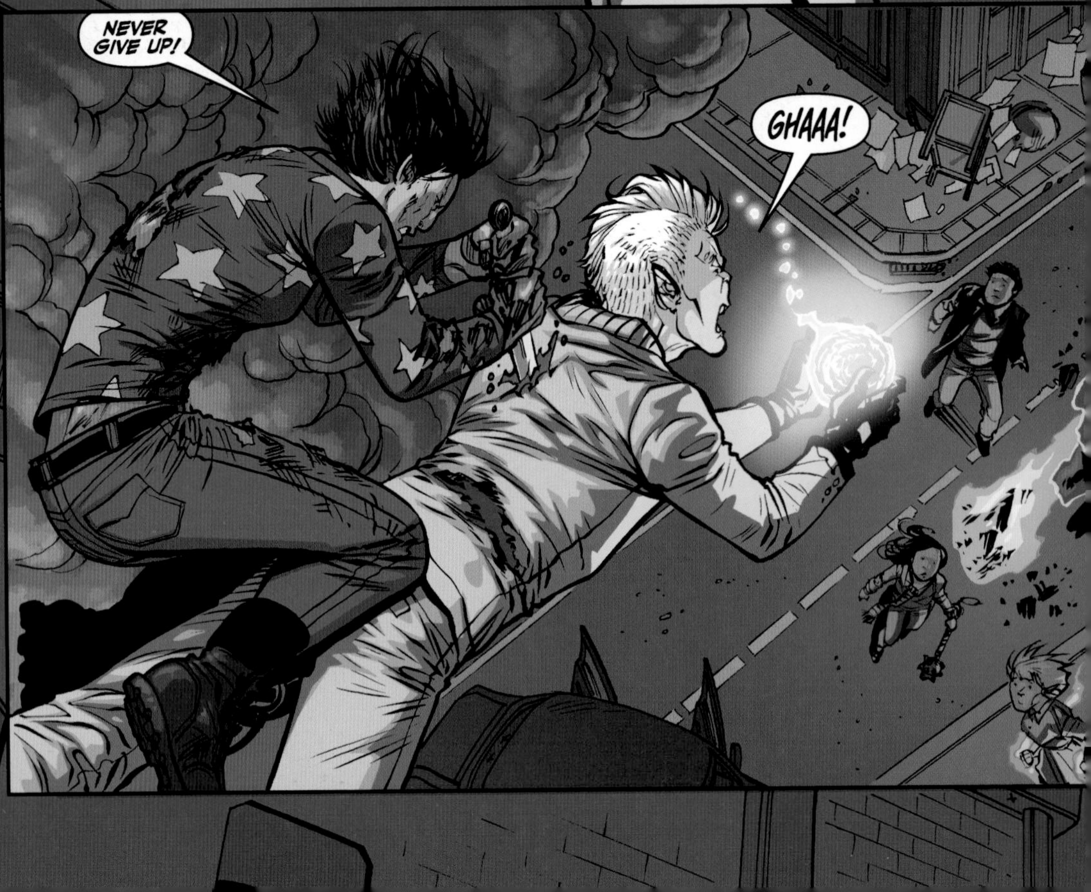
NEVER GIVE UP!
GHAAA!

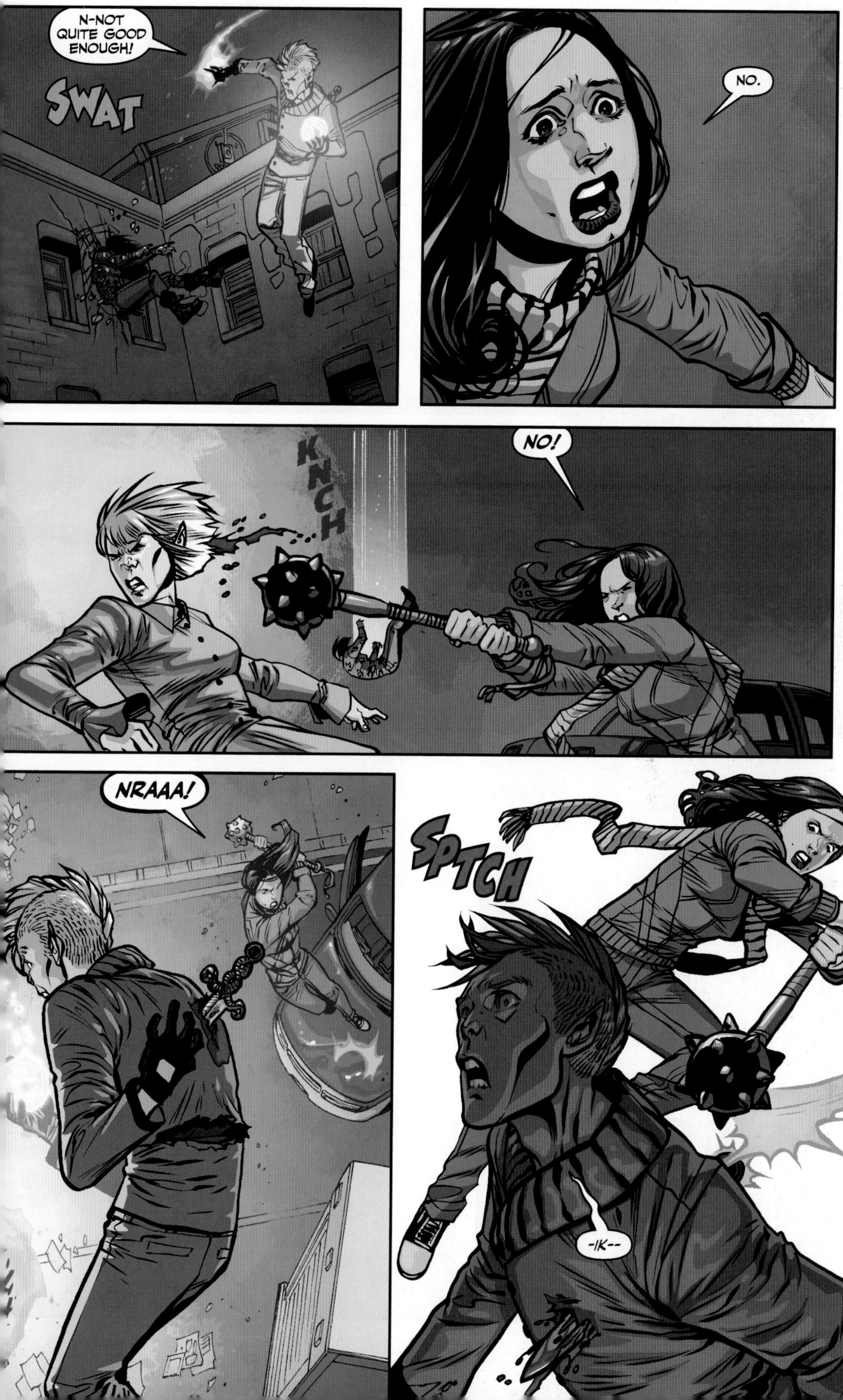
N-NOT QUITE GOOD ENOUGH!
SWAT
NO.
KNCH
NO!
NRAAA!
SPTCH
-IK--

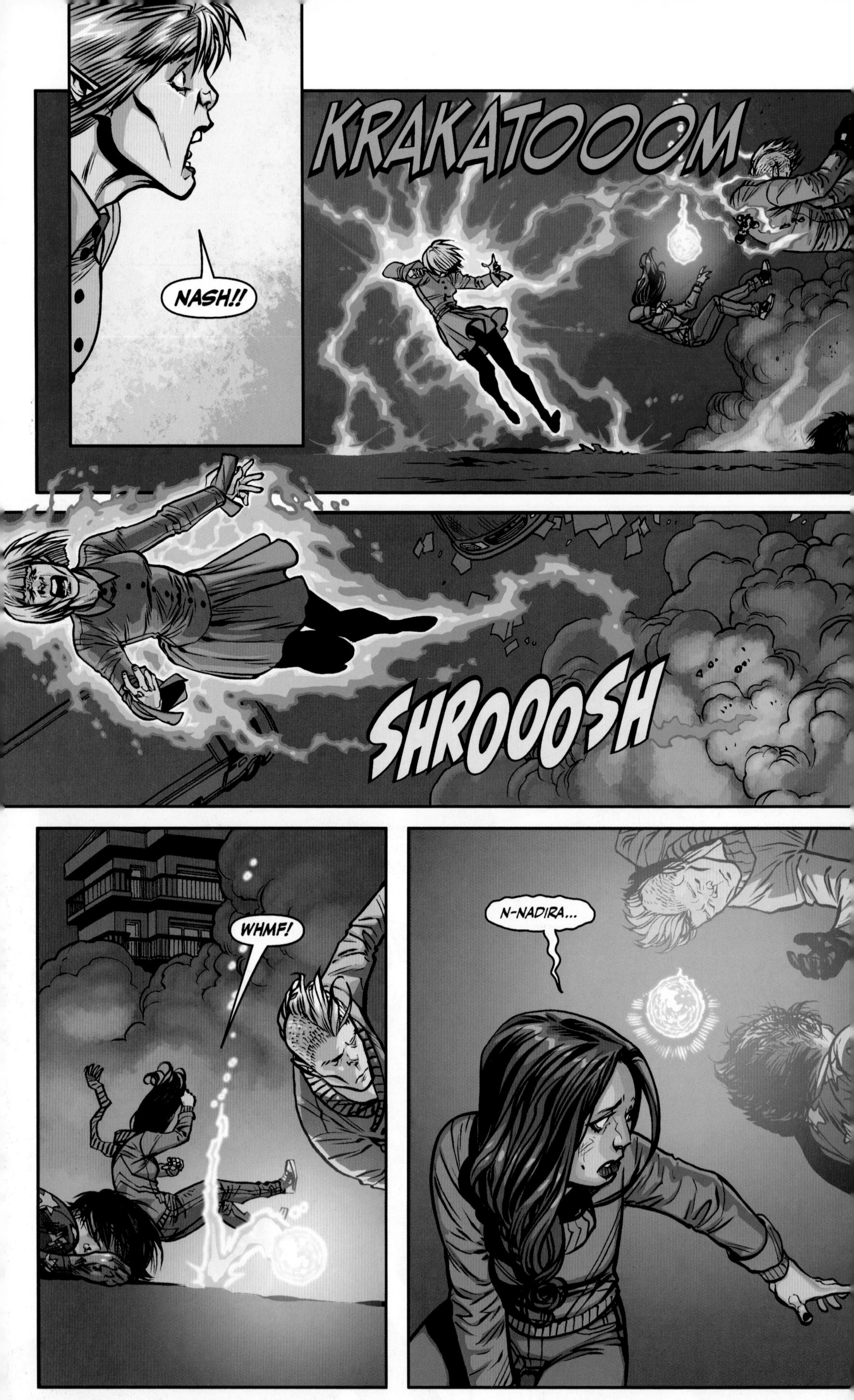
NASH!!
KRAKATOOOM
SHROOOSH
WHMF!
N-NADIRA...

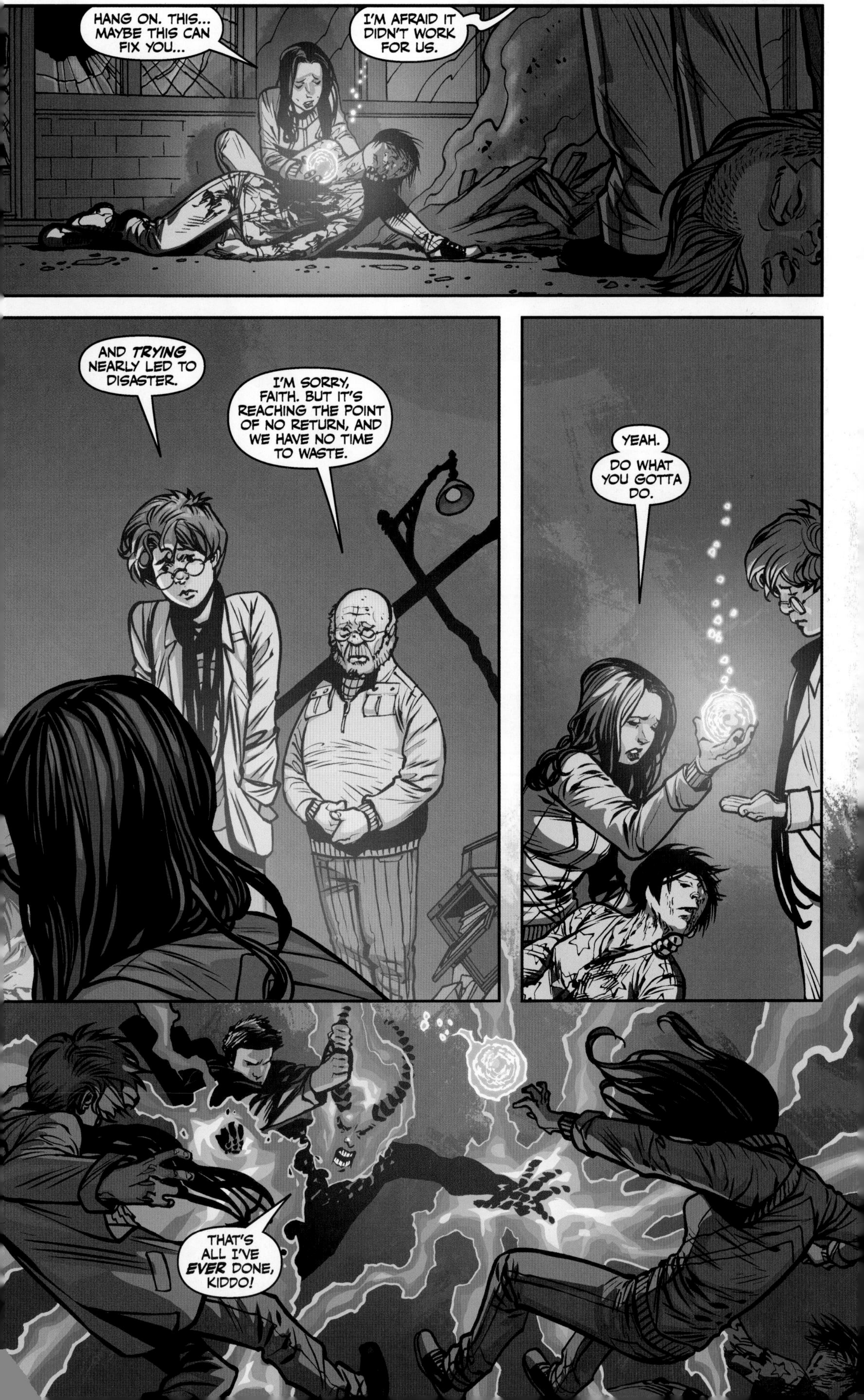
HANG ON. THIS... MAYBE THIS CAN FIX YOU...
I'M AFRAID IT DIDN'T WORK FOR US.
AND *TRYING* NEARLY LED TO DISASTER.
I'M SORRY, FAITH. BUT IT'S REACHING THE POINT OF NO RETURN, AND WE HAVE NO TIME TO WASTE.
YEAH. DO WHAT YOU GOTTA DO.
THAT'S ALL I'VE *EVER* DONE, KIDDO!

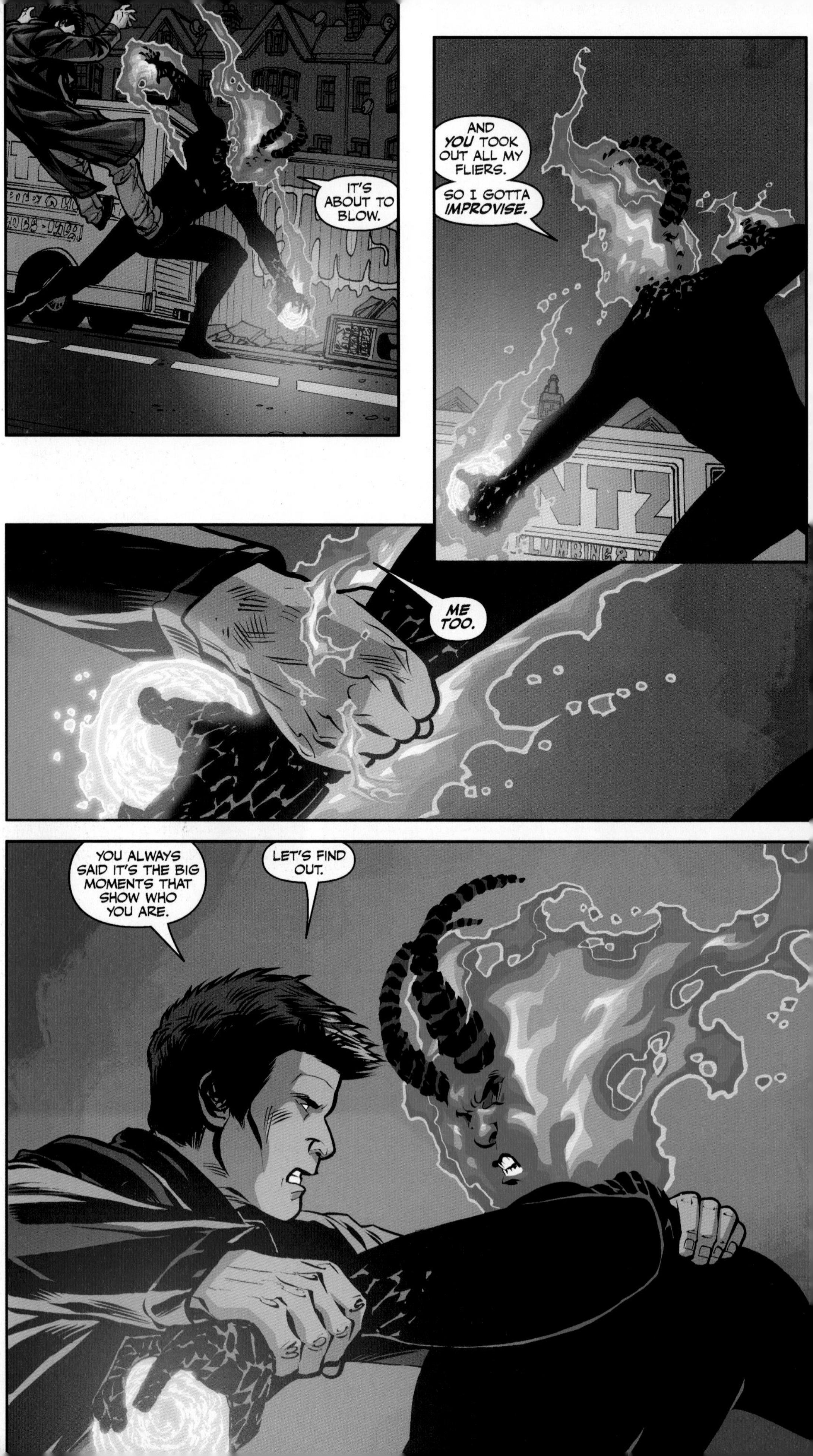
IT'S ABOUT TO BLOW.
AND *YOU* TOOK OUT ALL MY FLIERS.
SO I GOTTA *IMPROVISE.*
ME TOO.
YOU ALWAYS SAID IT'S THE BIG MOMENTS THAT SHOW WHO YOU ARE.
LET'S FIND OUT.

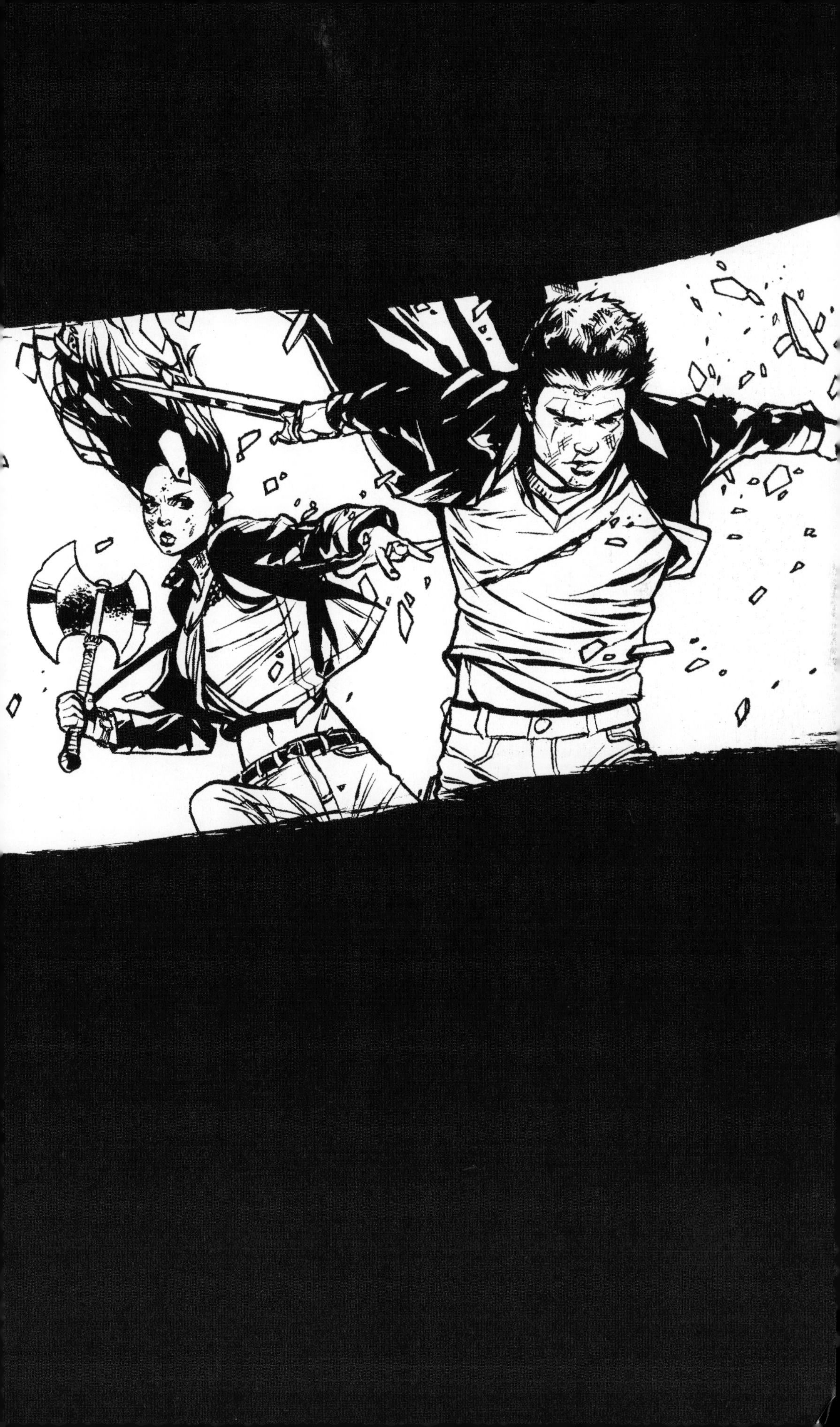

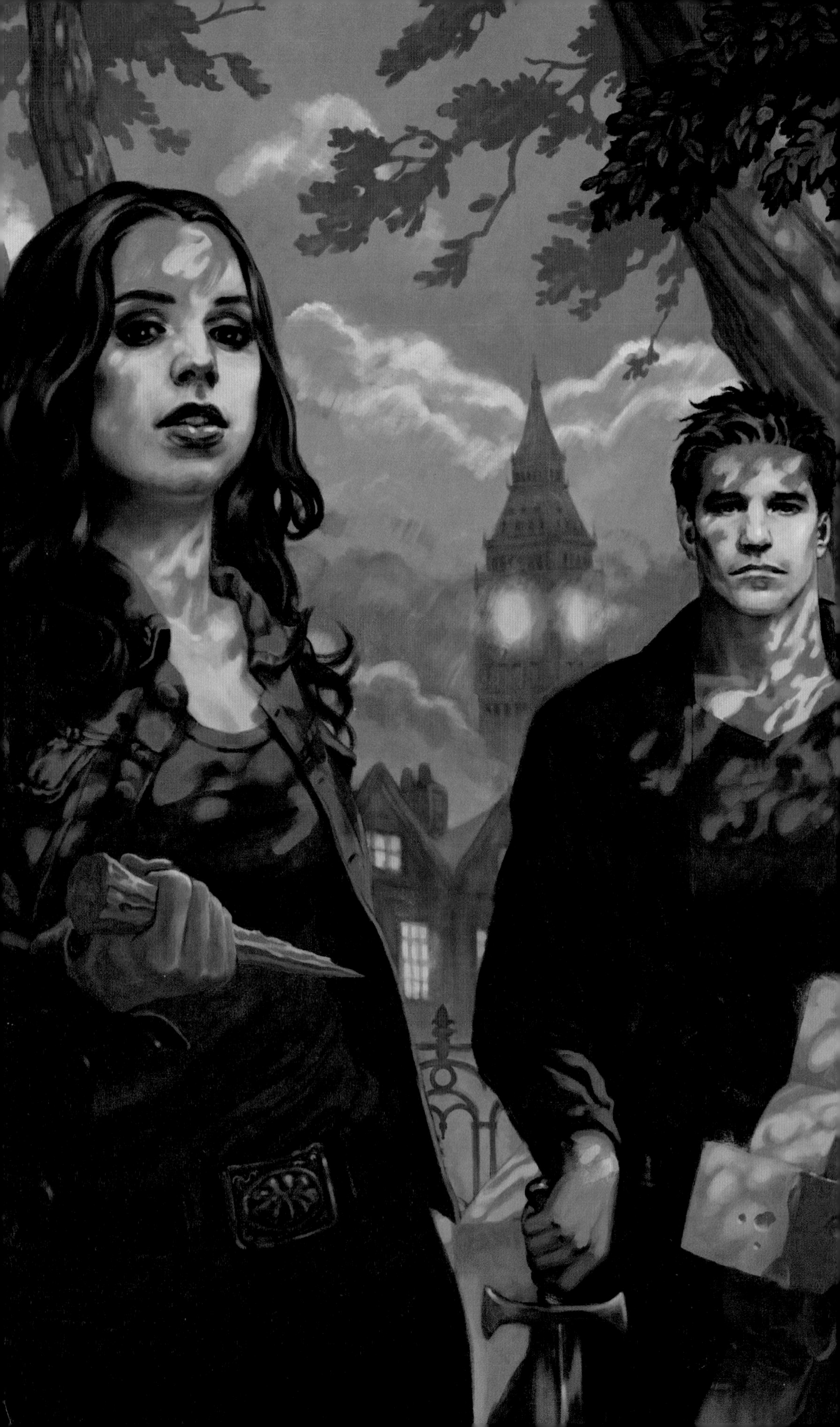

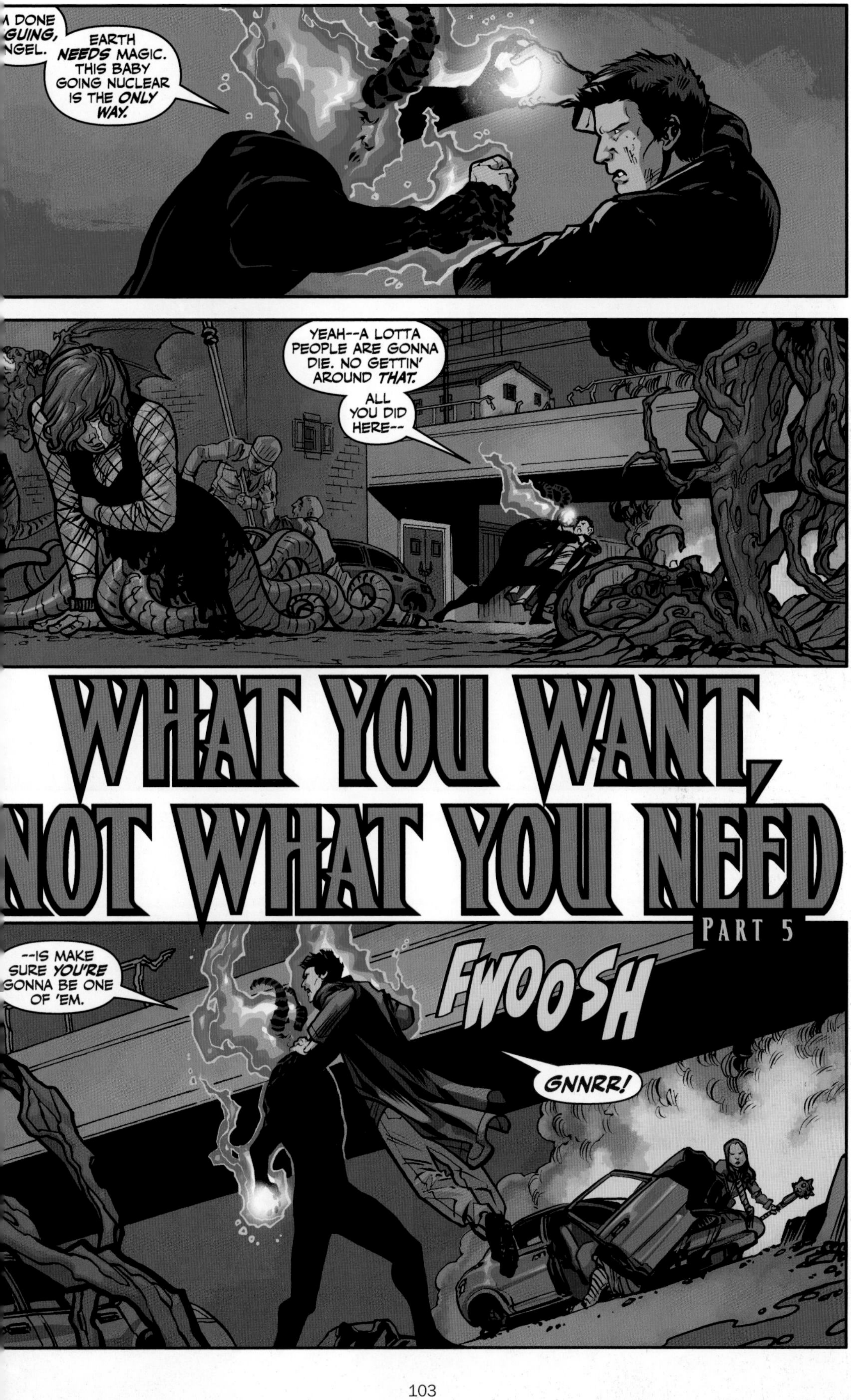
M DONE GUING, NGEL.
EARTH NEEDS MAGIC. THIS BABY GOING NUCLEAR IS THE ONLY WAY.
YEAH--A LOTTA PEOPLE ARE GONNA DIE. NO GETTIN' AROUND THAT.
ALL YOU DID HERE--
WHAT YOU WANT, NOT WHAT YOU NEED
PART 5
--IS MAKE SURE YOU'RE GONNA BE ONE OF 'EM.
FWOOSH
GNNRR!

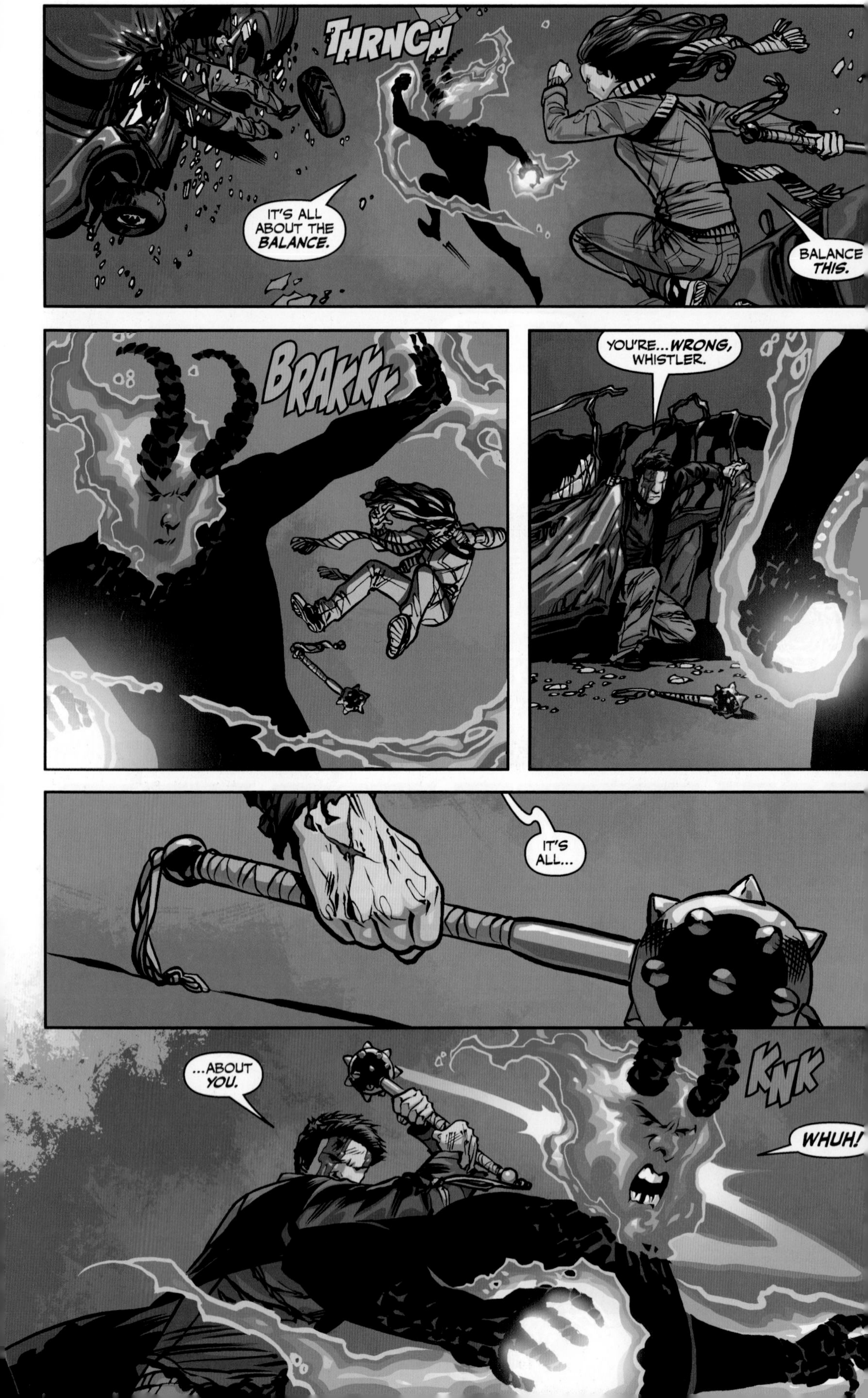
THRNCH
IT'S ALL ABOUT THE BALANCE.
BALANCE THIS.
BRAKKK
YOU'RE...WRONG, WHISTLER.
IT'S ALL...
...ABOUT YOU.
KNK
WHUH!

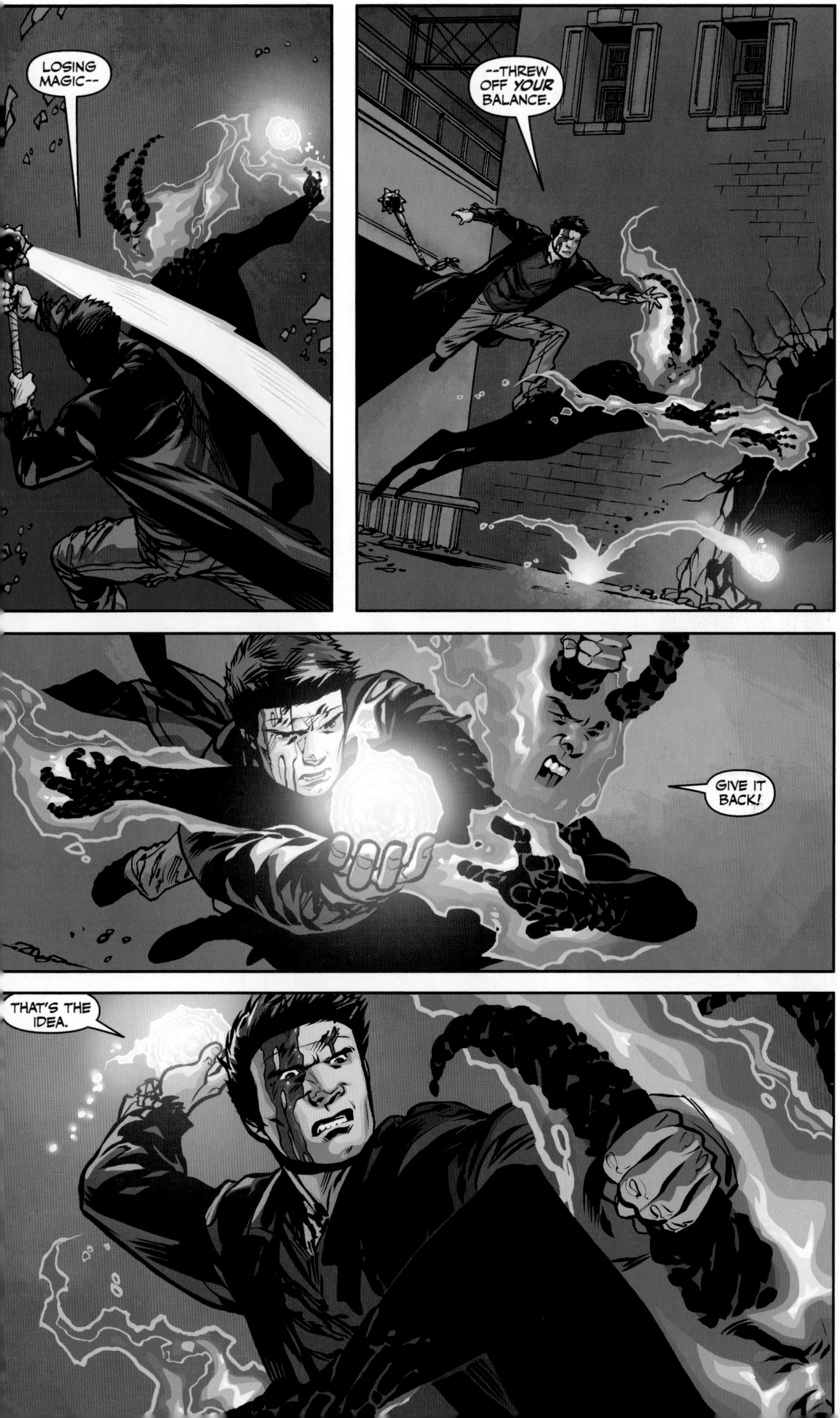
LOSING MAGIC--
--THREW OFF YOUR BALANCE.
GIVE IT BACK!
THAT'S THE IDEA.

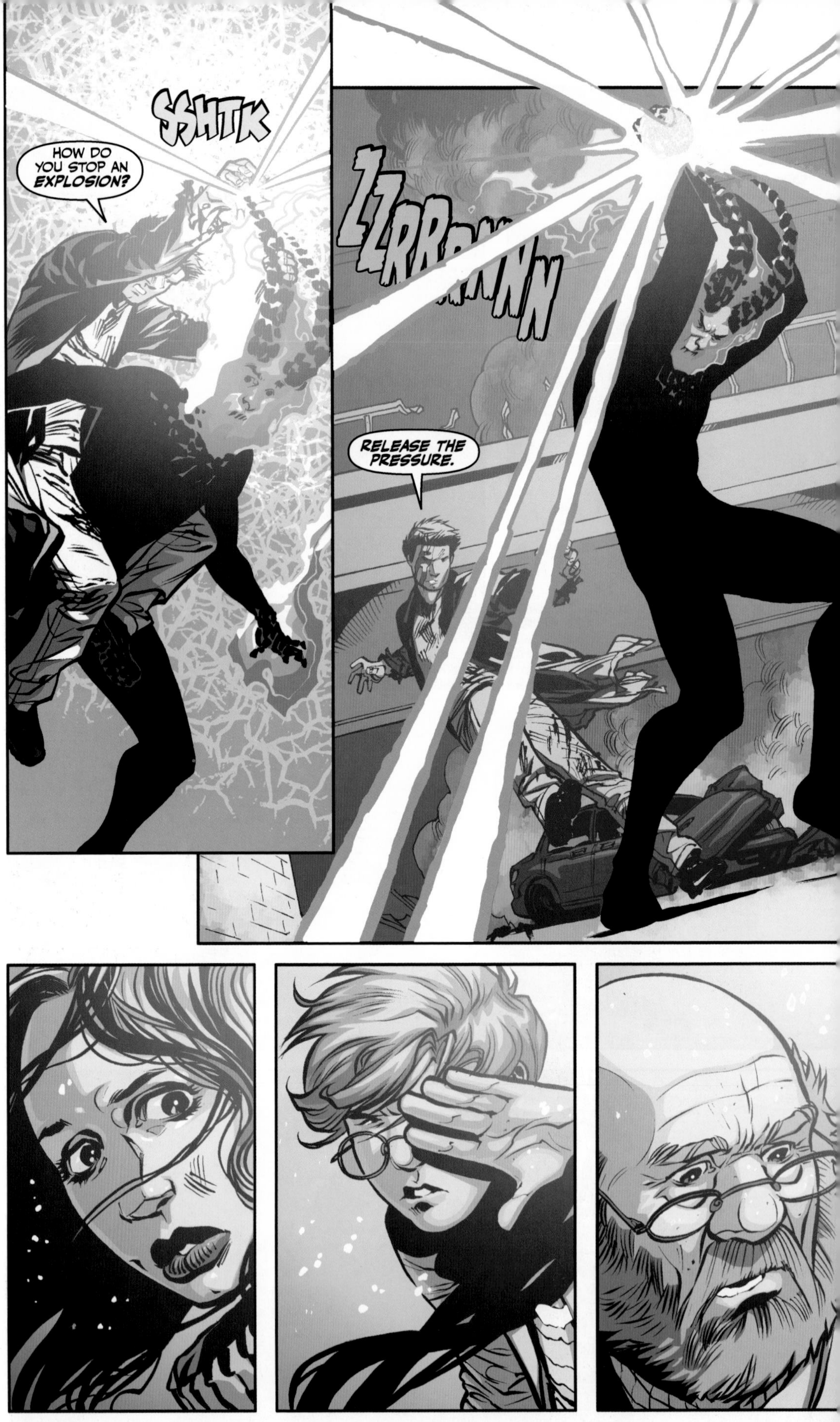
SSHTK
HOW DO YOU STOP AN *EXPLOSION?*
ZZRRRNNNN
RELEASE THE PRESSURE.

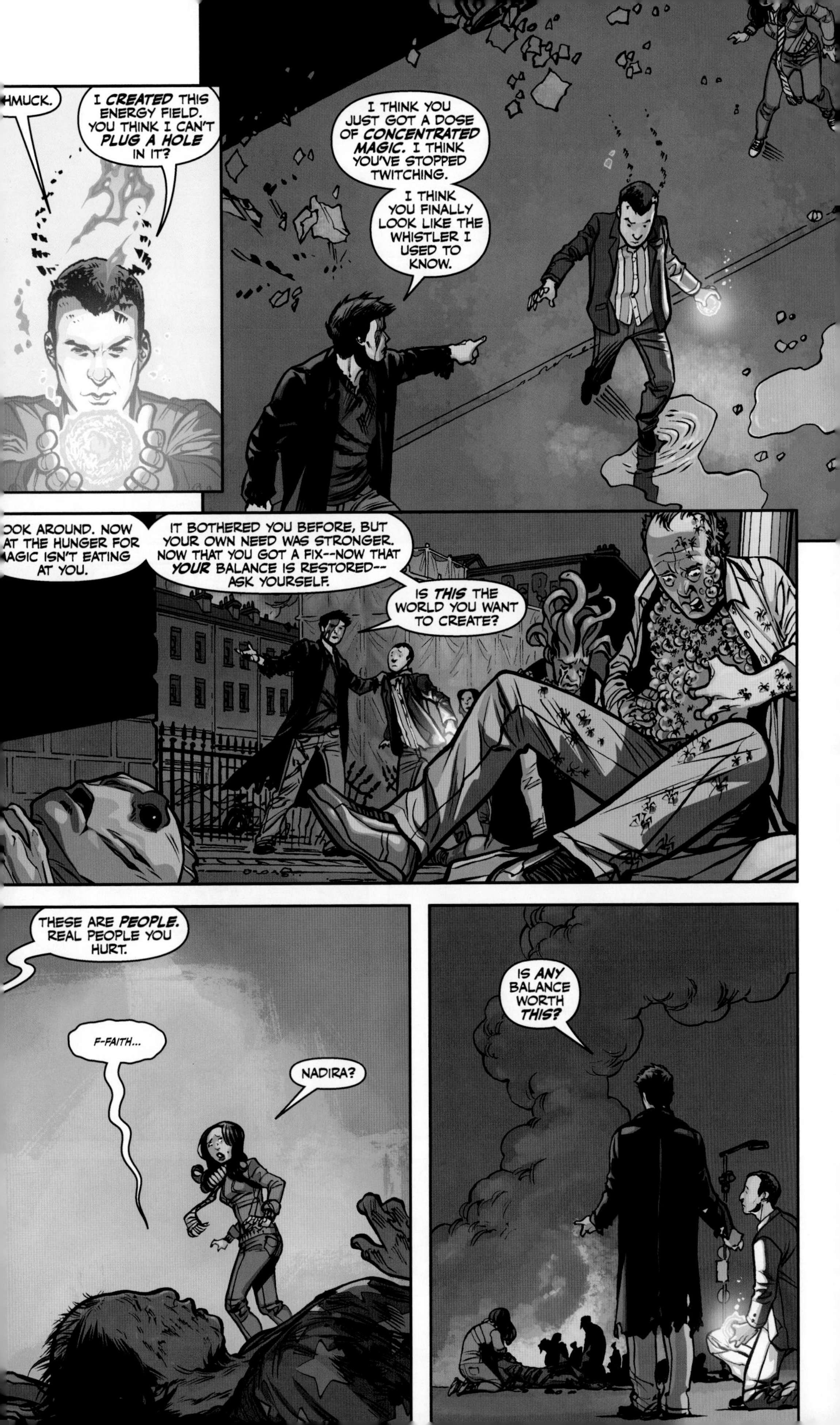
HMUCK.
I CREATED THIS ENERGY FIELD. YOU THINK I CAN'T PLUG A HOLE IN IT?
I THINK YOU JUST GOT A DOSE OF CONCENTRATED MAGIC. I THINK YOU'VE STOPPED TWITCHING.
I THINK YOU FINALLY LOOK LIKE THE WHISTLER I USED TO KNOW.
OOK AROUND. NOW AT THE HUNGER FOR AGIC ISN'T EATING AT YOU.
IT BOTHERED YOU BEFORE, BUT YOUR OWN NEED WAS STRONGER. NOW THAT YOU GOT A FIX--NOW THAT YOUR BALANCE IS RESTORED-- ASK YOURSELF.
IS THIS THE WORLD YOU WANT TO CREATE?
THESE ARE PEOPLE. REAL PEOPLE YOU HURT.
F-FAITH...
NADIRA?
IS ANY BALANCE WORTH THIS?

STAY WITH ME. HEY--YOU *DID* IT, GIRL.

YOU AVENGED YOUR SISTERS.

I... DID...?

HNH. ALL THAT HATE AND PAIN... FOR THIS...

YOU WERE RIGHT, FAITH.

IT WASN'T WORTH IT.

ANGEL... WHAT DID I DO?

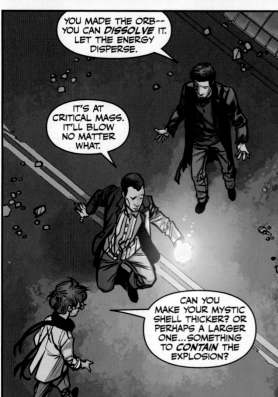

YOU MADE THE ORB-- YOU CAN *DISSOLVE* IT. LET THE ENERGY DISPERSE.

IT'S AT CRITICAL MASS. IT'LL BLOW NO MATTER WHAT.

CAN YOU MAKE YOUR MYSTIC SHELL THICKER? OR PERHAPS A LARGER ONE... SOMETHING TO *CONTAIN* THE EXPLOSION?

THAT'D TAKE ALL THE MAGIC I GOT IN ME. I'D BE SUCKED DRY AGAIN. JONESING.

RIGHT BACK WHERE WE STARTED.

THERE'S NO OTHER OPTION!

EXCEPT ONE.

BKKK

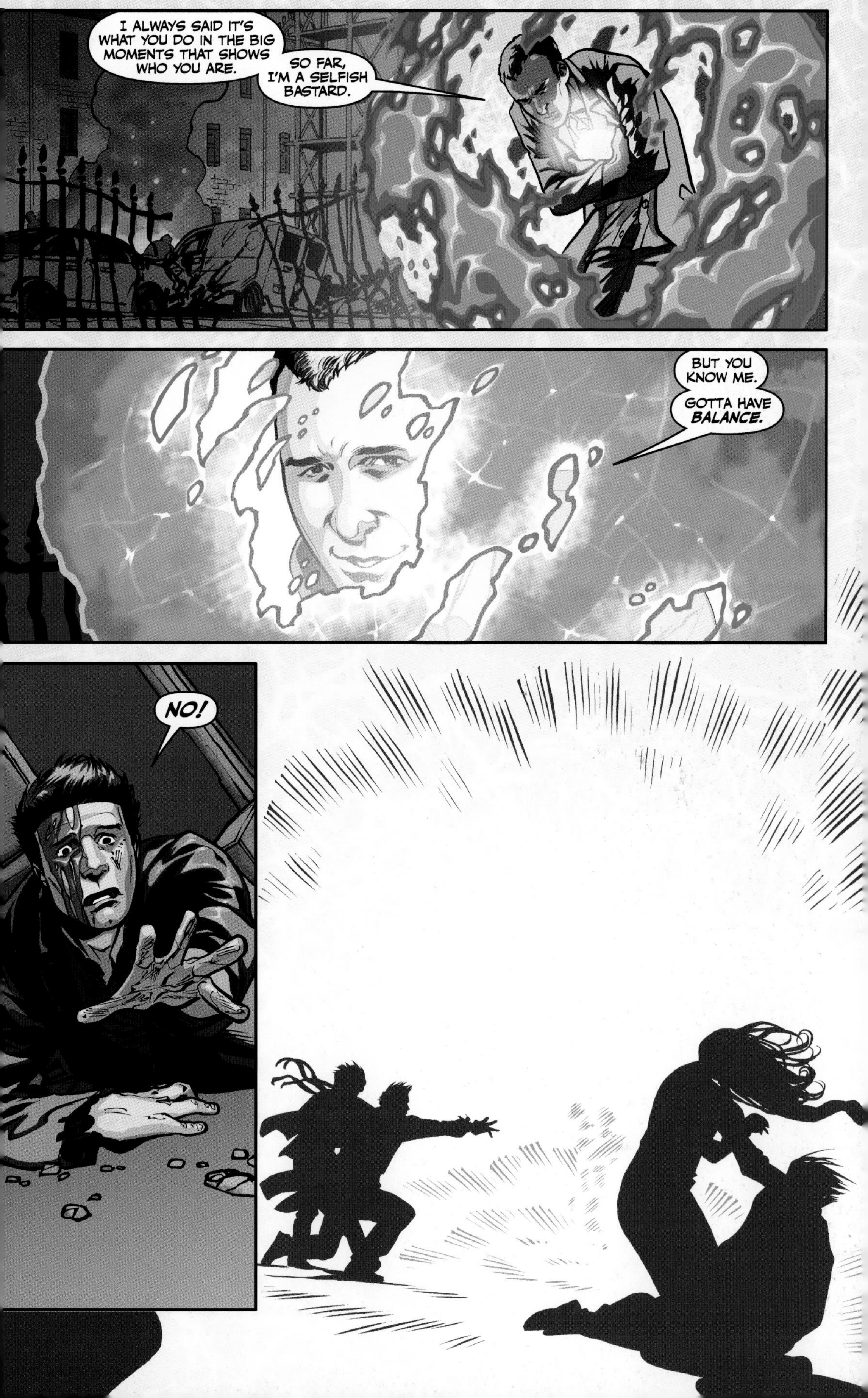
I ALWAYS SAID IT'S WHAT YOU DO IN THE BIG MOMENTS THAT SHOWS WHO YOU ARE.
SO FAR, I'M A SELFISH BASTARD.
BUT YOU KNOW ME.
GOTTA HAVE ***BALANCE.***
NO!

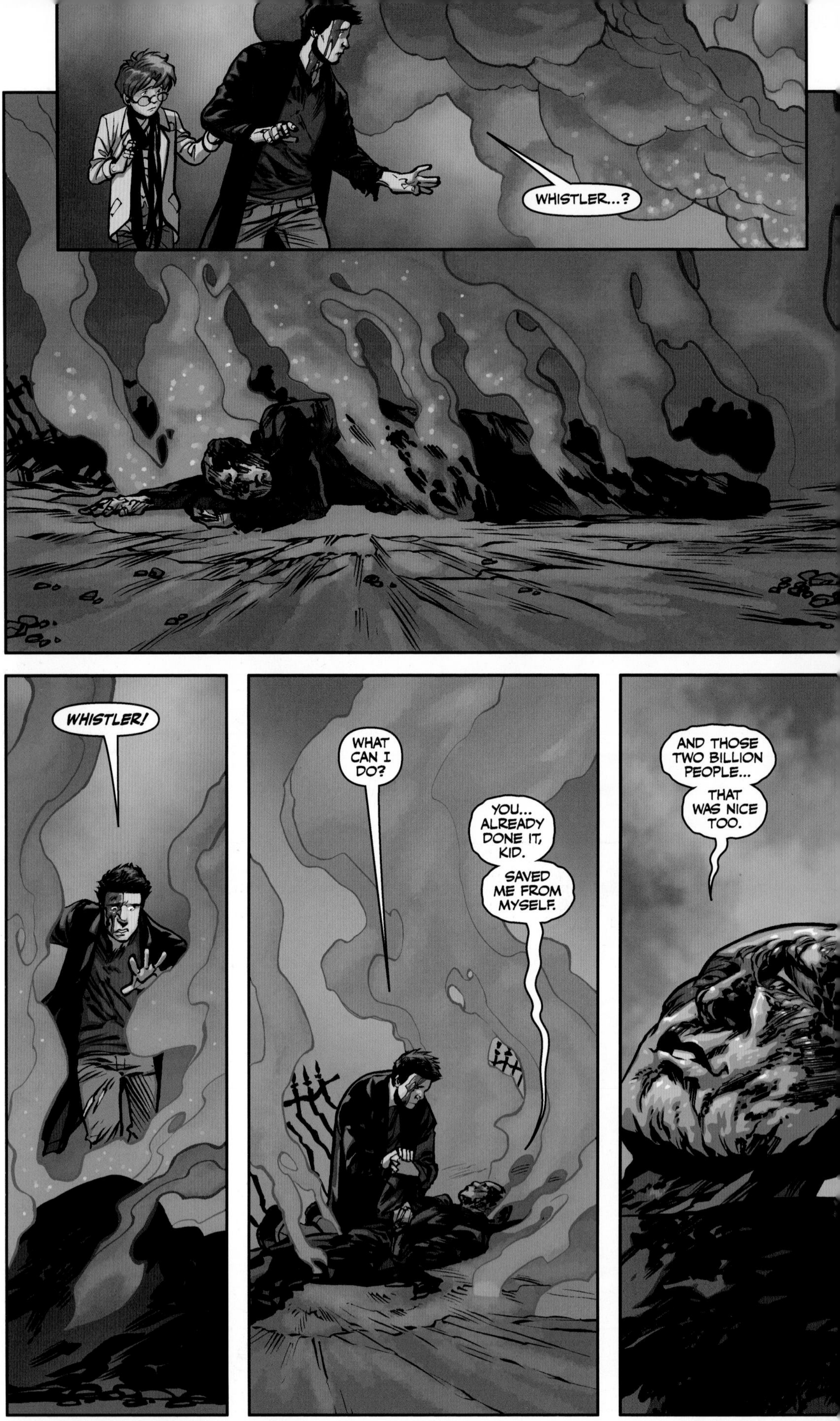
WHISTLER...?
WHISTLER!
WHAT CAN I DO?
YOU... ALREADY DONE IT, KID.
SAVED ME FROM MYSELF.
AND THOSE TWO BILLION PEOPLE...
THAT WAS NICE TOO.

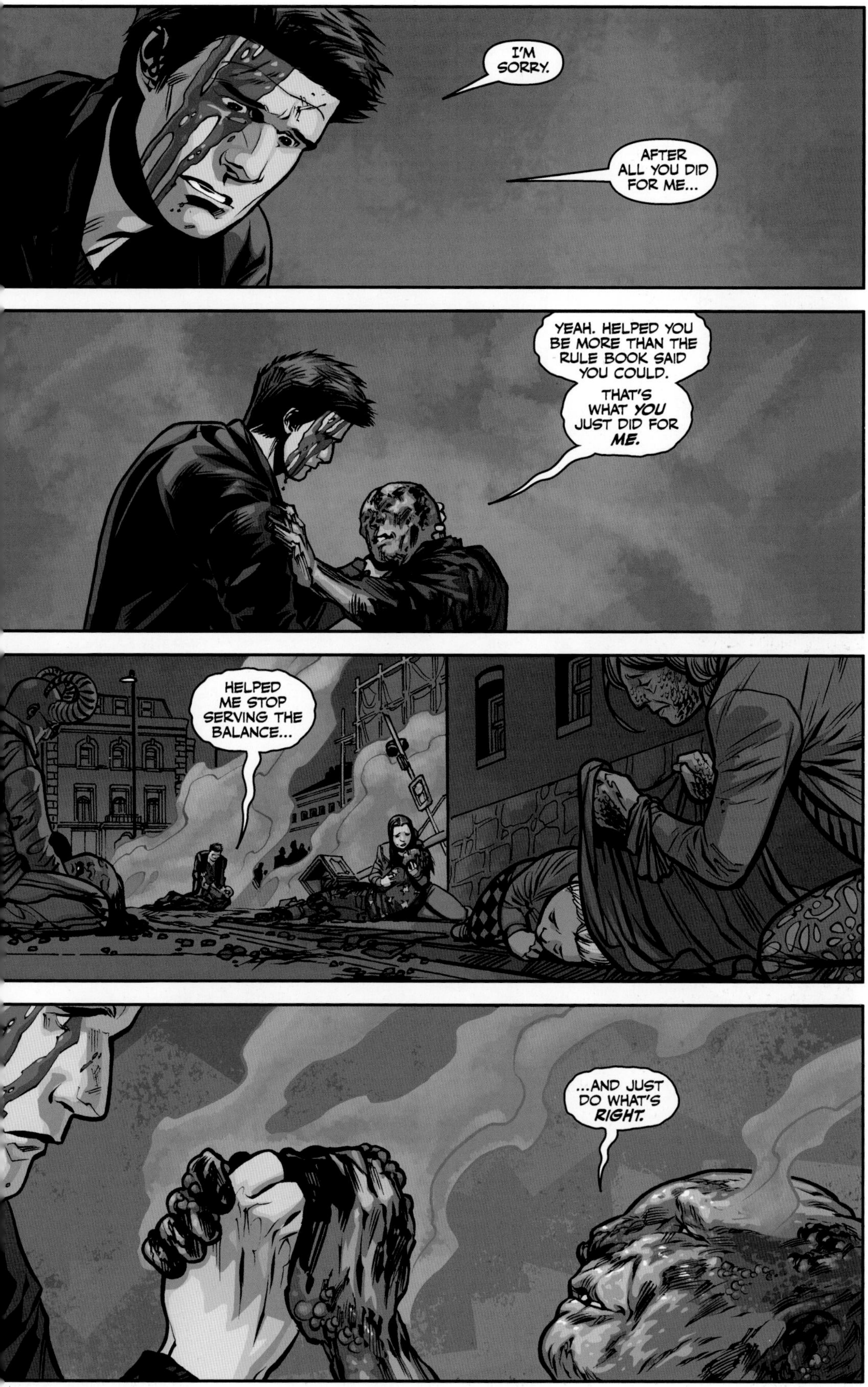
I'M SORRY.
AFTER ALL YOU DID FOR ME...
YEAH. HELPED YOU BE MORE THAN THE RULE BOOK SAID YOU COULD.
THAT'S WHAT *YOU* JUST DID FOR *ME.*
HELPED ME STOP SERVING THE BALANCE...
...AND JUST DO WHAT'S *RIGHT.*

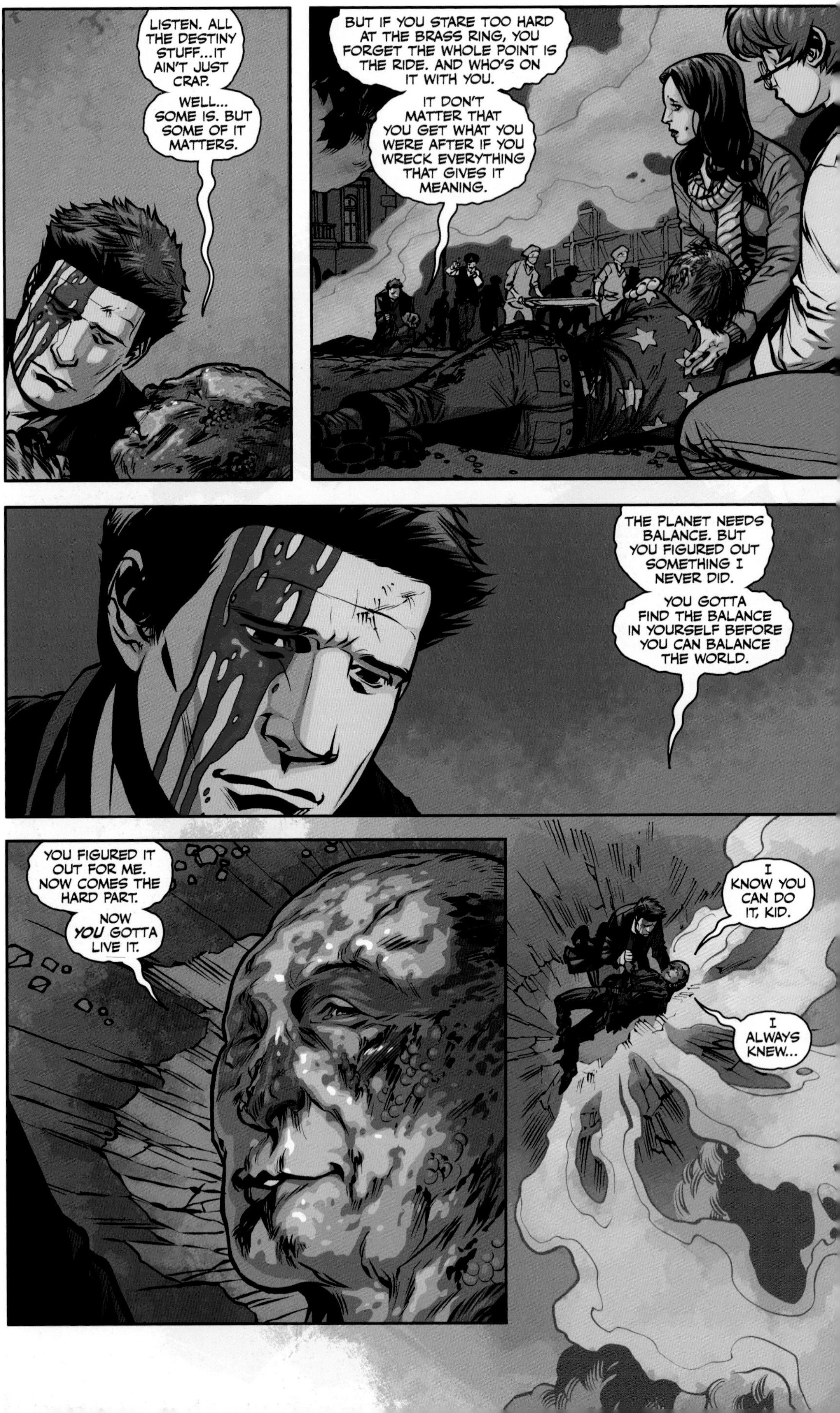
LISTEN. ALL THE DESTINY STUFF...IT AIN'T JUST CRAP.
WELL... SOME IS. BUT SOME OF IT MATTERS.
BUT IF YOU STARE TOO HARD AT THE BRASS RING, YOU FORGET THE WHOLE POINT IS THE RIDE. AND WHO'S ON IT WITH YOU.
IT DON'T MATTER THAT YOU GET WHAT YOU WERE AFTER IF YOU WRECK EVERYTHING THAT GIVES IT MEANING.
THE PLANET NEEDS BALANCE. BUT YOU FIGURED OUT SOMETHING I NEVER DID.
YOU GOTTA FIND THE BALANCE IN YOURSELF BEFORE YOU CAN BALANCE THE WORLD.
YOU FIGURED IT OUT FOR ME. NOW COMES THE HARD PART.
NOW *YOU* GOTTA LIVE IT.
I KNOW YOU CAN DO IT, KID.
I ALWAYS KNEW...

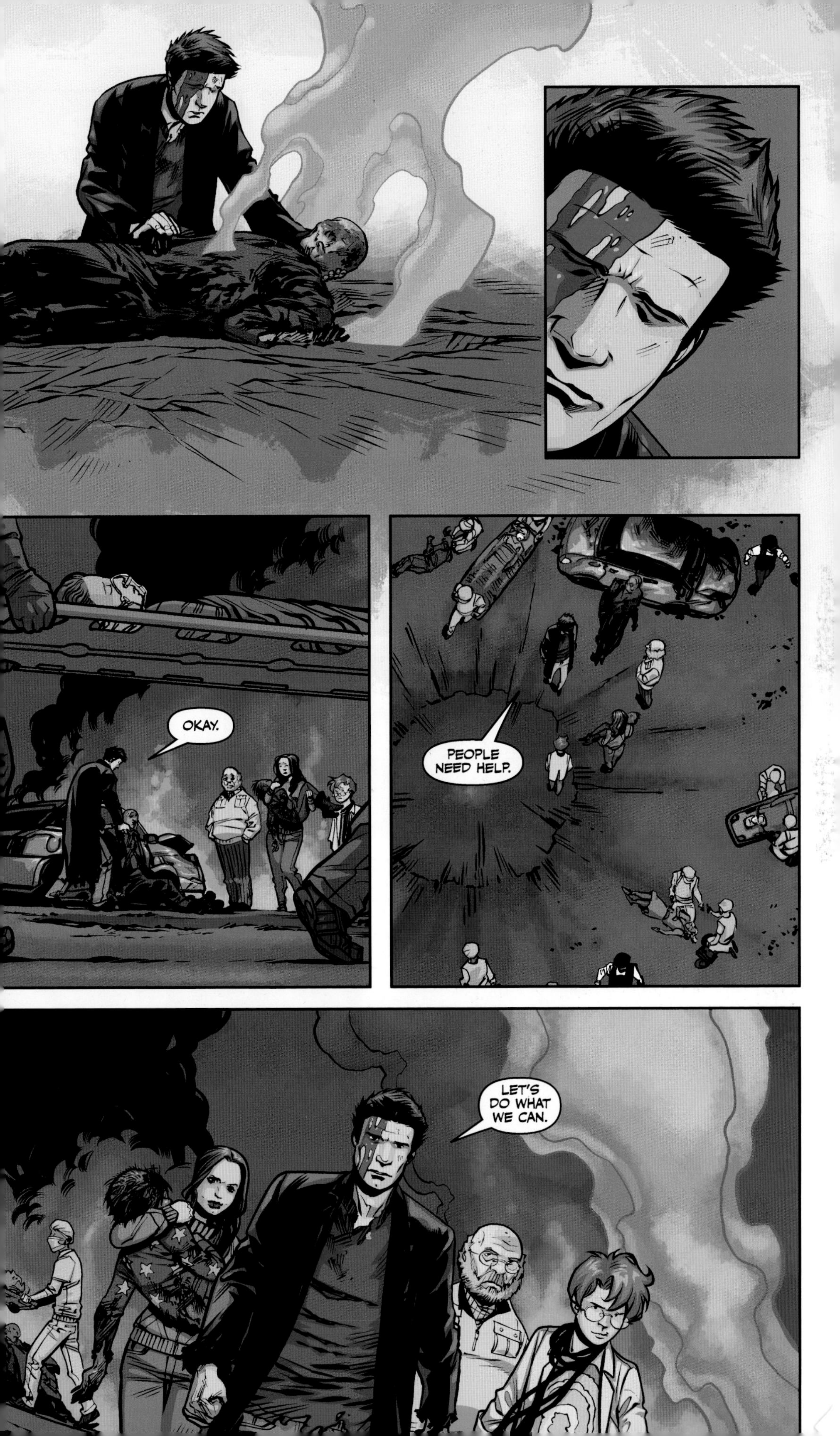
OKAY.
PEOPLE NEED HELP.
LET'S DO WHAT WE CAN.

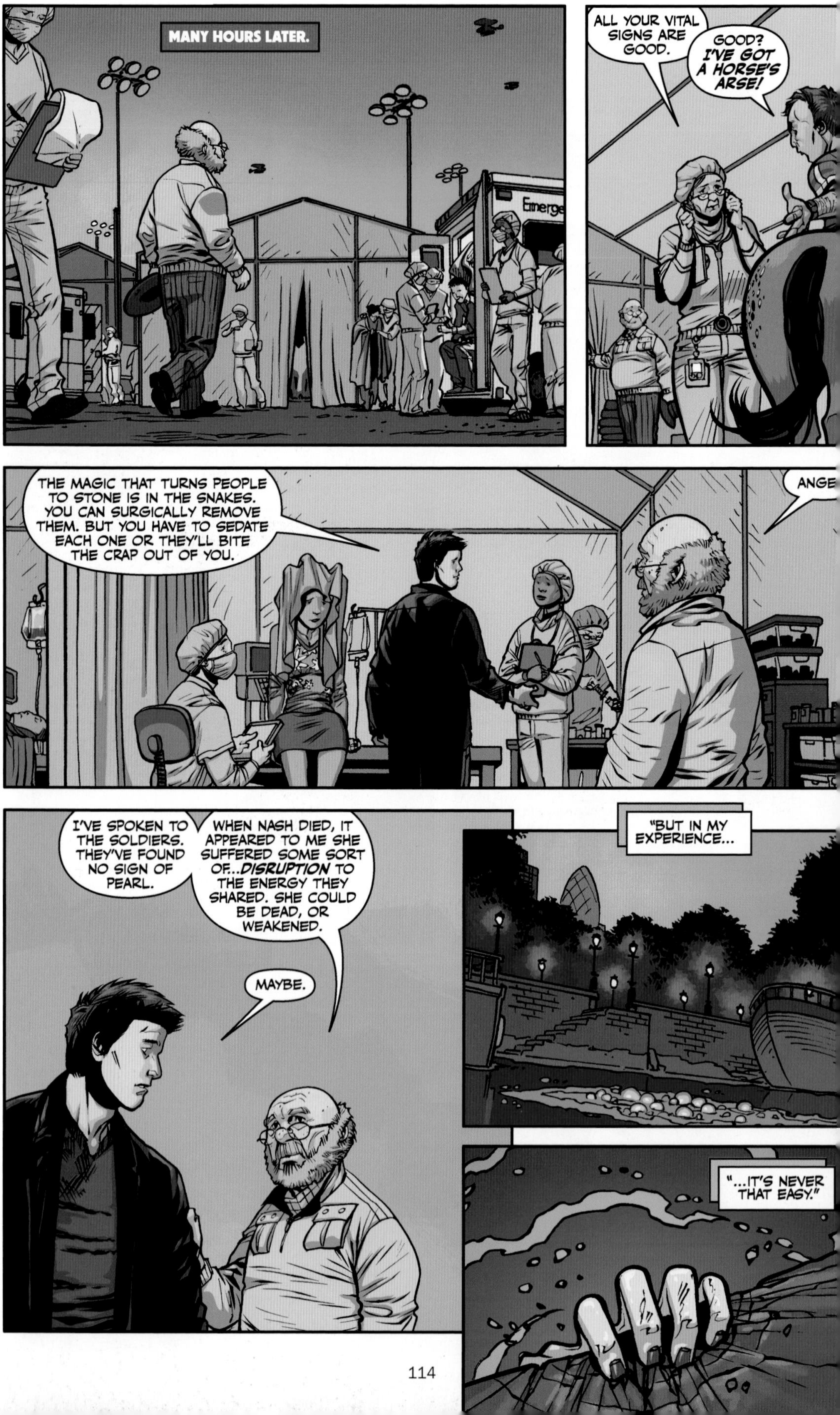
MANY HOURS LATER.
ALL YOUR VITAL SIGNS ARE GOOD.
GOOD? I'VE GOT A HORSE'S ARSE!
THE MAGIC THAT TURNS PEOPLE TO STONE IS IN THE SNAKES. YOU CAN SURGICALLY REMOVE THEM. BUT YOU HAVE TO SEDATE EACH ONE OR THEY'LL BITE THE CRAP OUT OF YOU.
ANGE
I'VE SPOKEN TO THE SOLDIERS. THEY'VE FOUND NO SIGN OF PEARL.
WHEN NASH DIED, IT APPEARED TO ME SHE SUFFERED SOME SORT OF...DISRUPTION TO THE ENERGY THEY SHARED. SHE COULD BE DEAD, OR WEAKENED.
MAYBE.
"BUT IN MY EXPERIENCE...
"...IT'S NEVER THAT EASY."

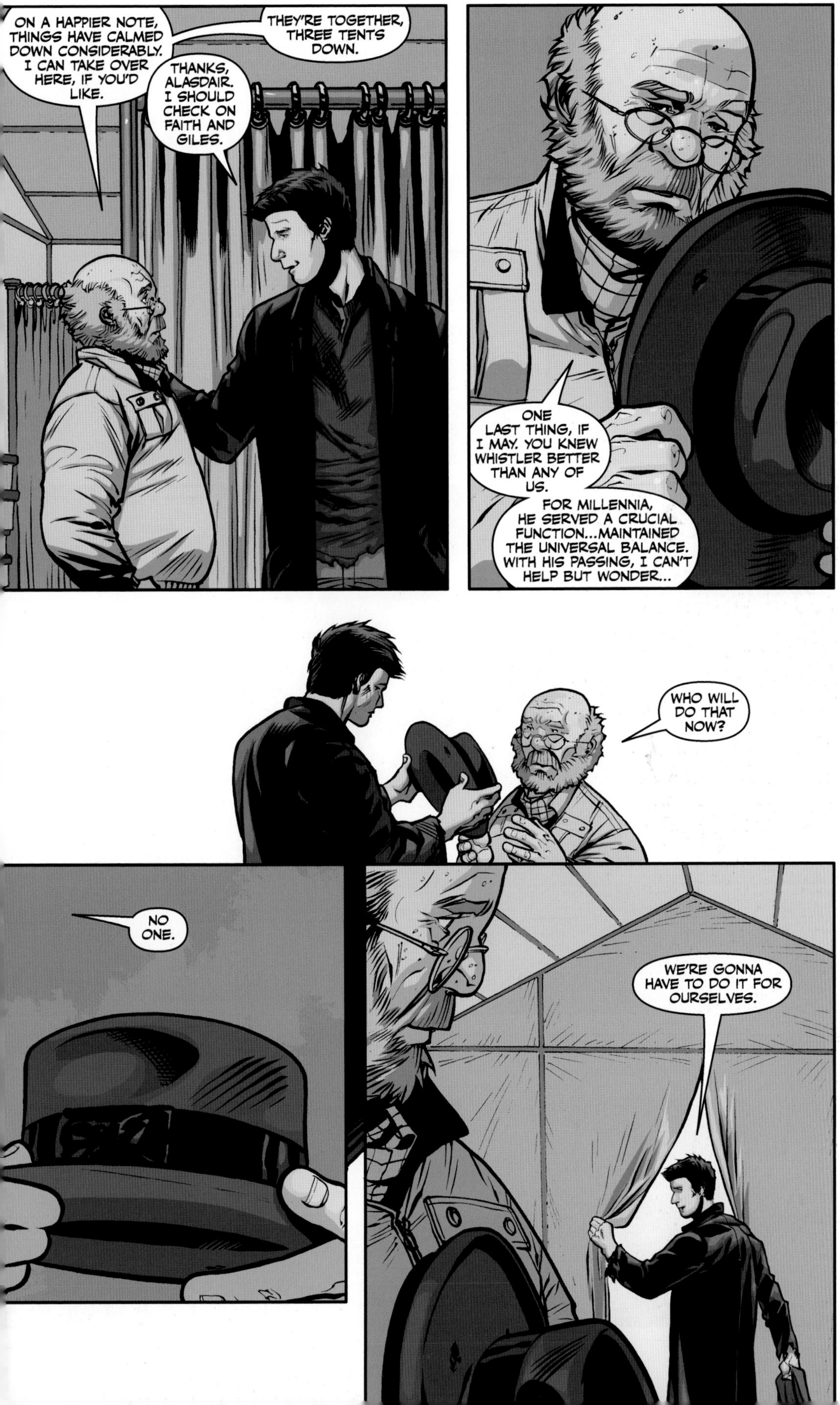
ON A HAPPIER NOTE, THINGS HAVE CALMED DOWN CONSIDERABLY. I CAN TAKE OVER HERE, IF YOU'D LIKE.
THEY'RE TOGETHER, THREE TENTS DOWN.
THANKS, ALASDAIR. I SHOULD CHECK ON FAITH AND GILES.
ONE LAST THING, IF I MAY. YOU KNEW WHISTLER BETTER THAN ANY OF US.
FOR MILLENNIA, HE SERVED A CRUCIAL FUNCTION...MAINTAINED THE UNIVERSAL BALANCE. WITH HIS PASSING, I CAN'T HELP BUT WONDER...
WHO WILL DO THAT NOW?
NO ONE.
WE'RE GONNA HAVE TO DO IT FOR OURSELVES.

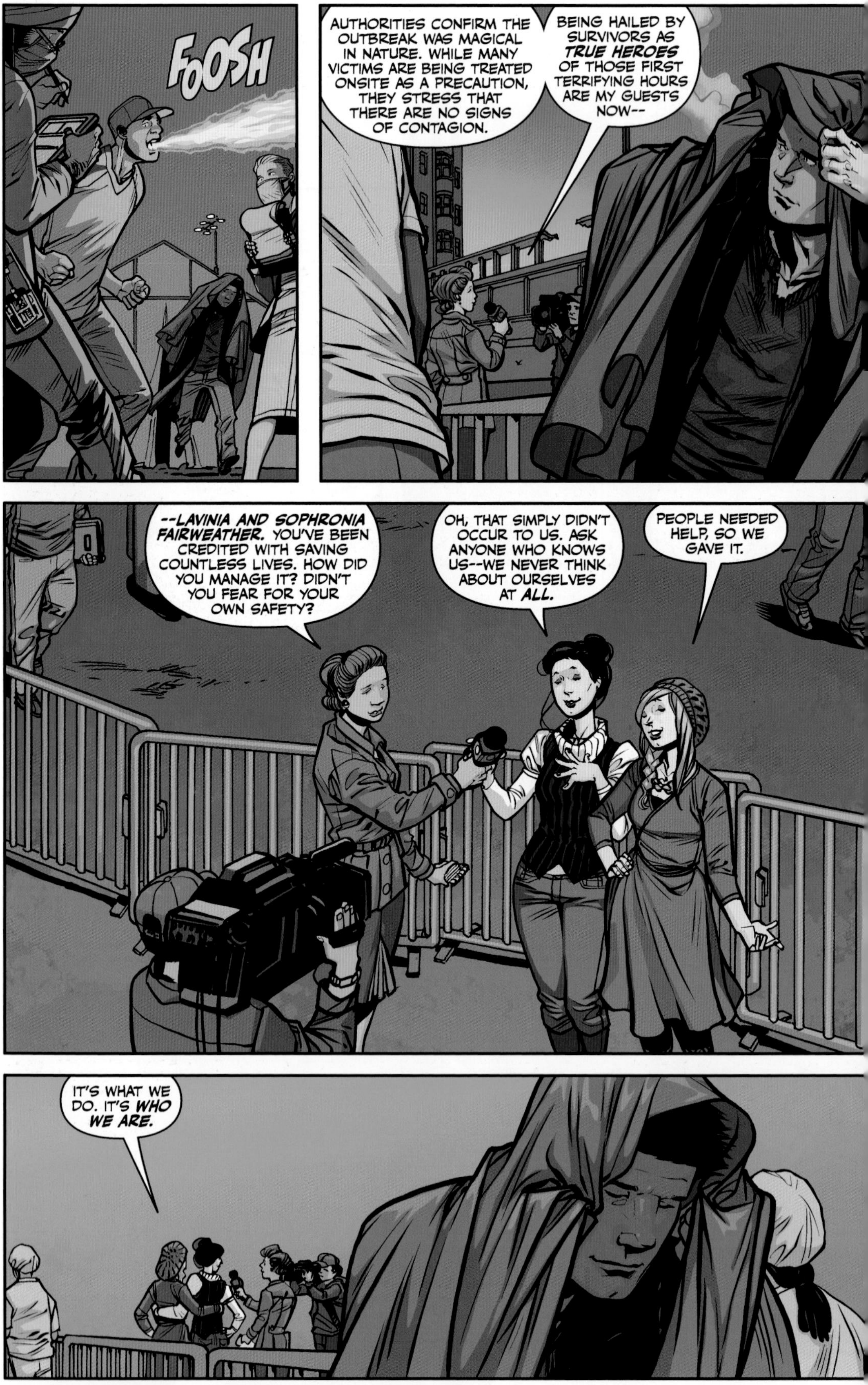
FOOSH
AUTHORITIES CONFIRM THE OUTBREAK WAS MAGICAL IN NATURE. WHILE MANY VICTIMS ARE BEING TREATED ONSITE AS A PRECAUTION, THEY STRESS THAT THERE ARE NO SIGNS OF CONTAGION.
BEING HAILED BY SURVIVORS AS TRUE HEROES OF THOSE FIRST TERRIFYING HOURS ARE MY GUESTS NOW--
--LAVINIA AND SOPHRONIA FAIRWEATHER. YOU'VE BEEN CREDITED WITH SAVING COUNTLESS LIVES. HOW DID YOU MANAGE IT? DIDN'T YOU FEAR FOR YOUR OWN SAFETY?
OH, THAT SIMPLY DIDN'T OCCUR TO US. ASK ANYONE WHO KNOWS US--WE NEVER THINK ABOUT OURSELVES AT ALL.
PEOPLE NEEDED HELP, SO WE GAVE IT.
IT'S WHAT WE DO. IT'S WHO WE ARE.

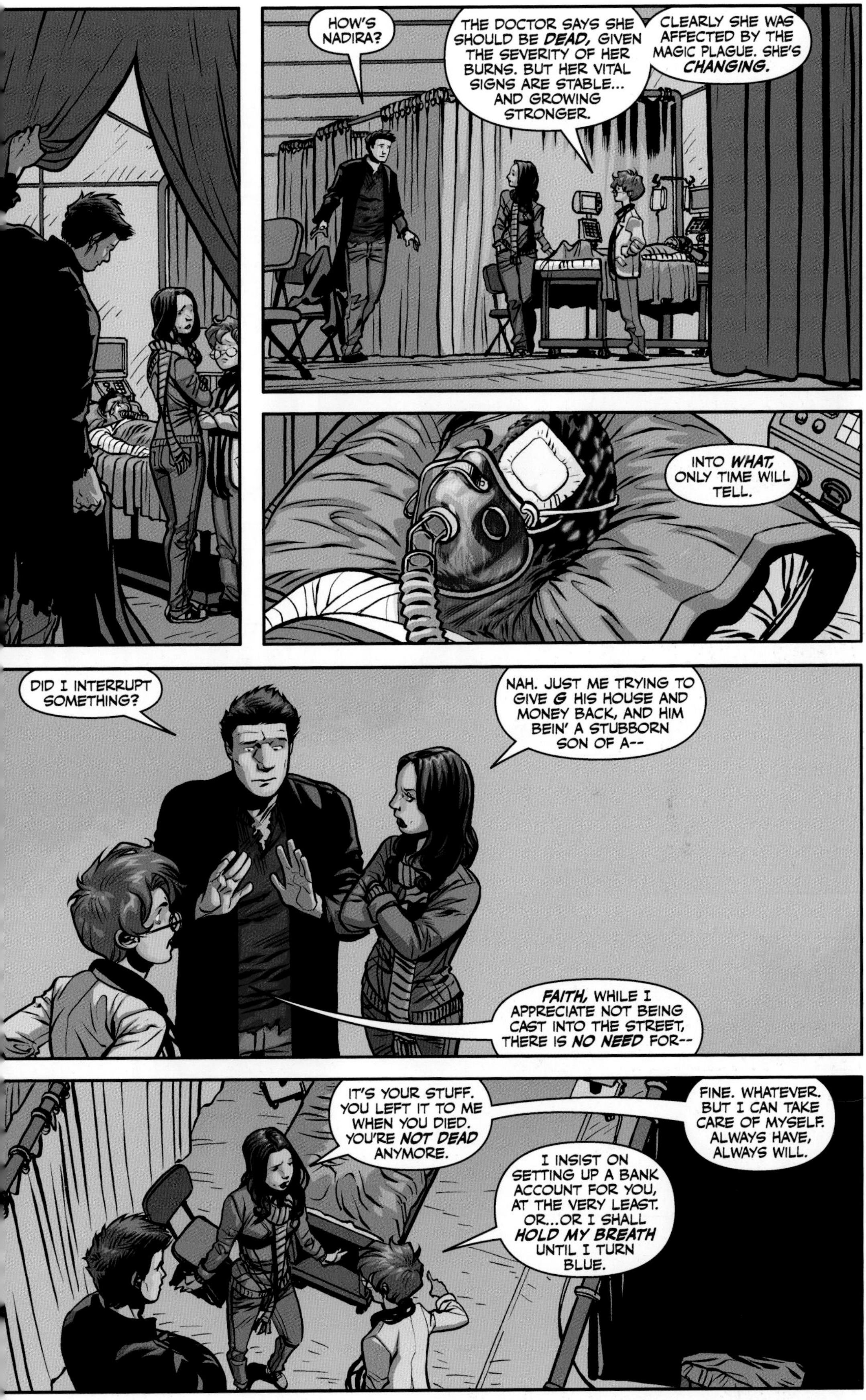
HOW'S NADIRA?
THE DOCTOR SAYS SHE SHOULD BE DEAD, GIVEN THE SEVERITY OF HER BURNS. BUT HER VITAL SIGNS ARE STABLE... AND GROWING STRONGER.
CLEARLY SHE WAS AFFECTED BY THE MAGIC PLAGUE. SHE'S CHANGING.
INTO WHAT, ONLY TIME WILL TELL.
DID I INTERRUPT SOMETHING?
NAH. JUST ME TRYING TO GIVE G HIS HOUSE AND MONEY BACK, AND HIM BEIN' A STUBBORN SON OF A--
FAITH, WHILE I APPRECIATE NOT BEING CAST INTO THE STREET, THERE IS NO NEED FOR--
IT'S YOUR STUFF. YOU LEFT IT TO ME WHEN YOU DIED. YOU'RE NOT DEAD ANYMORE.
I INSIST ON SETTING UP A BANK ACCOUNT FOR YOU, AT THE VERY LEAST. OR...OR I SHALL HOLD MY BREATH UNTIL I TURN BLUE.
FINE. WHATEVER. BUT I CAN TAKE CARE OF MYSELF. ALWAYS HAVE, ALWAYS WILL.

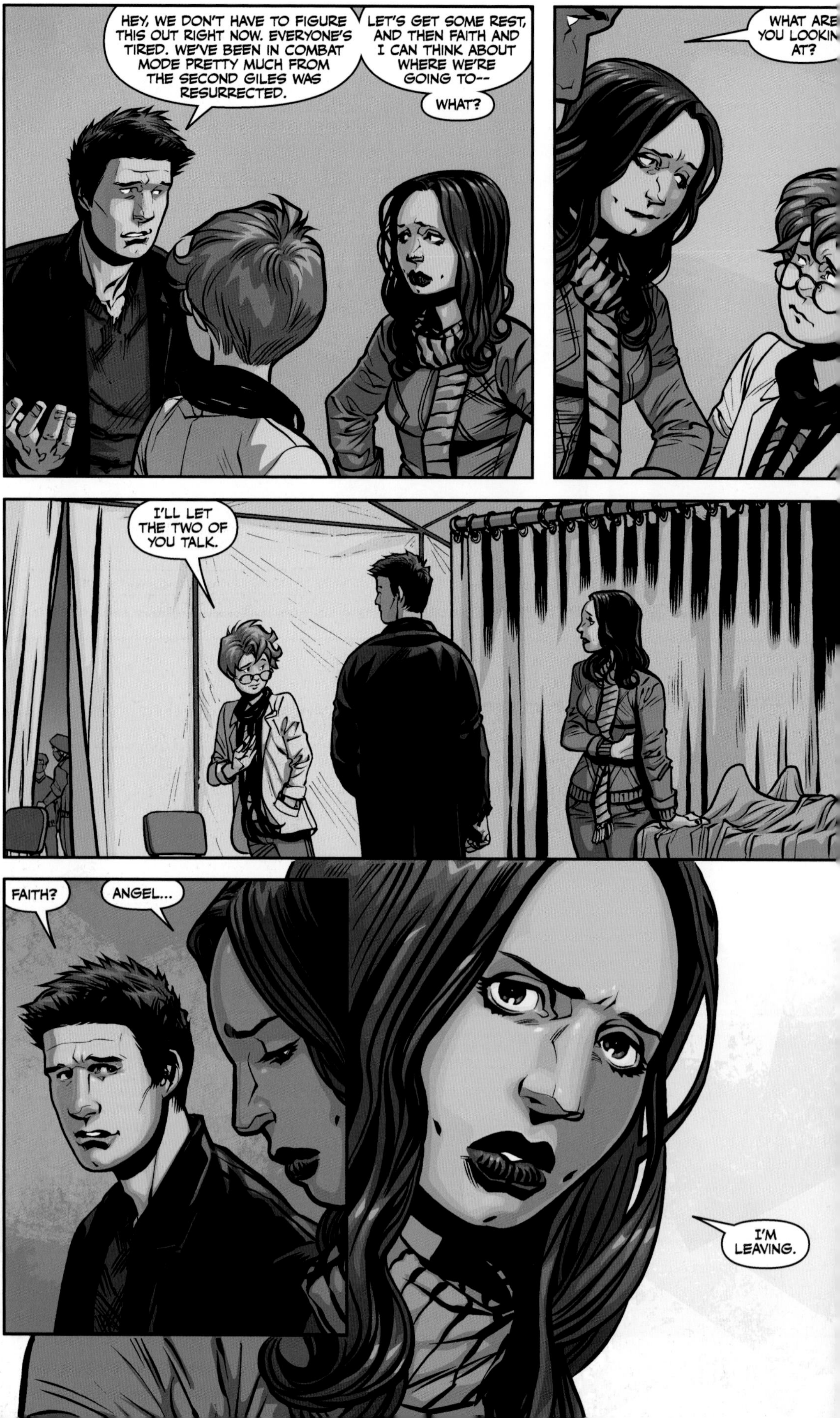
HEY, WE DON'T HAVE TO FIGURE THIS OUT RIGHT NOW. EVERYONE'S TIRED. WE'VE BEEN IN COMBAT MODE PRETTY MUCH FROM THE SECOND GILES WAS RESURRECTED.
LET'S GET SOME REST, AND THEN FAITH AND I CAN THINK ABOUT WHERE WE'RE GOING TO--
WHAT?
WHAT ARE YOU LOOKIN AT?
I'LL LET THE TWO OF YOU TALK.
FAITH?
ANGEL...
I'M LEAVING.

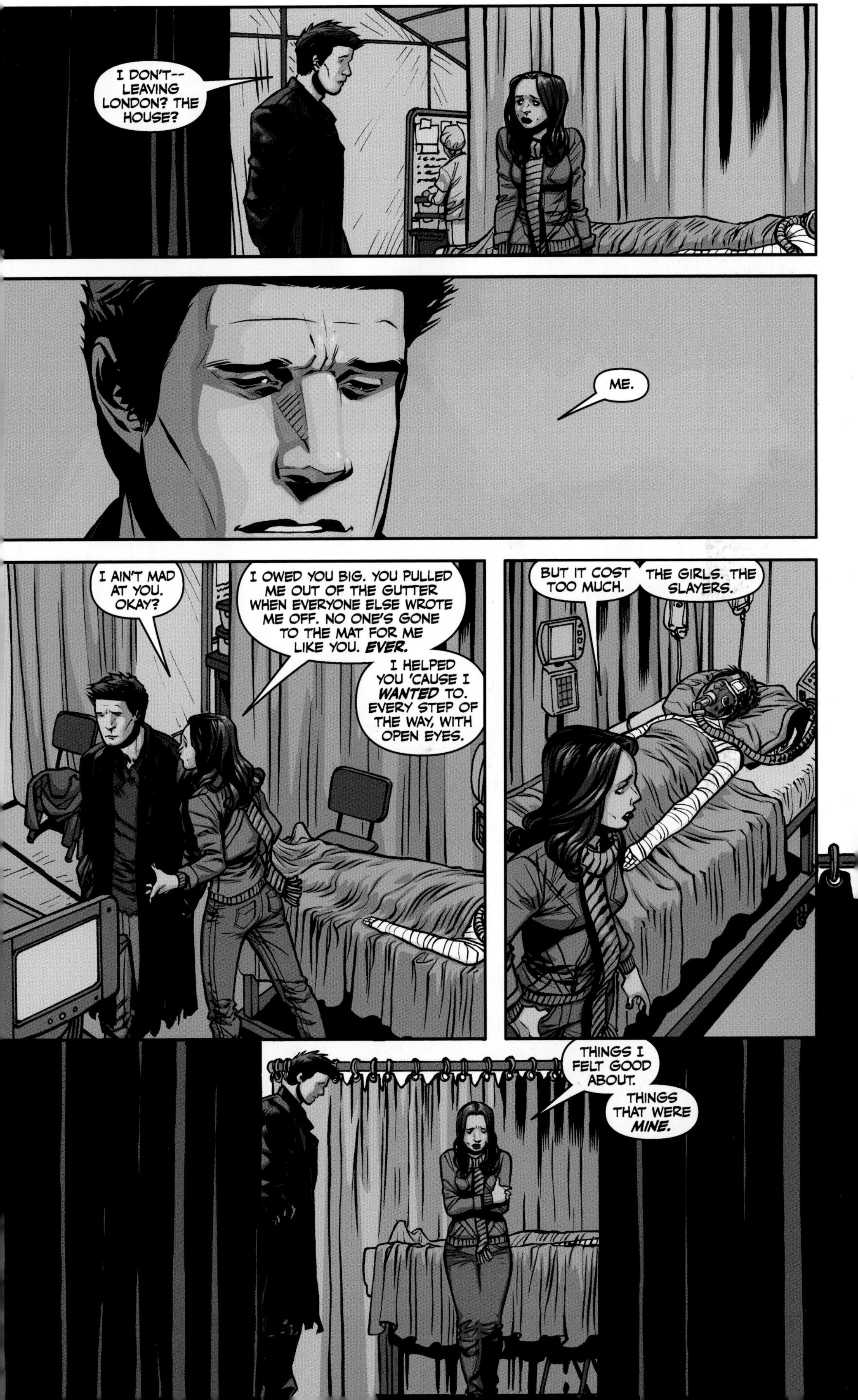
I DON'T--
LEAVING LONDON? THE HOUSE?
ME.
I AIN'T MAD AT YOU. OKAY?
I OWED YOU BIG. YOU PULLED ME OUT OF THE GUTTER WHEN EVERYONE ELSE WROTE ME OFF. NO ONE'S GONE TO THE MAT FOR ME LIKE YOU. EVER.
I HELPED YOU 'CAUSE I WANTED TO. EVERY STEP OF THE WAY, WITH OPEN EYES.
BUT IT COST TOO MUCH.
THE GIRLS. THE SLAYERS.
THINGS I FELT GOOD ABOUT.
THINGS THAT WERE MINE.

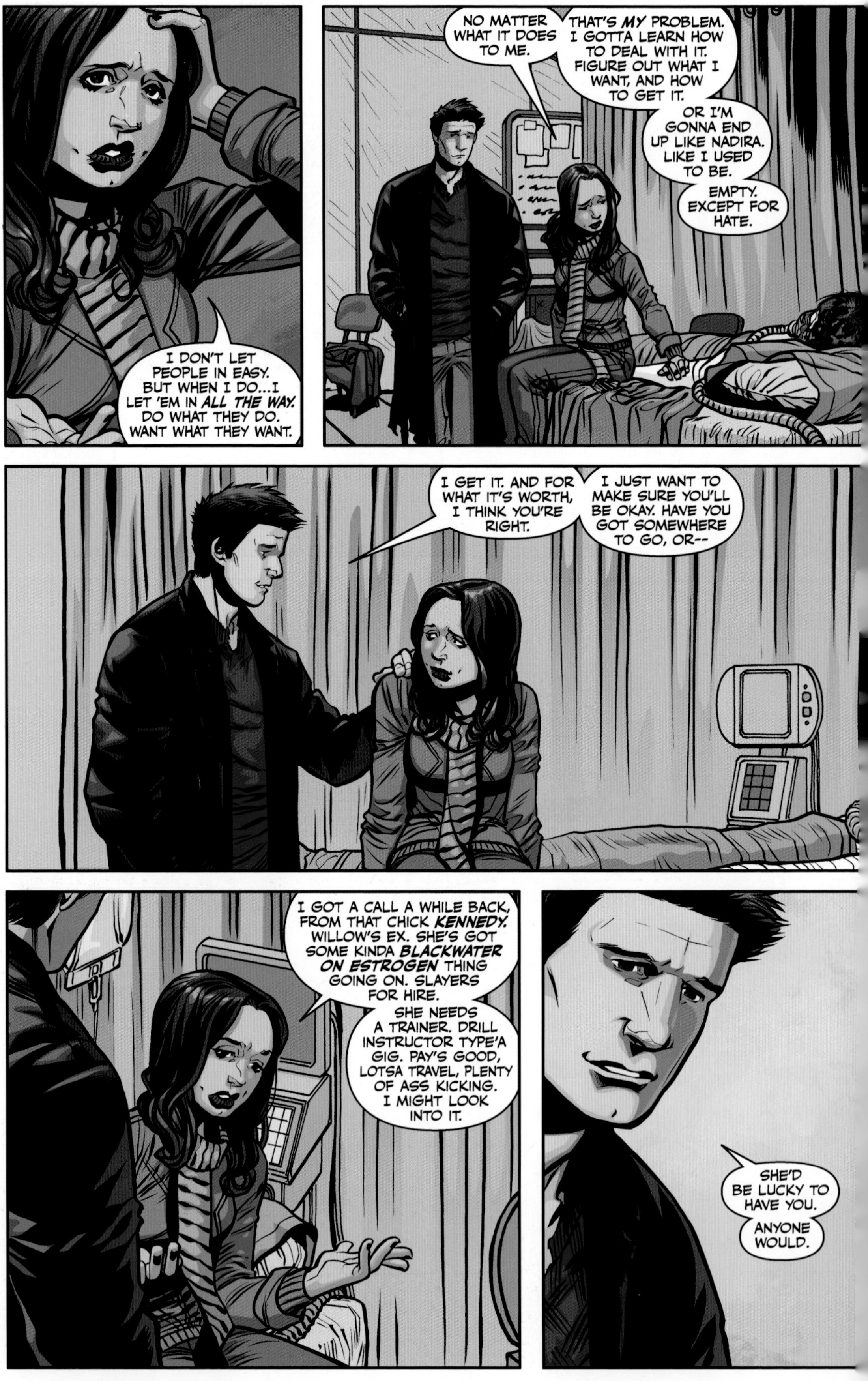
I DON'T LET PEOPLE IN EASY. BUT WHEN I DO...I LET 'EM IN ALL THE WAY. DO WHAT THEY DO. WANT WHAT THEY WANT.
NO MATTER WHAT IT DOES TO ME.
THAT'S MY PROBLEM. I GOTTA LEARN HOW TO DEAL WITH IT. FIGURE OUT WHAT I WANT, AND HOW TO GET IT.
OR I'M GONNA END UP LIKE NADIRA. LIKE I USED TO BE.
EMPTY. EXCEPT FOR HATE.
I GET IT. AND FOR WHAT IT'S WORTH, I THINK YOU'RE RIGHT.
I JUST WANT TO MAKE SURE YOU'LL BE OKAY. HAVE YOU GOT SOMEWHERE TO GO, OR--
I GOT A CALL A WHILE BACK, FROM THAT CHICK KENNEDY. WILLOW'S EX. SHE'S GOT SOME KINDA BLACKWATER ON ESTROGEN THING GOING ON. SLAYERS FOR HIRE.
SHE NEEDS A TRAINER. DRILL INSTRUCTOR TYPE'A GIG. PAY'S GOOD, LOTSA TRAVEL, PLENTY OF ASS KICKING. I MIGHT LOOK INTO IT.
SHE'D BE LUCKY TO HAVE YOU.
ANYONE WOULD.

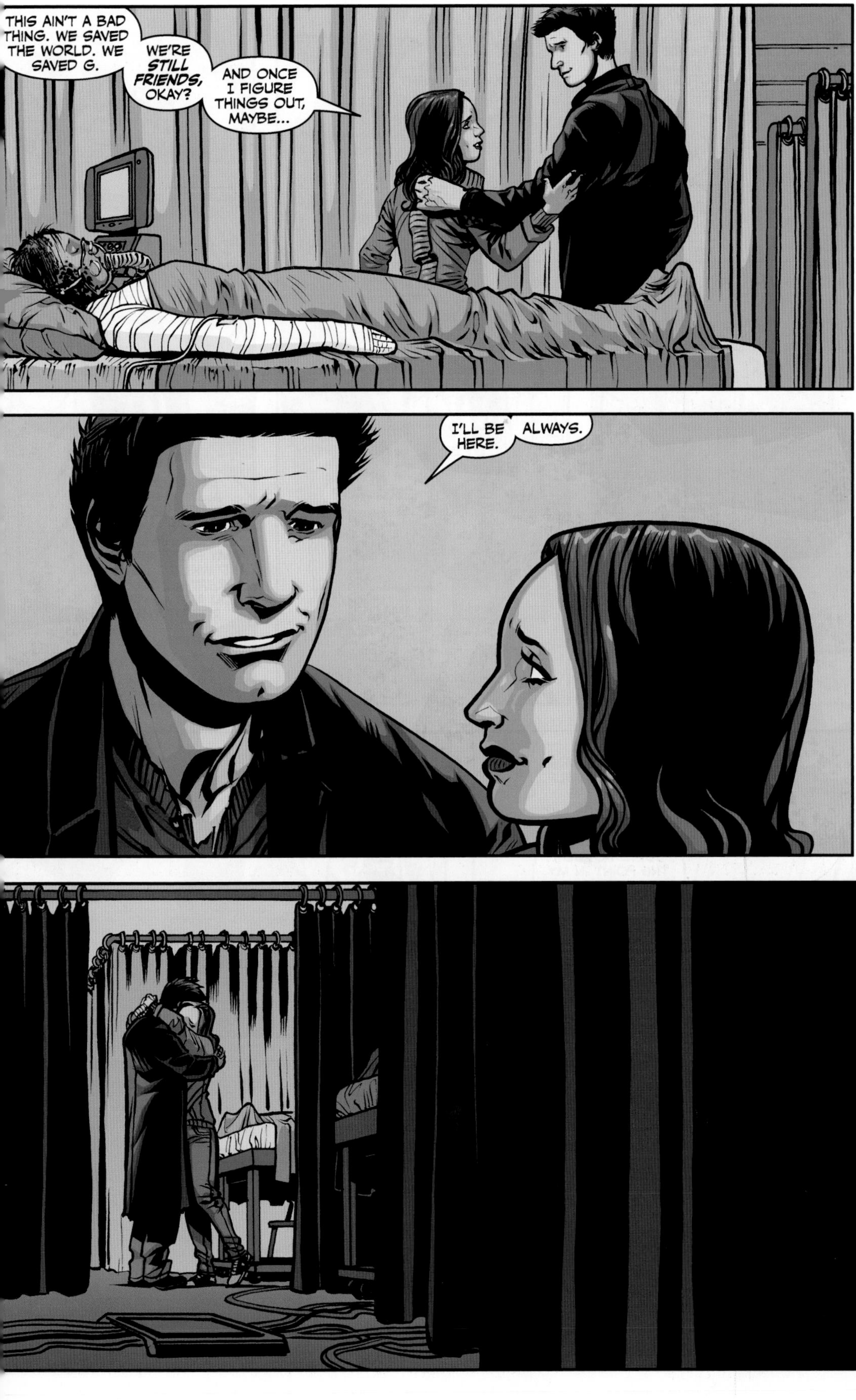
THIS AIN'T A BAD THING. WE SAVED THE WORLD. WE SAVED G.
WE'RE STILL FRIENDS, OKAY?
AND ONCE I FIGURE THINGS OUT, MAYBE...
I'LL BE HERE.
ALWAYS.

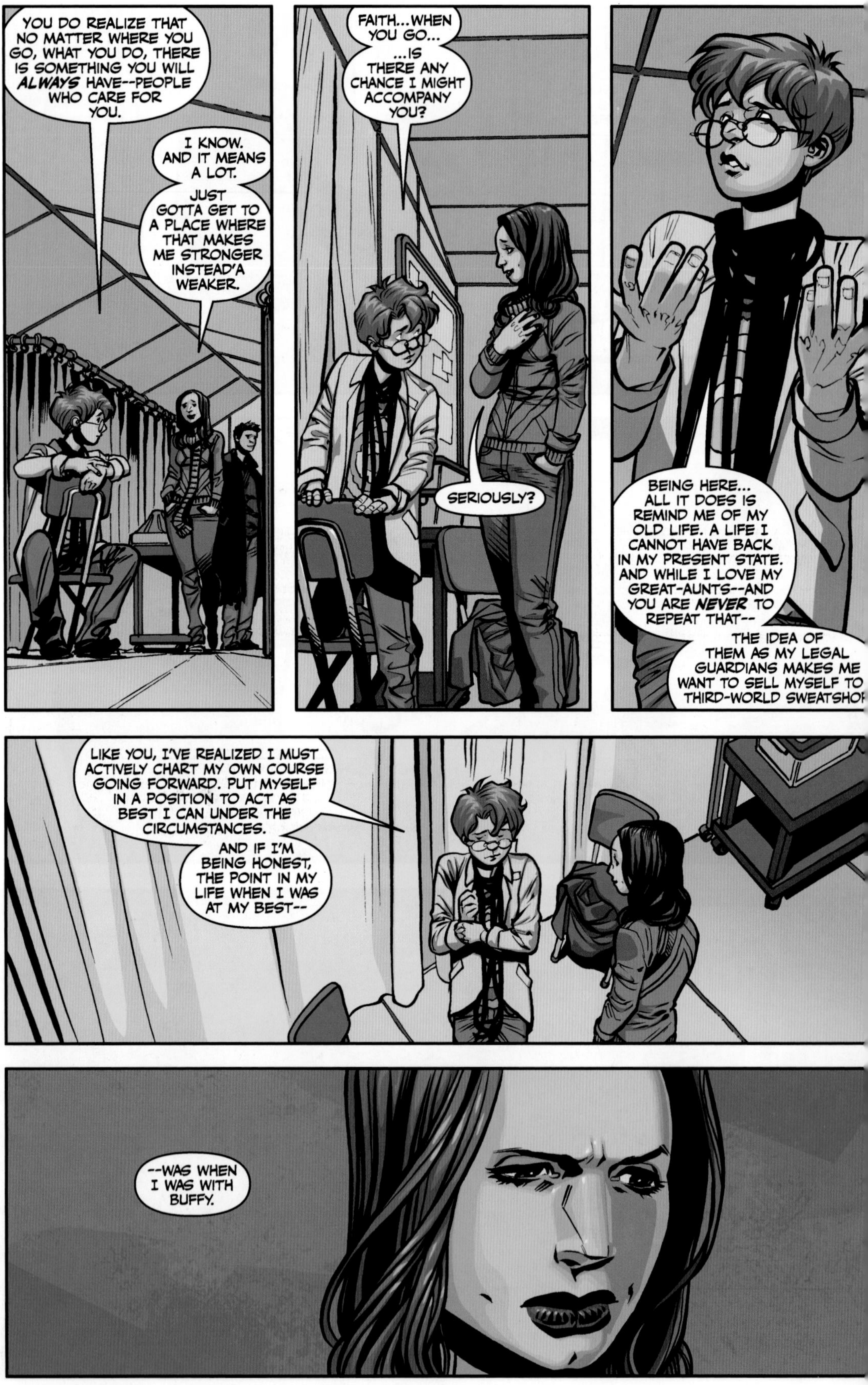

YOU DO REALIZE THAT NO MATTER WHERE YOU GO, WHAT YOU DO, THERE IS SOMETHING YOU WILL ALWAYS HAVE--PEOPLE WHO CARE FOR YOU.
I KNOW. AND IT MEANS A LOT.
JUST GOTTA GET TO A PLACE WHERE THAT MAKES ME STRONGER INSTEAD'A WEAKER.
FAITH...WHEN YOU GO...
...IS THERE ANY CHANCE I MIGHT ACCOMPANY YOU?
SERIOUSLY?
BEING HERE... ALL IT DOES IS REMIND ME OF MY OLD LIFE. A LIFE I CANNOT HAVE BACK IN MY PRESENT STATE. AND WHILE I LOVE MY GREAT-AUNTS--AND YOU ARE NEVER TO REPEAT THAT--
THE IDEA OF THEM AS MY LEGAL GUARDIANS MAKES ME WANT TO SELL MYSELF TO THIRD-WORLD SWEATSHO
LIKE YOU, I'VE REALIZED I MUST ACTIVELY CHART MY OWN COURSE GOING FORWARD. PUT MYSELF IN A POSITION TO ACT AS BEST I CAN UNDER THE CIRCUMSTANCES.
AND IF I'M BEING HONEST, THE POINT IN MY LIFE WHEN I WAS AT MY BEST--
--WAS WHEN I WAS WITH BUFFY.

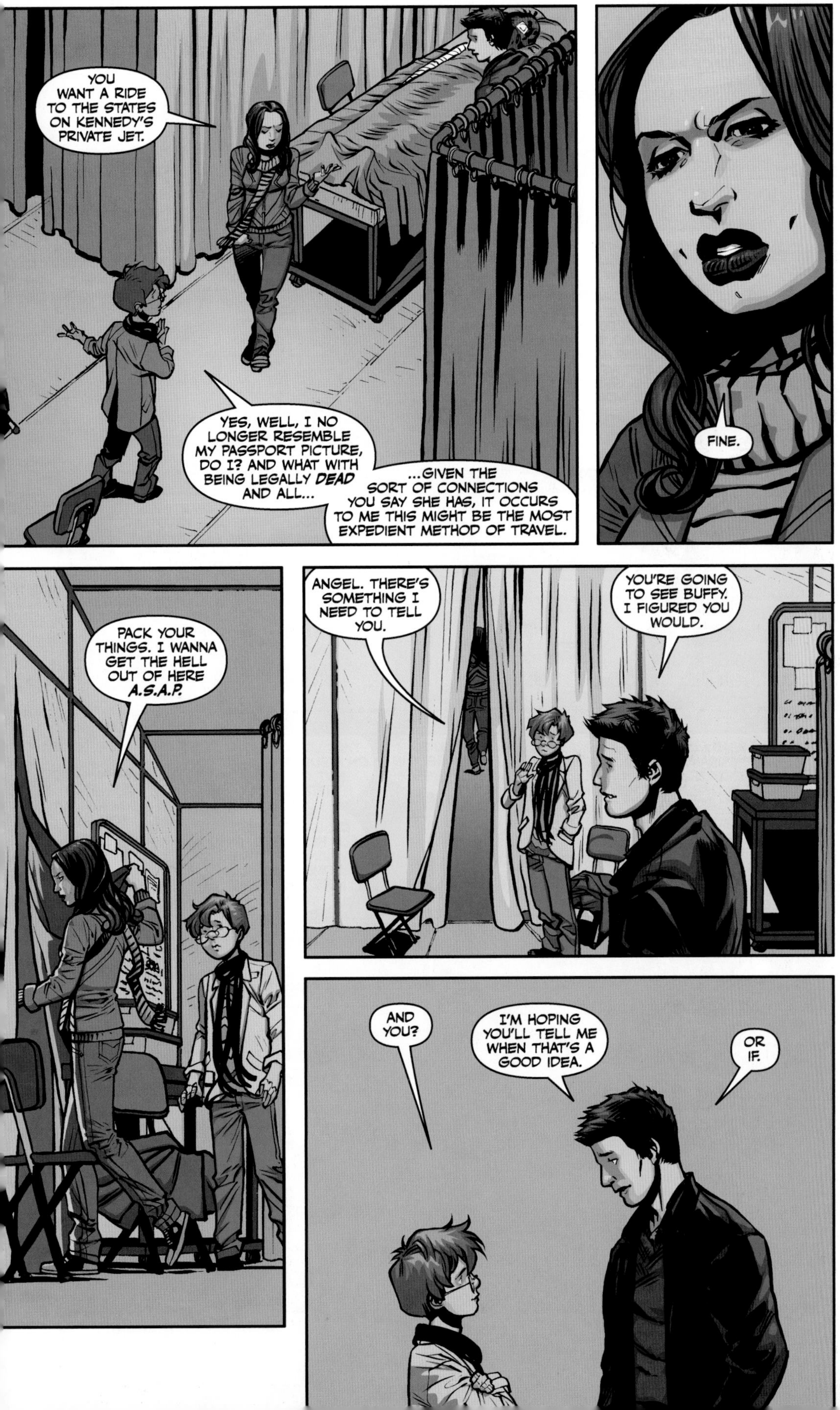

YOU WANT A RIDE TO THE STATES ON KENNEDY'S PRIVATE JET.
YES, WELL, I NO LONGER RESEMBLE MY PASSPORT PICTURE, DO I? AND WHAT WITH BEING LEGALLY *DEAD* AND ALL...
...GIVEN THE SORT OF CONNECTIONS YOU SAY SHE HAS, IT OCCURS TO ME THIS MIGHT BE THE MOST EXPEDIENT METHOD OF TRAVEL.
FINE.
PACK YOUR THINGS. I WANNA GET THE HELL OUT OF HERE *A.S.A.P.*
ANGEL. THERE'S SOMETHING I NEED TO TELL YOU.
YOU'RE GOING TO SEE BUFFY. I FIGURED YOU WOULD.
AND YOU?
I'M HOPING YOU'LL TELL ME WHEN THAT'S A GOOD IDEA.
OR IF.

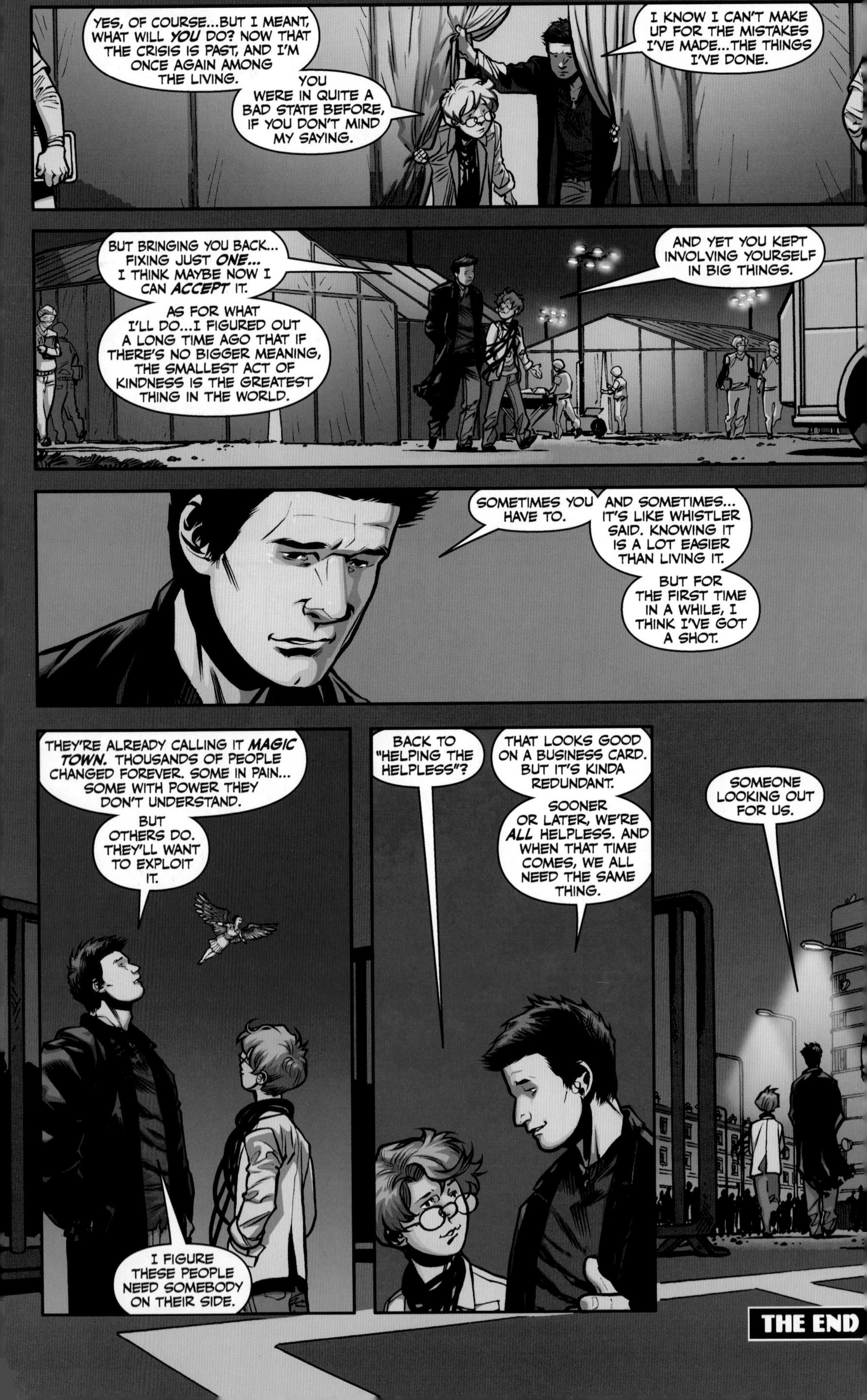
YES, OF COURSE...BUT I MEANT, WHAT WILL *YOU* DO? NOW THAT THE CRISIS IS PAST, AND I'M ONCE AGAIN AMONG THE LIVING.
YOU WERE IN QUITE A BAD STATE BEFORE, IF YOU DON'T MIND MY SAYING.
I KNOW I CAN'T MAKE UP FOR THE MISTAKES I'VE MADE...THE THINGS I'VE DONE.
BUT BRINGING YOU BACK... FIXING JUST *ONE...* I THINK MAYBE NOW I CAN *ACCEPT* IT.
AS FOR WHAT I'LL DO...I FIGURED OUT A LONG TIME AGO THAT IF THERE'S NO BIGGER MEANING, THE SMALLEST ACT OF KINDNESS IS THE GREATEST THING IN THE WORLD.
AND YET YOU KEPT INVOLVING YOURSELF IN BIG THINGS.
SOMETIMES YOU HAVE TO.
AND SOMETIMES... IT'S LIKE WHISTLER SAID. KNOWING IT IS A LOT EASIER THAN LIVING IT.
BUT FOR THE FIRST TIME IN A WHILE, I THINK I'VE GOT A SHOT.
THEY'RE ALREADY CALLING IT *MAGIC TOWN.* THOUSANDS OF PEOPLE CHANGED FOREVER. SOME IN PAIN... SOME WITH POWER THEY DON'T UNDERSTAND.
BUT OTHERS DO. THEY'LL WANT TO EXPLOIT IT.
I FIGURE THESE PEOPLE NEED SOMEBODY ON THEIR SIDE.
BACK TO "HELPING THE HELPLESS"?
THAT LOOKS GOOD ON A BUSINESS CARD. BUT IT'S KINDA REDUNDANT.
SOONER OR LATER, WE'RE *ALL* HELPLESS. AND WHEN THAT TIME COMES, WE ALL NEED THE SAME THING.
SOMEONE LOOKING OUT FOR US.
THE END

ANGEL & FAITH
COVER GALLERY
AND SKETCHBOOK
WITH NOTES FROM
REBEKAH ISAACS

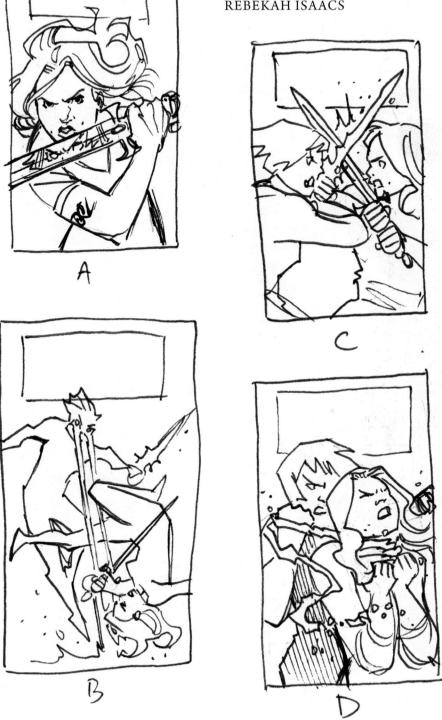

A

C

B

D

I feel like I must've pitched an "enemy reflected in the hero's blade" variation for every other cover . . . And it finally stuck! Every now and then it's fun to indulge in a cliché—especially the kind that I ran into the ground in my high school sketchbooks.

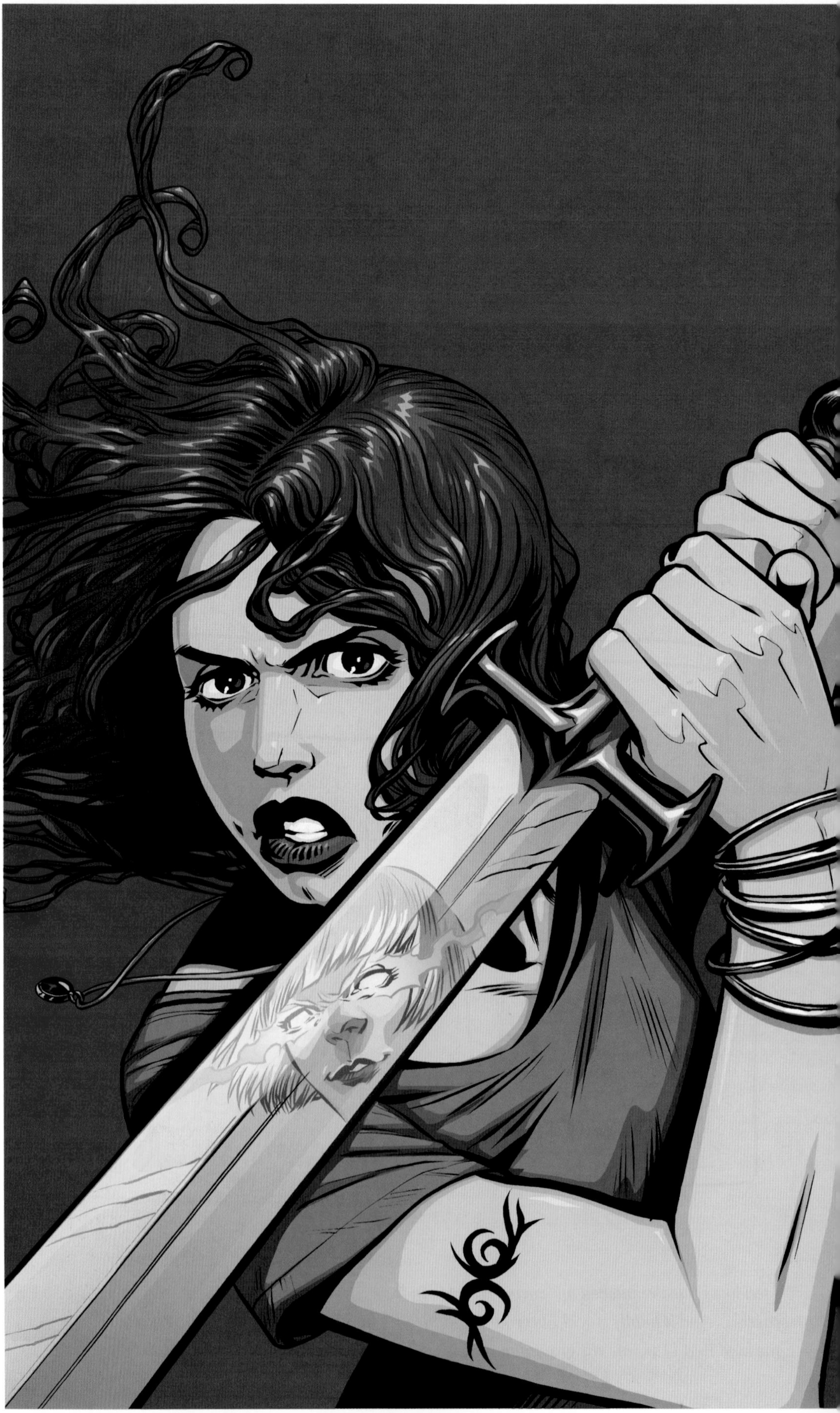

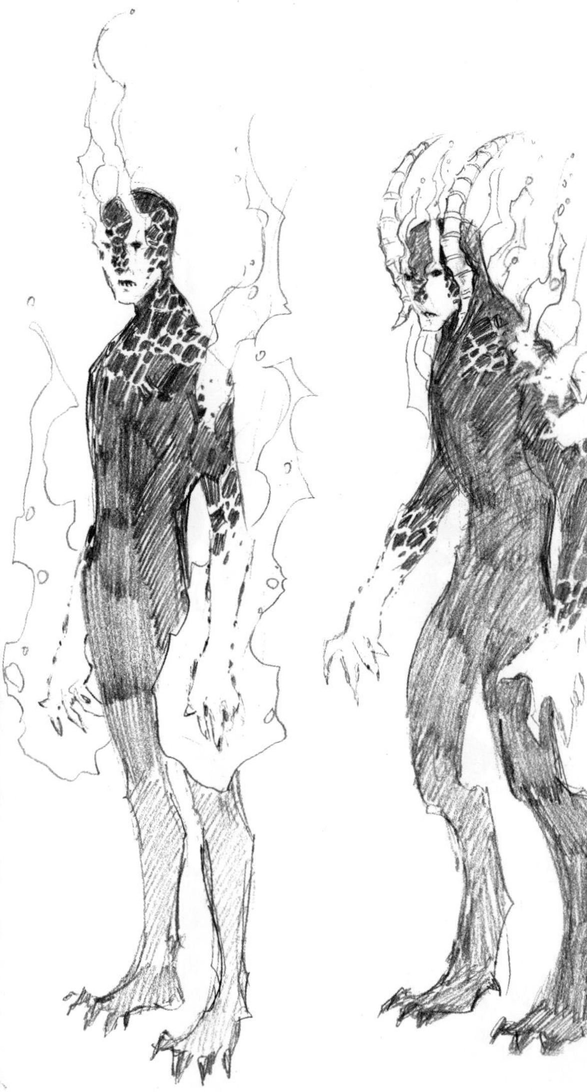

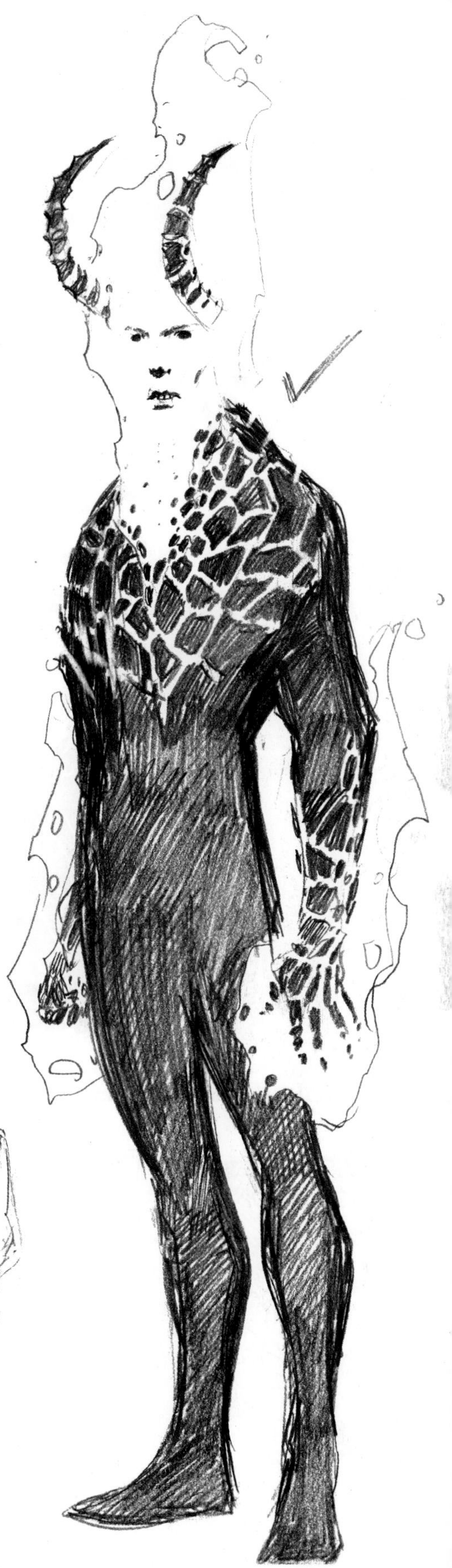

The Balrog in The Fellowship of the Ring *was a big inspiration for Whistler's demon/final boss/Super Saiyan form. Christos liked the final option for this one because, unlike many of my other demon designs, it seemed more otherworldly and not defined by animal-like characteristics, as befits Whistler being on a different level from man, beast, or common demon. This design relied a lot on color, and as usual, Dan knocked it out of the park.*

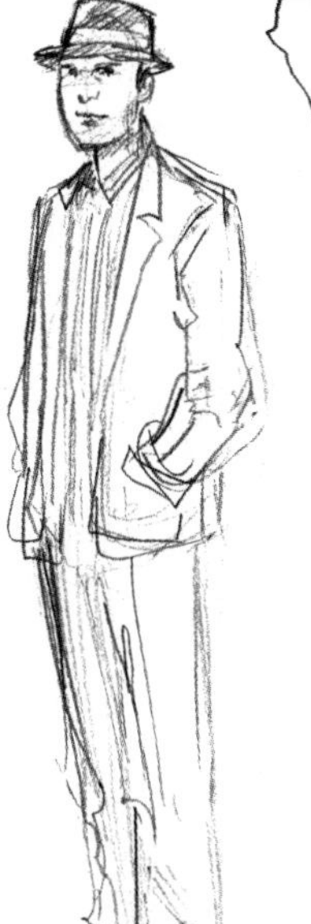

Facing page: *The variant cover art for issue #21.*

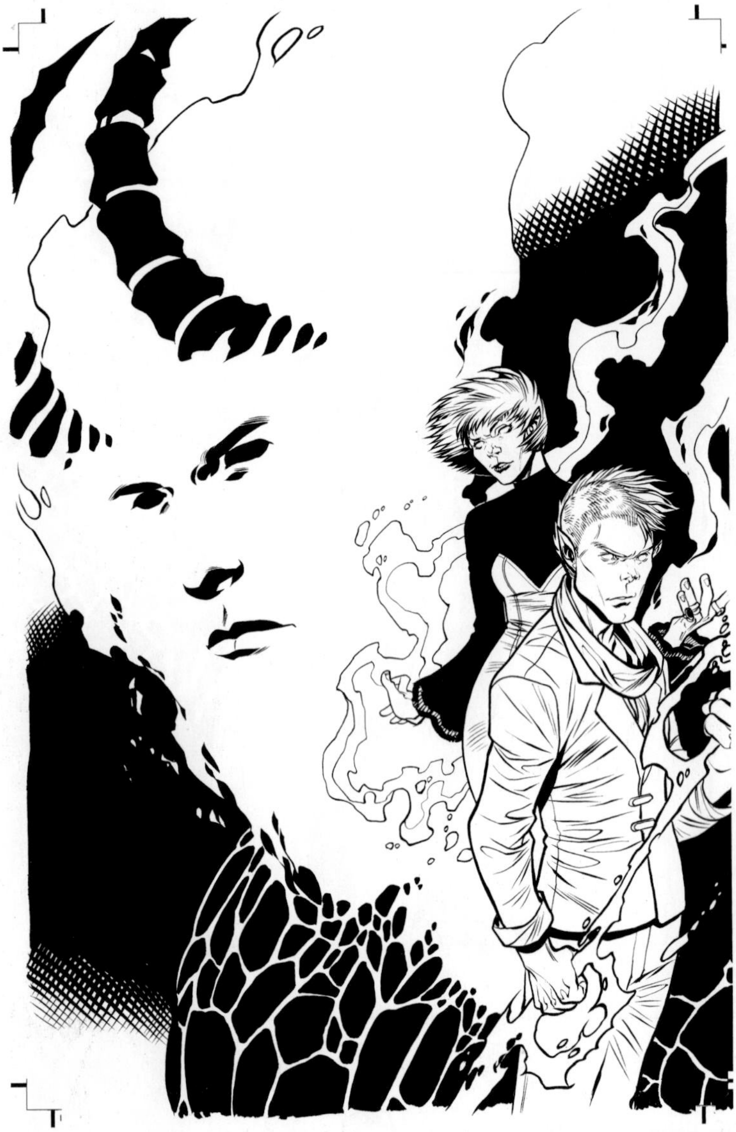

This page and the facing: *Sketches, inks, and final colors for the issue #22 variant cover.*

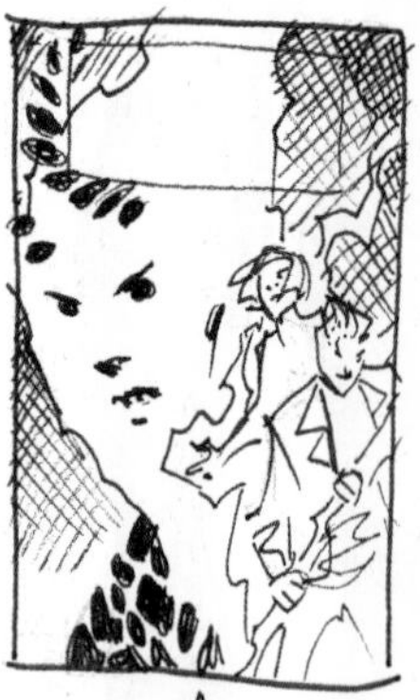

A

Movie-poster style!

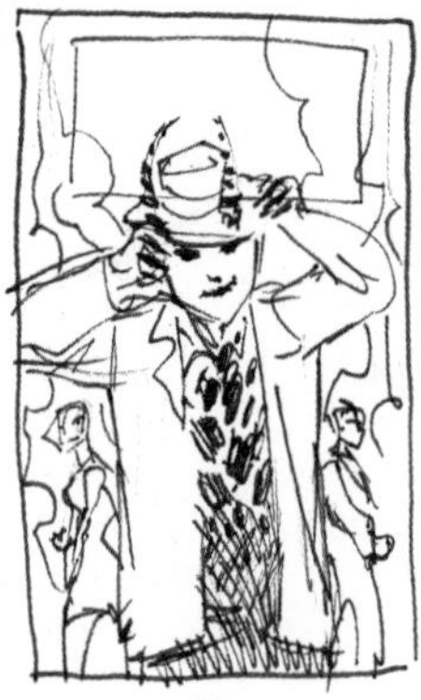

B

Whistler putting on or removing hat while transforming into demon form.

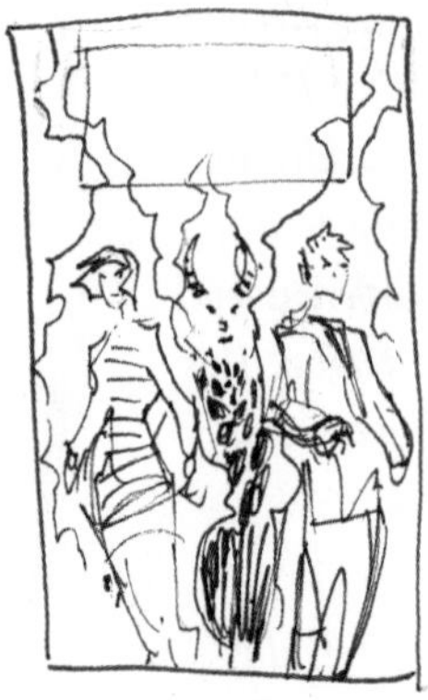

C

Whistler flanked by Pearl and Nash.

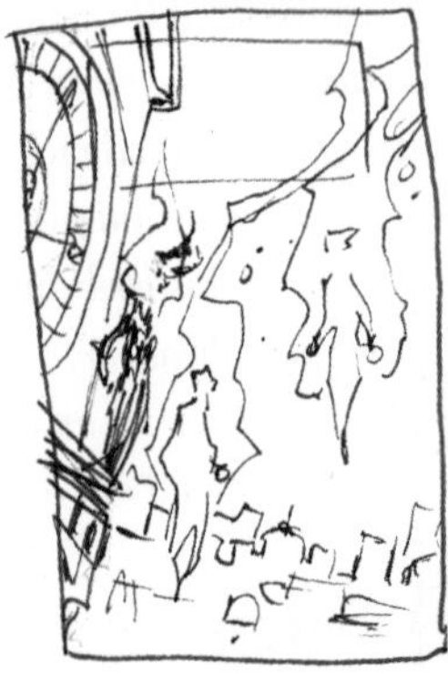

D

Looming over the London skyline at night, in full power.

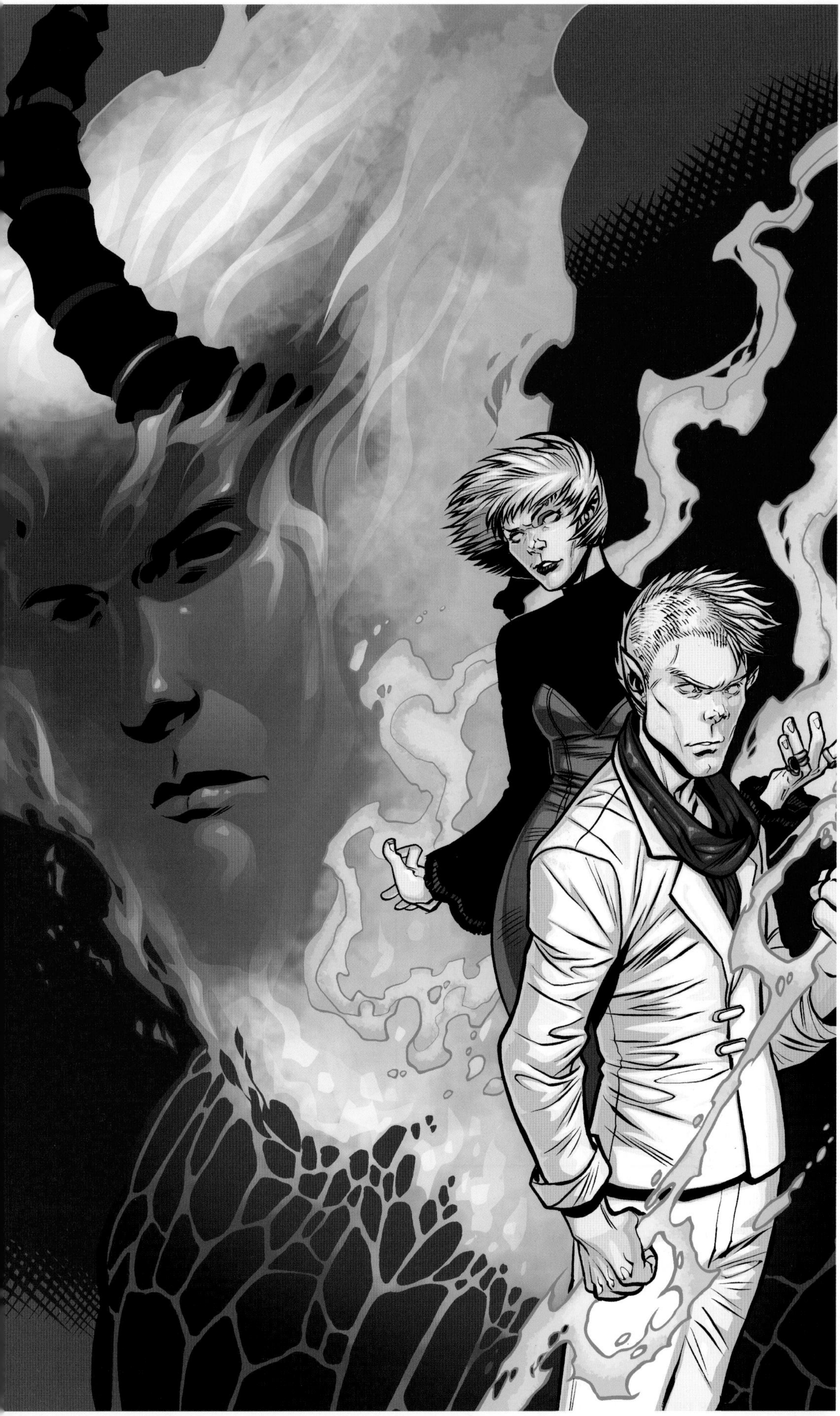

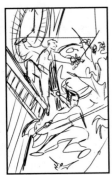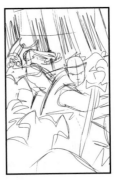

The prompt for this cover to issue #23 was "Iconic! Comic Booky! Huzzah." I feel like my best covers come from the most open-ended prompts, and this is one of my favorites! These flying beasties didn't end up making it into the interiors, but I could imagine they're still flapping around Magic Town somewhere.

The final variant cover art for Angel & Faith #23 is shown on page 2 of this collection.

Following pages: The variant cover art for issues #24 and #25.

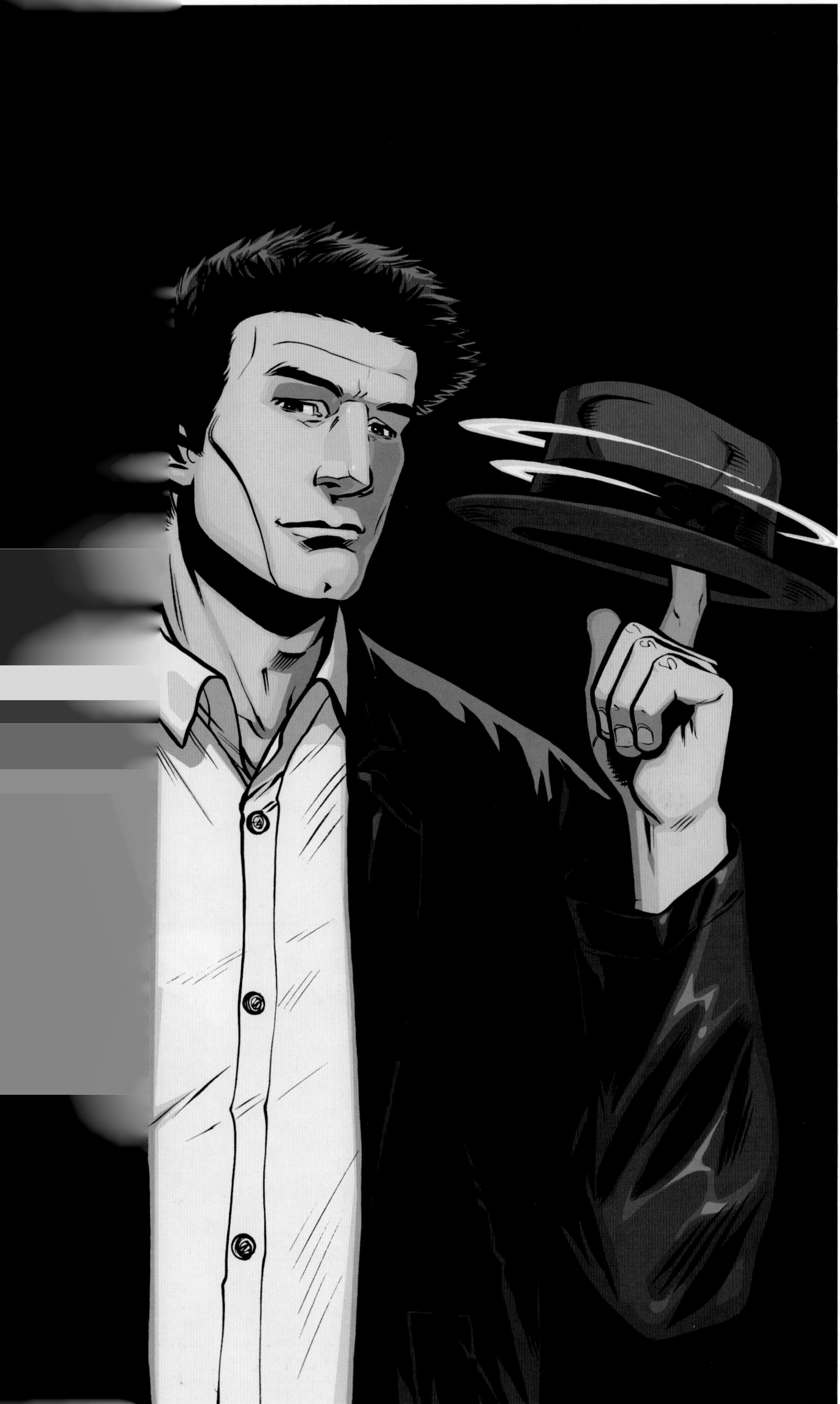

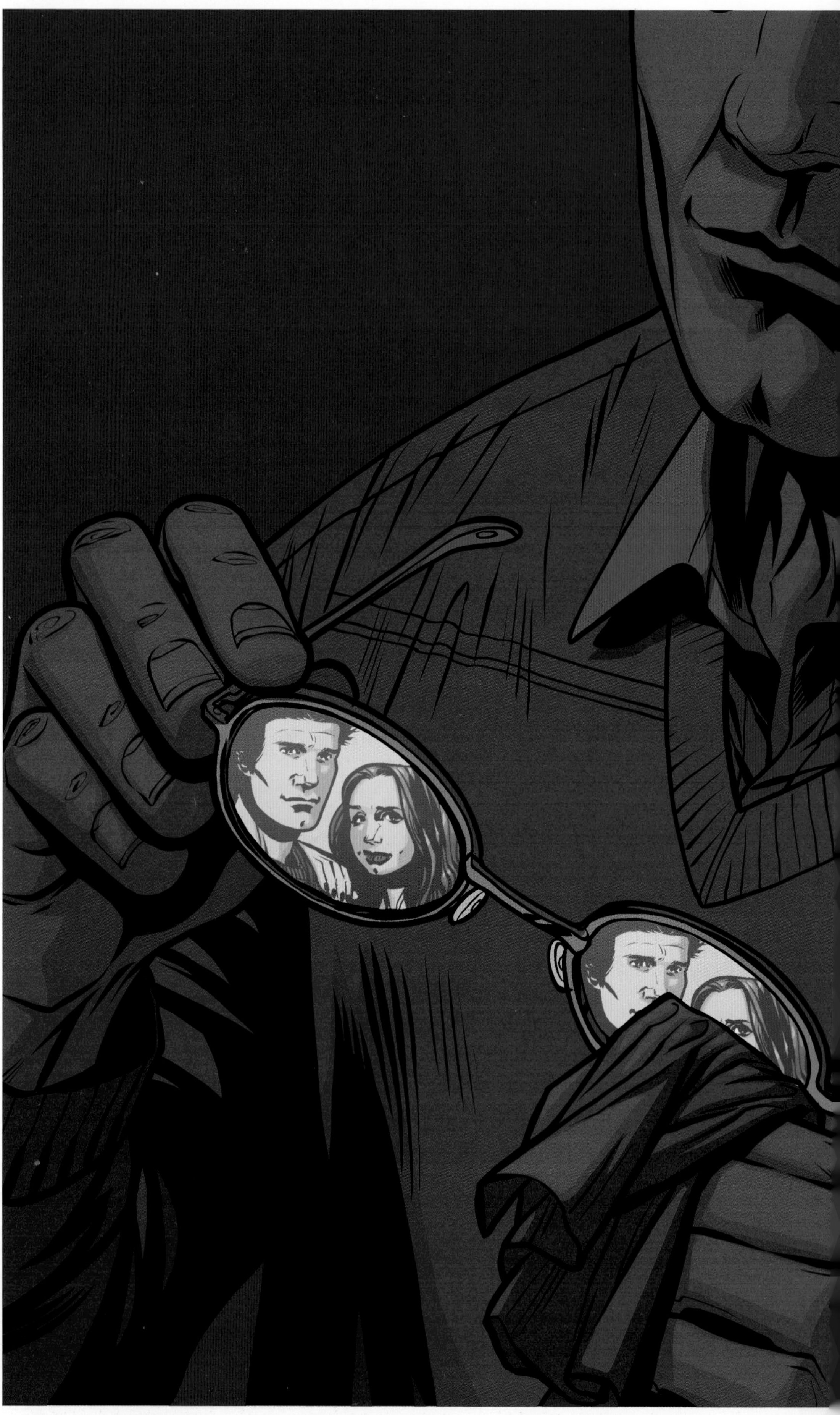

'ROM JOSS WHEDON

UFFY THE VAMPIRE SLAYER SEASON 8

'OLUME 1: THE LONG WAY HOME
ss Whedon and Georges Jeanty
BN 978-1-59307-822-5 | $15.99

'OLUME 2: NO FUTURE FOR YOU
rian K. Vaughan, Georges Jeanty, and Joss Whedon
BN 978-1-59307-963-5 | $15.99

'OLUME 3: WOLVES AT THE GATE
rew Goddard, Georges Jeanty, and Joss Whedon
BN 978-1-59582-165-2 | $15.99

'OLUME 4: TIME OF YOUR LIFE
ss Whedon, Jeph Loeb, Georges Jeanty, and others
BN 978-1-59582-310-6 | $15.99

'OLUME 5: PREDATORS AND PREY
ss Whedon, Jane Espenson, Georges Jeanty, Cliff Richards, and others
BN 978-1-59582-342-7 | $15.99

'OLUME 6: RETREAT
ss Whedon, Jane Espenson, Georges Jeanty, Karl Moline, and others
BN 978-1-59582-415-8 | $15.99

'OLUME 7: TWILIGHT
ss Whedon, Brad Meltzer, and Georges Jeanty
BN 978-1-59582-558-2 | $16.99

'OLUME 8: LAST GLEAMING
ss Whedon, Scott Allie, and Georges Jeanty
BN 978-1-59582-610-7 | $16.99

UFFY THE VAMPIRE SLAYER SEASON 8
IBRARY EDITION

OLUME 1
BN 978-1-59582-888-0 | $29.99

'OLUME 2
BN 978-1-59582-935-1 | $29.99

OLUME 3
BN 978-1-59582-978-8 | $29.99

OLUME 4
BN 978-1-61655-127-8 | $29.99

UFFY THE VAMPIRE SLAYER SEASON 9

OLUME 1: FREEFALL
ss Whedon, Andrew Chambliss, Georges Jeanty, and others
BN 978-1-59582-922-1 | $17.99

OLUME 2: ON YOUR OWN
ndrew Chambliss, Scott Allie, Georges Jeanty, and others
BN 978-1-59582-990-0 | $17.99

OLUME 3: GUARDED
ss Whedon, Jane Espenson, Drew Z. Greenberg,
eorges Jeanty, and others
BN 978-1-61655-099-8 | $17.99

OLUME 4: WELCOME TO THE TEAM
ndrew Chambliss, Georges Jeanty, Karl Moline, and others
BN 978-1-61655-166-7 | $17.99

OLUME 5: THE CORE
ndrew Chambliss, Georges Jeanty, and others
BN 978-1-61655-254-1 | $17.99

NGEL & FAITH

OLUME 1: LIVE THROUGH THIS
hristos Gage, Rebekah Isaacs, and Phil Noto
BN 978-1-59582-887-3 | $17.99

OLUME 2: DADDY ISSUES
hristos Gage, Rebekah Isaacs, and Chris Samnee
BN 978-1-59582-960-3 | $17.99

OLUME 3: FAMILY REUNION
hristos Gage, Rebekah Isaacs, Lee Garbett, and David Lapham
BN 978-1-61655-079-0 | $17.99

OLUME 4: DEATH AND CONSEQUENCES
hristos Gage and Rebekah Isaacs
BN 978-1-61655-165-0 | $17.99

OLUME 5: WHAT YOU WANT, NOT WHAT YOU NEED
hristos Gage and Rebekah Isaacs
BN 978-1-61655-253-4 | $17.99

PIKE

OLUME 1: A DARK PLACE
BN 978-1-61655-109-4 | $17.99

ILLOW

OLUME 1: WONDERLAND
BN 978-1-61655-145-2 | $17.99

Buffy the Vampire Slayer™

AVAILABLE AT YOUR LOCAL COMICS SHOP OR BOOKSTORE!

To find a comics shop in your area, call 1-888-266-4226. For more information or to order direct:
On the web: DarkHorse.com • E-mail: mailorder@darkhorse.com • Phone: 1-800-862-0052 Mon.–Fri. 9 AM to 5 PM Pacific Time

DARK HORSE BOOKS

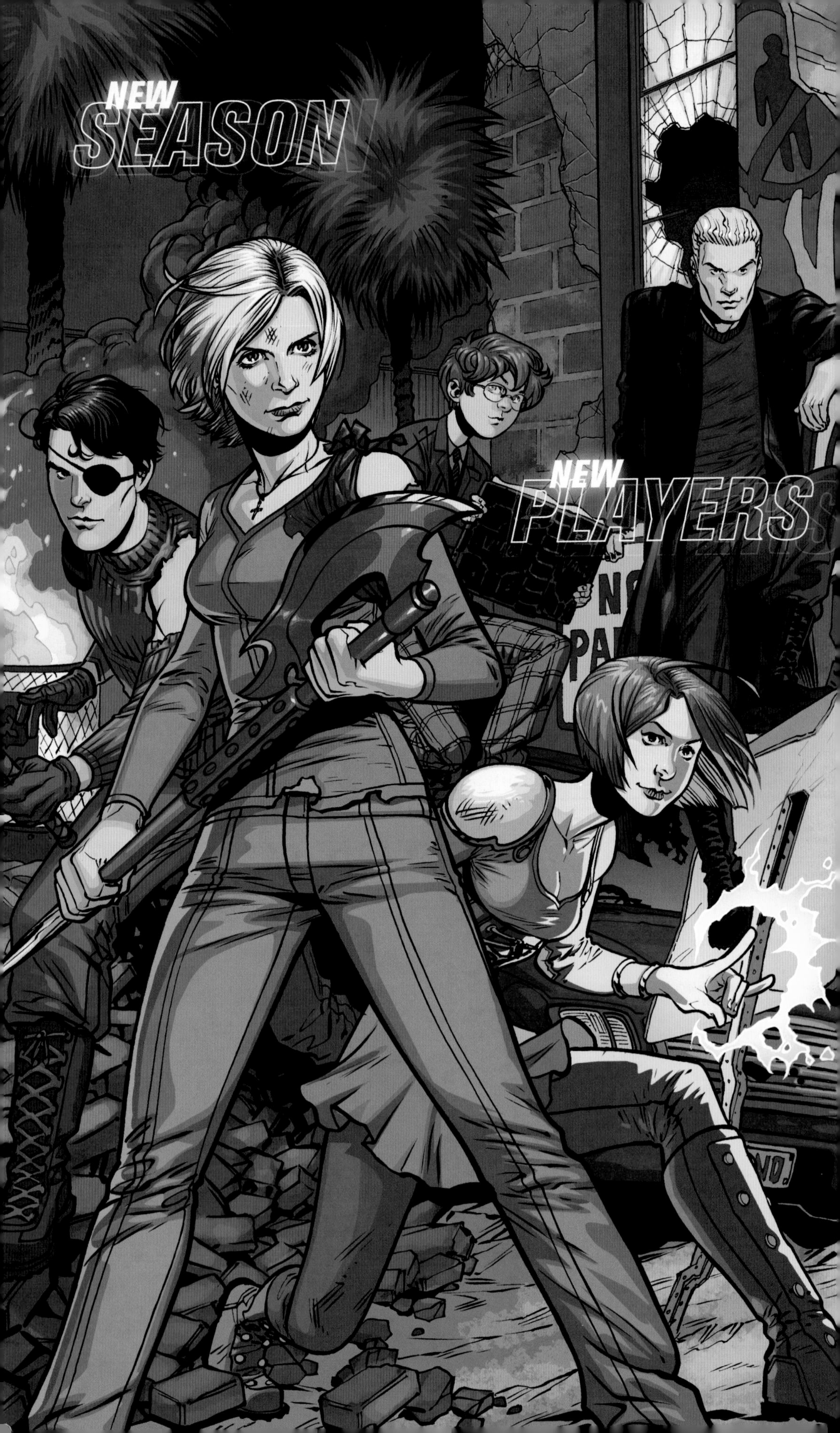
NEW SEASON
NEW PLAYERS

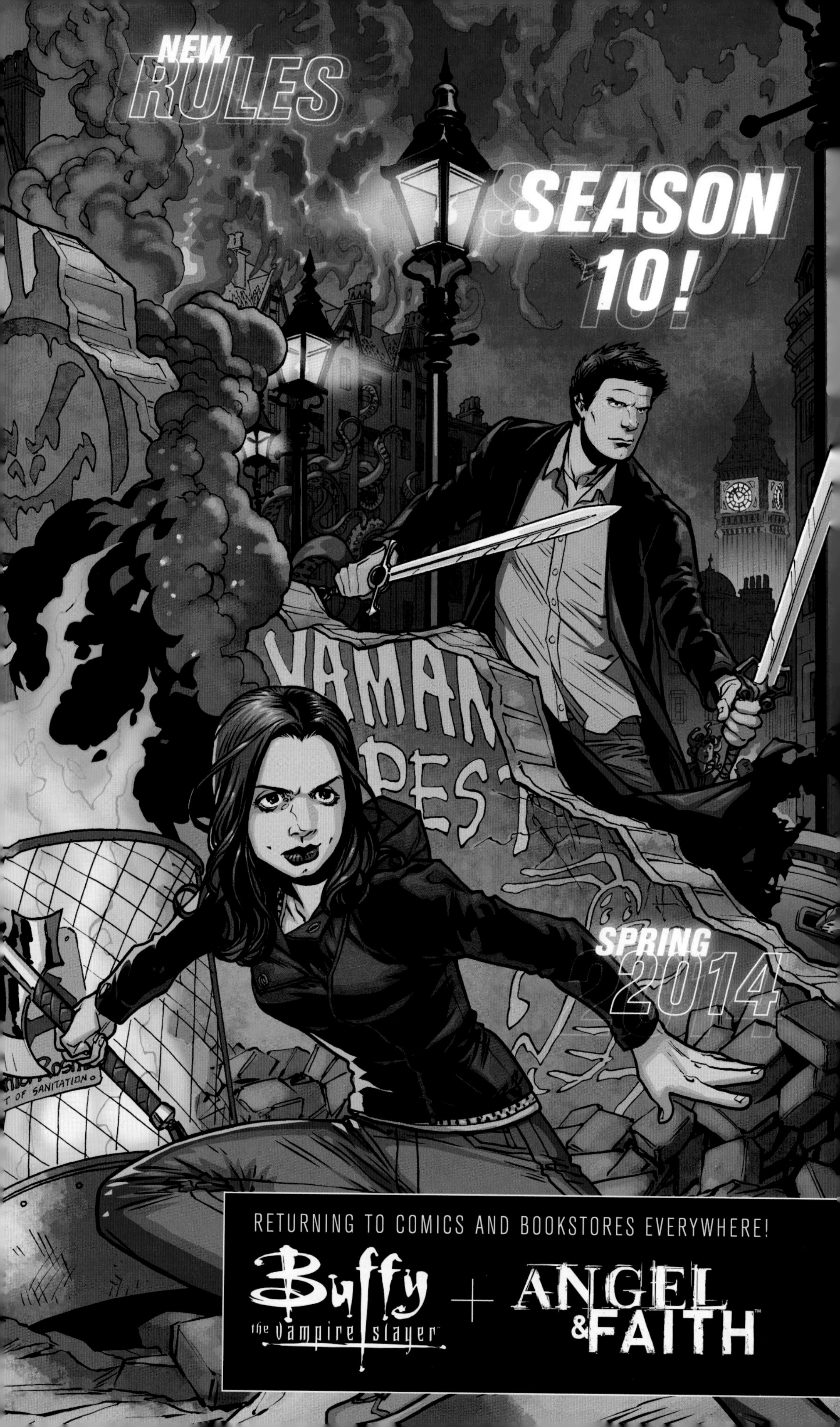

NEW RULES
SEASON 10!
SPRING 2014
RETURNING TO COMICS AND BOOKSTORES EVERYWHERE!
Buffy the vampire slayer
+
ANGEL & FAITH

JOSS WHEDON

Serenity
FIREFLY CLASS 03-K64
THOSE LEFT BEHIND

DR. HORRIBLE
AND OTHER HORRIBLE STORIES BY ZACK WHEDON
with Eric Canete, Farel Dalrymple, Jim Rugg, Joëlle Jones, and Scott Hepburn

JOSS WHEDON'S
dollhouse
EPITAPHS

Buffy
the vampire slayer
OMNIBUS
VOLUME 1

SERENITY VOLUME 1: THOSE LEFT BEHIND
Joss Whedon, Brett Matthews, and Will Conrad
978-1-59582-914-6 | $17.99

SERENITY VOLUME 2: BETTER DAYS AND OTHER STORIES
Joss Whedon, Patton Oswalt, Zack Whedon, Patric Reynolds, and others
978-1-59582-739-5 | $19.99

SERENITY VOLUME 3: THE SHEPHERD'S TALE
Joss Whedon, Zack Whedon, and Chris Samnee
978-1-59582-561-2 | $14.99

DR. HORRIBLE AND OTHER HORRIBLE STORIES
Joss Whedon, Zack Whedon, Joëlle Jones, and others
978-1-59582-577-3 | $9.99

DOLLHOUSE: EPITAPHS
Andrew Chambliss, Jed Whedon, Maurissa Tancharoen, and Cliff Richards
978-1-59582-863-7 | $18.99

TALES OF THE SLAYERS
Joss Whedon, Amber Benson, Gene Colan, P. Craig Russell, Tim Sale, and others
978-1-56971-605-2 | $14.99

TALES OF THE VAMPIRES
Joss Whedon, Brett Matthews, Cameron Stewart, and others
978-1-56971-749-3 | $15.99

BUFFY THE VAMPIRE SLAYER: TALES
978-1-59582-644-2 | $29.99

ANGEL OMNIBUS
Christopher Golden, Eric Powell, and others
978-1-59582-706-7 | $24.99

BUFFY THE VAMPIRE SLAYER OMNIBUS
Volume 1 978-1-59307-784-6 | $24.99
Volume 2 978-1-59307-826-3 | $24.99
Volume 3 978-1-59307-885-0 | $24.99
Volume 4 978-1-59307-968-0 | $24.99
Volume 5 978-1-59582-225-3 | $24.99
Volume 6 978-1-59582-242-0 | $24.99
Volume 7 978-1-59582-331-1 | $24.99

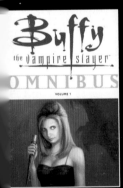

BUFFY THE VAMPIRE SLAYER: PANEL TO PANEL
978-1-59307-836-2 | $19.99